Labor Relations at the
New York Daily News

LABOR RELATIONS
at the
NEW YORK DAILY NEWS

Peripheral Bargaining and the 1990 Strike

KENNETH M. JENNINGS

Westport, Connecticut
London

Library of Congress Cataloging-in-Publication Data

Jennings, Kenneth M.
    Labor relations at the New York Daily News : peripheral bargaining
and the 1990 strike / Kenneth M. Jennings.
       p.   cm.
    Includes bibliographical references and index.
    ISBN 0-275-94587-1 (alk. paper)
    1. Collective bargaining—Newspapers—New York (N.Y.) 2. Strikes
and lockouts—Newspapers—New York (N.Y.) 3. Daily news (New York,
N.Y. : 1920)—Employees. I. Title.
HD6976.N392U615 1993
331.89′281071471—dc20   93-295

British Library Cataloguing in Publication Data is available.

Library of Congress Catalog Card Number: 93–295
ISBN: 0-275-94587-1

First published in 1993

Praeger Publishers, 88 Post Road West, Westport, CT 06881
An imprint of Greenwood Publishing Group, Inc.

Printed in the United States of America

The paper used in this book complies with the
Permanent Paper Standard issued by the National
Information Standards Organization (Z39.48-1984).

10 9 8 7 6 5 4 3 2 1

Contents

Acknowledgments

Many people have contributed to this book's contents. Betty Geitz has success-fully recreated her role as hardworking, constructively pushy "Mistress of Te-dium," who had to read handwritten material and handle six drafts and a log of more than 1,000 items. Ed Johnson, Dean of the College of Business, and Bob Pickhardt, Chairman of the Department of Management, Marketing and Busi-ness Law at the University of North Florida, gave me encouragement and finan-cial support to obtain necessary research materials. The University of North Florida library staff, including Jim Alderman, Signe Evans, and Sarah Philips through their courteous professionalism, enabled me to locate sources I would not have otherwise found. Several colleagues, notably Ron Adams, Bruce For-tado, and Paul Gerhart, generated enthusiasm and ideas for the project, while James Dunton, Andrew Schub, and Patricia Lorange Taylor at Praeger helped in this book's publication. Professor Milton Derber of the University of Illinois has always provided me with a teacher, scholar, and class-act role model. Finally, I mention my wife, Jackie, who radiates love through her efforts, sacrifice, and attitude, and to whom this book is dedicated.

Introduction

Some 160,000 negotiated labor–management agreements exist in the United States today. These agreements represent a significant social endeavor, yet one that is subject to internal uncertainties caused, in part, by market competition and opportunities. In many cases, these uncertainties extend to union and management officials in an organization, influencing their efforts to make joint decisions concerning compensation as well as the rights of employees and employers.

How might the interactions of these participants be altered by economic change and pressures? An evolving though unfortunate approach to emerging developments in the U.S. marketplace today is *peripheral bargaining,* which differs from traditional bargaining activities found in most previous labor–management relationships. The purpose of this book is to explore peripheral bargaining and its ultimate outcomes in depth.

Richard Walton and Robert McKersie's classic book, *A Behavioral Theory of Labor Negotiations,* maintained that traditional bargaining activities represent "the deliberate interaction of two or more complex social units which are attempting to define or redefine the terms of their interdependence." Moreover, the relationship between the parties to labor negotiations in usually unique, continuing, and long-term.

Hence, traditional bargaining focuses on the output of labor–management relationships and work rules, and usually features

- intensive efforts at the bargaining table by labor and management officials, who have joint goals of reaching agreement;
- a sense of mutual respect and trust between union and management negotiators;
- the realization that both parties have to live with each other after the labor agreement; and

- a nonreliance on, if not avoidance of, external bargaining tactics (such as appeals to public opinion) and outside organizations (such as the press, courts, or governmental agencies).

Peripheral bargaining has none of the aforementioned features of traditional bargaining. There is also very little, if any, focus on measurable bargaining issues such as wages, or containment of health costs. Instead, vague considerations such as personalities and principle are stressed by one or both parties. Thus, the parties are likely to spend little time in formulating, costing, and anticipating proposals in the prenegotiations stage. Any previous labor–management settlements that were amicably resolved between the parties are also ignored, while hostile negotiations and/or issues are emphasized.

One or both of the parties in peripheral bargaining might engage in dilatory maneuvers, surface bargaining, and other tactics that would violate their obligation under the National Labor Relations Act to bargain in good faith. This alternative bargaining approach might not include these tactics, however, and typically involves additional, broader considerations and behaviors. For example, management subscribing to peripheral bargaining would likely adopt tactics aimed at minimizing, if not destroying, union solidarity. This could apply to factions within a single union or to emphasizing differences between unions if more than one organization is involved in the negotiations. Back-to-work appeals engaging members to cross picket lines and/or hiring strike replacements are often employed by management to achieve this objective. There may also be more reliance on external agencies and individuals (courts, the National Labor Relations Board, elected government officials, and public hearings) because the need for suasion increases as negotiations proceed with few, if any, tangible bargaining results. One, likely both, of the parties will attempt to use the media, which reinforces peripheral bargaining as these organizations and related publicity intensify union–management differences and divert attention away from potential bargaining table issues. Management and union negotiators rely on press clippings and other external means of bargaining "success" and attempted face-saving approaches without having to justify the lack of bargaining results to their bargaining constituents (stockholders and union members).

A bargaining impasse is almost inevitable in peripheral bargaining, therefore, as union leaders do not have measurable accomplishments to give to their members that justify a ratified labor agreement. Each party then focuses on blaming the other party for this situation instead of looking for superordinate goals and other factors that could end the dispute. Under an extreme application of peripheral bargaining, as with the recent situation at Eastern Airlines, for example, "outsiders," such as those involved in bankruptcy proceedings, instead of bargaining table participants might resolve the impasse.

One or both parties might adopt a peripheral bargaining approach because each perceives the other either wants an impasse and/or will not bargain in good faith. Yet, management officials will more likely be the initiator and dominant player in peripheral bargaining, since they represent the ultimate grantor — there are very few, if any, working conditions that union officials obtain for their members without management's acquiescence. Management may adopt the peripheral bargaining approach for several reasons. It might believe there are more pressing organization concerns that require their attention. Or, management might regard the union as unable to deliver successfully on an obtained bargaining settlement to the membership. Management might also be out to either break the union or force the union members to work under working conditions that are extremely favorable to themselves.

Whatever the reason, the union's reactive response is not likely exemplary. Instead of attempting to structure some continuing relationships with appropriate management officials and seeking solutions to the bargaining impasse, union officials often join the external fight with various public relations campaigns, demonstrations, and boycotts. Directed against management officials and other individuals, the rhetoric of union leaders can often precipitate physically aggressive, violent actions that remove the parties even farther from the bargaining table.

The bargaining experience of the *New York Daily News* with ten unions from 1990 to 1993 represents a vivid, most recent example of peripheral bargaining. In the text, this situation will be rather fully explored through consideration of more that 1,000 written articles and related documents on the subject. Chapter 1 examines bargaining influences that affected the beginning of these negotiations, while Chapter 2 pertains to union and management's bargaining expectations around the expiration date of the 1990 labor agreement. Chapter 3 focuses on the incident that provoked the strike at the *News,* and Chapters 4 and 5 reveal many peripheral bargaining considerations and behaviors that occurred during the strike's first 100 days. The transitions from peripheral bargaining to traditional bargaining table behaviors and results, which occurred under Robert Maxwell's purchase of the *News,* are discussed in Chapter 6, while developments after the sale of the *News* to Maxwell are discussed in Chapters 7 and 8. A final chapter furnishes some observations into the *Daily News*'s experience and implications for subsequent peripheral bargaining that might occur in other organizations in the United States.

Influences Affecting the 1990 *Daily News* Negotiations

The 1990 labor-management negotiations at the *New York Daily News* were influenced by management's financial concerns and the expectations of the union members and leaders involved. Negotiations were also affected by at least three preceding collective bargaining experiences. The first negotiations discussed in this chapter occurred in 1985 between three unions and management at the *Chicago Tribune*, a newspaper that, along with the *Daily News*, was owned by the Chicago Tribune Company. The 1985 negotiations influenced the 1990 *News's* negotiations in at least two ways. Charles Brumback, a *Tribune* management executive, was strongly associated with management's collective bargaining approach in both situations. Also, many of the peripheral bargaining activities and concerns that figured in the 1985 experience at the *Tribune* were mirrored in the 1990 experience at the *News*.

Next discussed in this chapter will be *News's* labor–management negotiations in 1982 and 1987, which suggested a partial tradition of bargaining table emphasis and resolution at the newspaper. In addition to previously experienced peripheral bargaining at the *Tribune* and nonperipheral bargaining at the *News*, two other potential influences existed in the 1990 *News's* negotiations, namely, a decision issued by the National Labor Relations Board; and economic conditions that existed after the 1987 labor agreement was reached at the *News*.

THE 1985 *CHICAGO TRIBUNE* COLLECTIVE BARGAINING EXPERIENCE

Charles Brumback's Accession

Charles Brumback was the *Tribune* executive most identified with the organization's collective bargaining stance in 1985. He became president and chief operating officer of the Tribune Company, which owned the *New York Daily News* in 1989 and thereafter influenced management's bargaining stance in the *News's* 1990 negotiations. Brumback had obtained an undergraduate degree in economics from Princeton and worked at Arthur Young and Company before joining Sentinel Star, publisher of the *Orlando Sentinel* in 1957, where he served as controller, business manager, and general manager. The Tribune Company purchased the *Orlando Sentinel* in 1965; there Brumback eventually became president and chief executive officer (CEO) before assuming those same positions at the *Chicago Tribune* in 1981. (On August 1, 1990, he became CEO of the Chicago Tribune Company, which owned the *Chicago Tribune* and the *New York Daily News*.)

Brumback enjoyed a good reputation among stock analysts for his efficient, cost-control measures. A profile in *Crain's Chicago Business* further indicated that he would be "vilified" by union leaders, but "lionized" by newspaper analysts and "loved" by stockholders. At least one individual, however, indicated that Brumback did not understand his organization's product, newspapers, and presumably the employees and unions responsible for its publication:

> Brumback is not a newspaperman. He doesn't know how to cover a fire, a homicide, or a war. He can't edit copy. He could never make a living writing headlines. Nor is he a New Yorker who grew up with the *Daily News* as part of the texture of life itself. He is an accountant from Toledo, Ohio.[1]

Brumback also had a reputation for being blunt and tough. One of his "admiring" associates noted that a confrontation by Brumback would feature a "punch in the face," not a stab in the back.

Brumback's reputational dimensions affected a 1985 labor dispute at the *Chicago Tribune*. His desire for savings, coupled with a hard-nosed approach with seemingly little empathy for those who produce the newspaper, influenced the impasse and its results, which no doubt shaped management's bargaining approach in the 1990 negotiations with the *News's* unions.

Early Bargaining Issues and Dissension

In early June 1985, the Chicago Typographical Union Local 16 (CTU), the Chicago Mailers' Union Local 2, and the Chicago Web Printing Pressmen's Union Local No. 7 took lopsided strike votes (301–5, 305–2, and 278–2 respectively) against the Tribune Company. The votes reflected resentment toward the bargaining process and lack of bargaining results. For example, the printers represented by the CTU had last received a wage increase in August 1982, while the mailers' last wage increase had occurred in April 1983.

The printers had obtained lifetime employment guarantees in the 1975 labor–management agreement in exchange for wide-ranging concessions that allowed the *Tribune* to introduce state-of-the-art technology and automation efficiently. There were some 600 printers employed at the *Tribune* at the time this provision was negotiated. Retirements and employee buy-outs (as high as $90,000) reduced this figure to about 230 at the time of the strike votes; however, *Tribune* representatives maintained that rapid technological advances made many of the remaining printers unnecessary in their present work assignments.

Management's major bargaining concern was obtaining discretion to transfer employees to other departments when jobs became obsolete because of automation or other industry changes. Union workers were not unalterably opposed to this action; however, they wanted the process to be slower and feature their input.

Union requests appeared consistent with other adjustments to technological change at some 432 newspapers surveyed by the Rand Corporation (*Bargaining Responses to the Technology Revolution: The Case of the Newspaper Industry*). One conclusion of the study is that unions generally have not been an obstacle to technological change largely because many newspaper firms do not resort to massive, uncompensated layoffs when labor-saving technologies are introduced. Instead, management typically reduced staffing levels through natural attrition, buy-outs, and/or retraining.

An impasse over technological change at the Tribune Company was reached by October 24 and dramatized a few days before the strike vote, when management told the least senior member of the CTU that either he would have to choose another department to work in or he would be assigned one. When the employee refused to make a choice, he was assigned to the mailroom, a department represented by the mailers' union.

This singular move quickly precipitated the previously cited, lopsided strike votes among three unions. Mailers and pressmen opposed this action because they did not want their jurisdictions invaded by members of another union. A vice president of the International Typographical Union (ITU) agreed with the mailers and pressmen, and indicated that no union could exist under management's unilateral action. He further suggested that his union might accept printers in the mailroom *if* management negotiated this issue with both unions.

Management did not believe this issue warranted a work stoppage; however, it stressed its intent to hire strike replacements and continue operations should this event occur. This decision was likely made easier by a prior agreement with the *Chicago Sun-Times* to make press capacity available to print the *Tribune* in the case of a strike.

Both management and union representatives no doubt assessed the role of the Teamsters' Union in calculating the strike's likelihood and success. The Teamsters represented *Tribune* drivers who were working under an unexpired labor agreement that prohibited sympathy strikes supporting other *Tribune* employees' unions. However, Jackie Presser, president of the International Brotherhood of Teamsters, was favoring a merger with the financially troubled International Typographical Union, and some thought that he could effectively persuade the *Tribune*'s drivers to honor the other union's pickets should a strike occur.

The Strike's Initiation

The printers, pressmen, and mailers coordinated bargaining efforts through a "Unity Committee," a coalition of all unions representing *Tribune* employees that set a strike date of July 7 if the bargaining impasse was not resolved. Collective bargaining continued beyond the strike deadline; however, a strike began on July 18. Charles Brumback expressed management's surprise over this development, since he had thought management was close to a settlement with the pressmen, and had negotiated with the printers until 5:30 P.M. the day of the strike.

The unions admitted the strike's timing was intended as a surprise in response to the strong actions taken by the company on the eve of the publicized strike deadline (July 7). An official of the pressmen's union noted that company guards stormed into the printing plant and ordered presses shut down:

When the shutdown was completed, security personnel – brandishing guns and clubs and accompanied by vicious dogs – herded the employees into the cafeteria and restrained them against their will. Quite frankly, we were not going to give (Tribune Company president) Charlie Brumback a chance to do that again.[2]

At least one union official, aware that the printers had been without a labor agreement for two-and-a-half years, countered Brumback's reaction:

After two weeks of negotiation . . . we've had two meetings and there has been no motion. We've been negotiating for three years. It's more of the same. They just don't move very fast. . . . They're playing games with us, and that's why we're out on the street.[3]

Both sides reacted quickly to the strike announcement. Unions considered a twofold boycott of the *Chicago Tribune:* that letters be sent to some 450,000 households having at least one union member; and that efforts be made urging *Tribune* advertisers not to continue their activities. Management threatened printing, mailing, and press employees with strike replacements during bargaining sessions, and sent letters to employees after the strike announcement that warned that the company would seek strike replacements for any employees who did not report for their next work shift. Union leaders conceded that printers and mailers could be easily replaced but pressmen would be more difficult because of the technical nature of their jobs. Management's strike replacement approach was further reflected in a *Chicago Tribune* editorial which indicated that newspapers were different from other businesses because they are obligated to furnish "free and independent flow of information back and forth between the government and the governed." The editorial further noted that continued publishing of a struck newspaper, while neither comfortable nor profitable, "is out of commitment to that obligation, not disrespect for the right of production unions to strike, that the *Chicago Tribune* will continue to make efforts to do so, no matter what."[4]

Negotiations were scheduled with the three unions about a week after the strike began. At least three negotiation areas remained between management and the pressmen. The union requested an extra employee be brought in if a press broke down, while management sought more discretion in reducing staffing levels (ranging from four to nine employees) for a press.

A second issue involved the company's desire to assume more discretion over hiring decisions. Management proposed the elimination of the union's hiring hall or "call room," which traditionally referred new hires to the company. Finally, the union, while agreeing with management's right to remove supervisors from the bargaining unit, wanted assurances that these individuals could not subsequently perform bargaining unit work, thereby diluting the union's strength. The second and third issues applied to the mailers' union as well.

The printers announced a day after the strike began that they had made a major concession that *Tribune* management dismissed out of hand. The printers had offered to allow the newspaper to transfer employees out of the composing room if they were given a buy-out option.

Management did not rely on two law firms used in previous collective bargaining efforts. Instead, L. Michael Zinser, an attorney for the Nashville law firm of King, Ballow and Little, became a prominent figure in the negotiations. Indeed, the presence of Zinser prompted the pressmen's union to postpone the bargaining session. A union leader objected not only to being kept waiting for 50 minutes, but also to being surprised with a management lawyer because the union was without its attorney; moreover, the union leader contended that Zinser was a member of the "biggest union-busting law firm in America."

More than 700 striking *Tribune* employees called a week after the strike and heard union leaders urge a consumer boycott of the paper. Union officials reported that some 15,000 subscription cancellations had been made and maintained that a goal of 100,000 canceled subscriptions was attainable. Management indicated that fewer than 2,000 subscriptions were lost. Also in attendance were leaders of the American Federation of Labor and Congress of Industrial Organizations (AFL-CIO) and three unions representing other *Tribune* employees: the photoengravers, electricians, and paperhandlers, who were in turn urged to honor the picket lines. Officials of the Teamsters, however, were conspicuous by their absence. Strikers continually interrupted rally speakers with shouts of "Where are you, drivers?" Yet, an official of the ITU said they had not been invited in order to give them some time and leeway "to solve their problem."

Approximately a week after the strike's initiation, management did offer the unions proposals that included a wage increase. Some of the printers who were offered a transfer could receive a one-time termination incentive of $30,000, while printers with verifiable medical or physical handicaps could receive an additional retirement benefit of $400 per month for a period up to five years. Another company action, allowing striking employees to remain on their group insurance plans if they paid full premiums, was lauded by union leaders as a "goodwill gesture." Yet, there was not sufficient bargaining progress to prompt a settlement between the *Tribune* and any of the three unions.

Extension of Peripheral Bargaining

Peripheral bargaining occurred before the strike (in the absence of bargaining table efforts and boycott strategy, for example) and in the days and months following the strike. At least two outside sources were related to the unions' bargaining efforts during the strike's first days. Lane Kirkland, then president of the AFL-CIO, attended a rally supporting the strikers and stated:

The question is whether this newspaper, for so many years a Chicago institution, can get away with kicking workers in the teeth. If they can get away with that in the great working man's city of Chicago, there's no place they can't get away with it.[5]

Alderman Edward Vrdolyak introduced a resolution in the Chicago City Council that denounced *Tribune* management for not bargaining in good faith and for violating a city ordinance barring Chicago firms from importing workers from outside the city during a strike. Several legal experts and a spokesman for Mayor Harold Washington felt that the ordinance prompting Vrdolyak's resolution was probably unconstitutional.

Vrdolyak also criticized other unions, particularly the Teamsters' union, for not honoring the picket lines. This latter inaction reflected and enhanced a feud between Jackie Presser and printers' union officials. While the proposed merger vote between the teamsters and typographers (printers) was still being conducted, Presser indicated that ITU's national president, Robert McMichen, and other leaders opposed to the merger used the *Tribune* strike as a tactic to arouse "anti-teamster sentiment" in the election. Possible tactics notwithstanding, the proposed merger was eventually defeated. The Teamsters continued delivery of *Tribune* newspapers, reduced the striking unions' bargaining power, and generated deep-seated acrimony. The coordinator for the strike unity council reflected on the Teamsters' inaction:

The easiest way to end the strike early would be to stop delivery. If they [the Teamsters] had gone out, we'd have never forgotten them. Well, they didn't go out—and we'll never forget them.[6]

Management also emphasized outside sources in its bargaining/strike strategy. Striking mailers, who were predominantly white males making $14 an hour plus benefits, were mainly replaced with women and/or African Americans who received $8 an hour with no benefits. Moreover, management sent letters to members of the Newspaper Personnel Relations Association. The letters sought help in finding offset press operator replacements and read, in part,

We have operated normally since the strike began (July 18), but I really, really need your help, if you can.

Yes, we would even like to have someone from your newspaper if they are qualified and it is truly an opportunity for them, and you could lose them without it hurting you seriously.

No, press operators are probably not going to live downtown, but they can live in some truly great suburbs and still enjoy all the fantastic stuff a city like Chicago offers from the sports teams to the art museum to the Chicago Symphony to Lake Michigan and so forth.[7]

Bargaining sessions continued in September with little success. The mailers' union contended that management intended to staff the mailroom entirely with part-time employees, while an official of the printers' union claimed management's three-tier hourly salary offer ($8.16, $10.88, and $13.60) made to strikers who had earned $12.94 an hour a "big step backwards." Violence was limited during the first two-and-one-half months of the strike although an average of 20–25 *Tribune* vending boxes were vandalized (jammed with a wad of paper and a washer) or defaced. One related arrest involved a striking pressman.

During this time period, the *Sun-Times* severed its joint bargaining arrangement with the *Tribune* and the printers who had been without a labor agreement for some two-and-a-half years at both organizations. The printers and other major unions traditionally bargained with an employer umbrella group, the Chicago Newspaper Publishing Association. Two unions, the mailers and pressmen, opted out of the agreement in 1985 and settled with the *Sun-Times;* however, the printers continued to work without an agreement at that organization. A union official for the printers stressed that this separation was made by the *Sun-Times,* which could no longer tolerate the *Tribune*'s "unfair demands and union bashing." Shortly after the separation, the *Sun-Times* reached a six-year contract settlement with what the printers' union called a "very fair" series of annual wage increases retroactive to 1983.

Bargaining became increasingly peripheral four months after the strike began. No success resulted from internal bargaining. Further, management thought a mediator would be unnecessary in this dispute since the issues were clearly established. Union support came from a wide variety of outsiders. For example, Cardinal Joseph Bernardin admitted that he was not "fully informed on strike issues" but contended that "a successful outcome seems urgent for our city at this time." United Farm Workers founder Cesar Chavez accused the newspaper of "trying to destroy the unions"; and Ed Asner, president of the Screen Actors Guild and star of the television series "Lou Grant," walked the picket line outside the Tribune Tower one morning. Union leaders also met with Mayor Washington, who avoided any immediate commitments. Edward Brabec, president of the Chicago Federation of Labor, labeled *Tribune* management as "the greediest employer I've come across in my life" and pledged $5,000 to the unions' Christmas strike fund.

Unions continued to urge the boycott of the *Tribune,* although subscription cancellations were estimated to remain at the 2,000 level. This statistic suggested that reader loyalty is hard to break, even among staunch unionists. Some maintain that a successful boycott requires substantial preparation and communication efforts to convince the public that they should change their ingrained purchasing habits because the unions' case is both clear and just.

Management–union bargaining efforts appeared almost entirely devoted to outside factors as the strike tallied six months in January 1986. Around this time period, the unions and management began filing unfair labor practice charges against each other. The National Labor Relations Board (NLRB) regional office issued four related complaints against the company and dismissed the company's charges against the unions. (Tentative results of these charges occurred in 1990 and will be discussed later in the text.)

Management also resorted to outside sources in the bargaining process when it filed suit against three striking production unions seeking to block mass picketing in front of the Tribune Tower and the newspaper's printing plant. The suit alleged employees had rapidly escalated their picketing efforts at both locations in recent months, used vile language, and threw objects at people leaving and entering the building.

While this suit was being considered, another Circuit Court judge approved an agreement between management and three striking unions to ensure a peaceful unionist rally at the newspaper's printing plant. The rally was attended by some 5,000 to 10,000 strikers and strike sympathizers and did feature some violence such as brick and rock throwing incidents and damage of at least one *Tribune* delivery truck. Some 37 people were arrested for their actions.

A restraining order was issued that enjoined the striking unions from engaging in violence or intimidation on the two picket lines. A management representative indicated that legal action was mandated by the rally's mob violence, which he thought was more associated with Libya or Iran instead of Chicago's streets. This rationale was countered by a union attorney, who claimed that managers were seeking an injunction because they failed to stop a legitimate protest and were desperately blaming the unions for the acts of unidentified individuals; moreover, the attorney thought this legal movement was intended to assuage the egos of *Tribune* executives, who knew they were losing the strike, and to deplete the strikers' morale.

One bargaining development did occur during this time period—the return of 63 printers to work. The *Tribune* had notified the union of these vacancies and had created a preferential hiring list for the remainder of the printers in case of future openings. This situation did not apparently create substantial animosity among fellow printers who remained on the picket line and the pressmen and the mailers who were not recalled. For example, the president of the pressmen's union stressed that this action would "not destroy the unity among our three unions." The return of some printers also did not result in any immediate collective bargaining settlement, which eventually occurred some three years later.

The Strike at One Year and Implications for the 1990
Daily News Negotiations

Few if any other tangible results were reached through bargaining sessions occurring through the strike's first year. Ed Brabec, president of the Chicago Federation of Labor, indicated that the negotiations were going nowhere, as management's seeming agreements on some bargaining issues were forgotten in subsequent sessions.

Striking mailers and pressmen, while receiving weekly payments of $70 or $250 from their unions, had almost all of their jobs assumed by permanent replacements. In addition to the 63 printers who returned to work, there were 55 supervisors who had carried union cards and did not strike, while 50 union members either did not strike or returned shortly after the walkout began. Moreover, the *Tribune*'s reporters not represented by a union as well as eight unions representing *Tribune* employees (drivers, machinists, electricians, paperhandlers, mechanics, engravers, operating engineers, and elevator operators) did not honor picket lines and continued to work during the strike.

The strikers might have consoled themselves that the *Tribune* had to hire far more employees to get the paper out since the pressroom crew increased from a prestrike level of 7 or 8, to 12 or 13. Yet, the wages of the replacements were much lower. Even Theodore Kheel, advisor to the *New York Daily News* unions in the 1990 negotiations, thought the *Tribune* was "winning" the dispute, because the newspaper was being produced at half the cost.

James Squires, editor of the *Tribune* at the time, maintained, however, that management did not break the unions; instead the unions "ran themselves out" with internal quarreling. Kheel agreed with Squires's assessment; he blamed some of the *Tribune*'s union leaders acting "like a bunch of jerks" in this situation. George McDonald, head of the New York's Allied Printing Trades Council (APTC)—an umbrella organization representing ten unions at the *Daily News*, also criticized the Chicago unions for not coordinating themselves better before the strike took place and for not being able to shut the *Chicago Tribune* down in order to win their bargaining position. McDonald's observations were seconded by a newspaper industry analyst who contended that unions had no power if the company controlled its newspaper distribution.

The Tribune Company realized at least short-term benefits from this bargaining inactivity, as record profits of $241 million were announced for 1985 with even better results predicted for 1986. Managers at other newspapers closely monitored the *Tribune*'s accomplishments through peripheral bargaining. They realized that their organizations could not move to another location if labor costs became too high since their businesses were rooted in the city where they published. A *Tribune* bargaining victory in a strong blue-collar town like Chicago would generate hope for their operations.

As they approached their own negotiations in early 1990, the *Daily News* unions and management responded to what they felt were several implications for bargaining strategy and related tactics suggested by the 1985 *Chicago Tribune* negotiations. Management had emphasized peripheral collective bargaining efforts in 1985. Bargaining issues had not been clearly defined in the initial bargaining stages for the printers and never clarified for the mailers and the pressmen. Moreover, the employees in the job classifications realized no tangible bargaining issue resolutions and/or mutually agreed-upon steps for impasse resolution.

Management's peripheral bargaining strategy forced the unions to revert to tactics away from the bargaining table with no resultant success. The printers, mailers and pressmen could not unify other *Tribune* unions, including the Teamsters, that had labor agreements in force with the newspaper. Union members' appeals for a boycott of the *Tribune* did not alter the company's bargaining stance. Management contended only 5,200 lost subscriptions were lost through this campaign, a minuscule figure when compared to the *Tribune*'s circulation figures (1,163,983 on Sunday and 760,031 daily). Moreover, the advertising lineage actually increased during the strike.

Unions were equally ineffective in working Chicago's political infrastructure to alter the dispute in their favor. No elected official could order a private sector company such as the *Tribune* to settle its collective bargaining differences. However, these officials could at least structure public opinion by suggesting that the unions had a legitimate position and that a collective bargaining impasse would be against the public interest.

Mayor Harold Washington maintained a hands-off approach to the *Tribune*'s bargaining impasse resolution. This situation may have been attributed in part to the lack of union support for Washington's candidacy and/or the hierarchies of the *Tribune*'s unions, which were dominated by whites (Washington was black). Whatever the reason, Washington did not personally intervene in the *Tribune*'s labor dispute, an approach to labor problems different from that of one of his predecessors, Richard Daley. Chicago Federation of Labor president Ed Brabec indicated that no union leader had wanted to receive Daley's lecture on possible responsibility for an unacceptable bargaining stance/impasse, which, in Daley's terms, would give Chicago a "black eye."

Unfair labor practices filed by the mailers and the pressmen were not resolved during Brumback's first year as CEO, and *Tribune* management appeared to use peripheral bargaining effectively. A labor agreement was obtained from the printers on terms acceptable, if not favorable, to the *Tribune*. The jobs with pressmen and mailers classifications were staffed with strike replacements who had far lower wages and no union representation. There were some 375 members of the pressmen's union before the 1985 strike. Five years later, there were 27 members in the pressmen's union.

Management could therefore take full advantage of some $200 million in new technology by slashing some 400 jobs (more than 25 percent of the production work force) as well as operating costs by 50 percent. A senior executive at a rival newspaper labeled the *Tribune*'s sixfold earnings increase after its 1985 strike, "one of the great successes in newspaper publishing."

UNION AND BARGAINING TRADITIONS
IN NEW YORK CITY

New York City's Unionized Atmosphere

Brumback made no secret about his unhappiness with the *New York Daily News* and likely agreed with his predecessor, Stanton R. Cook, who regarded not making progress at the *News* as "the No. 1 disappointment." Brumback appeared so intent on replicating his 1985 *Chicago Tribune* bargaining "success" at the *News* that some of his colleagues labeled the 1990 labor–management confrontation, "Charlie II." A former editor of the *Tribune* also predicted that Brumback would not be muscled by New York unions.

Newspaper delivery is the key to successful publishing during a strike. This operation would pose a formidable challenge if a strike occurred in New York City because some 800,000 newspapers have to be delivered to 10,000 vendors during a two-hour period each morning. Some union leaders strongly maintained that nonunion newspaper delivery during a strike could not take place in New York City. Publishing insider Rupert Murdoch agreed with this assessment, particularly if the nonunion distribution of newspapers occurred without police protection, and his sentiment was supported by past experience. Previous newspaper strikes in New York City during the 1960s had hastened the demise of the *Herald Tribune*, the *Mirror*, the *Journal American* and the *World-Telegram and Sun*. The *News* had also experienced a strike in 1978 when delivery was impeded by rock throwing, firebombed trucks, and numerous arrests. When *News* reporters went on strike, the newspaper hit the stands for two days until drivers joined the strike and brought circulation to a halt. After this strike, some 12 percent of the paper's circulation never returned. A union spokesperson suggested the circulation reduction reflected that New Yorkers, although a diverse group, "will not buy a scab newspaper."

Successful publishing of the *News* during a strike in 1990 would pertain to the extent that New York City is a "union town," in attitude and in number. Much of New York City's population recognizes, even appreciates, organized labor's legitimacy. This attitude typically assumes that the individual employee is helpless when confronting a large organization and that only through collective action can employees express their needs and gain their ends. Thus, a union town would stress "solidarity" in a labor dispute and regard strikebreaking, with its "Screw you, Jack, I'll get mine" mentality, as an ugly indifference and threat to long-standing concerns of employees.

Holders of this attitude would tend to support the strikers, and this support might include boycotting the organization's products, urging elected officials to end the dispute, and ignoring or even condoning strikers' hostile actions, particularly if they occur against the organization and/or strike replacements. The impact of this attitude on a labor dispute depends on the number of individuals who believe it to be correct and applicable to the specific dispute in question. A strong union town would likely have a large population base either belonging to unions or being in a household having at least one union member.

Some academicians and union officials question whether New York City would become a strong union town if a strike occurred. A large employment shift occurred in New York City during the 1980s. Some 150,000 manufacturing (and mostly unionized) jobs were eliminated during this time period while more than 350,000 new (and mostly nonunionized jobs) were added in service industries such as insurance, banking, and real estate.

Also, New York City's overall economic conditions as the 1990 labor agreement expired might not have engendered a favorable public sentiment/solidarity to the *News's* unions particularly if they engaged in a work stoppage. At this time, for example, the city threatened to lay off more than 30,000 employees. One observer puts this situation into perspective:

I would easily guess that the public is not going to be particularly distressed that *The Daily News* is considered to be antiunion in this particular dispute.

The general public tenor is, "If I'm not protected, so why should you be?" There are hundreds if not thousands of people waiting on line to take blue-collar jobs, so the ability of unions to rally people in their favor has declined.[8]

In summary, the 1985 *Chicago Tribune* bargaining approach would not automatically work if applied to the *Daily News's* negotiations in 1990. Some thought the newspaper's populace reflected a union town, one that would support employees if they struck, thereby hindering, if not eliminating, the delivery and/or sale of the paper. Others suggested that this description no longer applied to New York City because union members could not enlist public support for their causes.

While New York City's influence in a potential 1990 *News* strike was debatable, union and management negotiators knew that successful public relations efforts concerning bargaining goals/activities would yield beneficial, if not essential, support. This realization had been reinforced by the 1982 and 1987 collective bargaining settlements at the *News,* which, at a minimum, were not hindered by the larger community. These situations will now be briefly summarized since they represented an alternative bargaining approach to the 1985 *Chicago Tribune* experience.

1982 Collective Bargaining at the *Daily News*

Before the Tribune Company went public, management in Chicago tried to sell the *Daily News;* however, it could not literally give the newspaper away because of enormous severance pay and unfunded pension obligations that any new owner would have to assume. Early in 1982, the Tribune Company announced it would rather sell the *Daily News* than invest $60 million in new equipment considered necessary for the newspaper's profitability. The *News* had lost $12 million in 1981 and at that time was estimating losses of $30 million and $50 million in 1982 and 1983 respectively. Daily and Sunday circulation had dropped from 2 million and 2.8 million in 1974 to 1.5 and 2 million by 1982.

The Allied Printing Trades Council (APTC), an umbrella organization of ten newspaper unions in New York City that represented employees at the *News,* (see Exhibit 1.1) indicated that it would be willing to discuss potential cost-cutting concessions as well as establish a trust so that employees could help raise capital for needed improvements. Stanton Cook, the *Tribune's* CEO, thought the

Exhibit 1.1
Summary of the *News*'s Ten Unions Represented by the Allied Printing Trades Council (APTC) 1990*

International Brotherhood of Electrical Workers, Local 3
   Membership: 43; Function: Electrical Maintenance
   President: Dennis McSpedon

International Typographical Union, Local 6
   Membership: 199; Function: Typesetters and Composing Room Employees
   President: James Grottola

Machinists Local 434
   Membership: 32; Function: Maintain Presses and Other Equipment
   President: Joseph Armao

Newspaper Guild of New York
   Membership: 786; Function: Newsroom and Advertising Employees
   President: Barry Lipton

Newspaper and Mail Deliverers Union of New York and Vicinity
   Members: 743; Function: Drivers
   President: Michael Alvino

Newspaper Printing Pressmen's Union No. 2
   Members: 410; Function: Operate the Presses
   President: Jack Kennedy

New York Mailers, Union Local 6
   Members: 116; Function: Bundle and Prepare Newspapers for Delivery
   President: George McDonald

Paperhandlers Union
   Membership: 79; Function: Load And Unload Paper Rolls onto Printing Presses
   President: Pat Flannery

Photoengravers Union Local 1-P
   Membership: 16; Function: Take Pictures of Completed Pages
   President: Stan Aslanian

Stereotypers Union Local 1
   Membership: 37; Function: Use Film to Make Plates for Presses
   President: Jack Kennedy (not same as Pressmen's president)

Source: Harry Berkowitz, "Unions Vow to Bring News 'To Its Knees'; Guild Members Join Strike Upon Word of Mass Firings," *Newsday,* October 27, 1990.

*The International Typographical Union, Local 6 was no longer in the APTC when it did not join the other 9 unions in the strike.

unions' "cooperative attitude" expressed in these actions would help the organization find a qualified buyer.

Joe Allbritton, the chairman of Allbritton Communications Company, announced on April 1, 1982, his intent to purchase the *News,* an acquisition he made contingent on reaching $70 million in cost concessions with the unions by

April 25. One of Allbritton's aides indicated that Allbritton wanted to be represented by Robert Ballow in related negotiations with the unions, but *Tribune* management refused this request, indicating that unions would regard Ballow's hiring as "inflammatory." This view of course suggests that Brumback's 1985 hiring of Ballow to handle collective bargaining at the *Tribune* was deliberately intended to send the unions a message that the previous bargaining relationship was significantly altered if not ended.

Allbritton introduced the first two negotiation sessions by indicating that neither he nor the union would be negotiating through the media. In addition, he informed the unions that he wanted the current contract, scheduled to expire in 1984, extended to 1987. Unions were expected to forego scheduled wage increases in 1982 and 1983 in exchange for a 20 percent share of future profits, and determine among themselves how 1,600 jobs (about a third of the payroll) would be eliminated. The wage concessions would save some $50 million over the extended agreement.

Bargaining continued to avoid the media although this process ceased on April 22. The printers' union was concerned about salary payments to its members who had lifetime employment guarantees. Bertram Powers, president of the printers' union, invited Rupert Murdoch, publisher of the *New York Post,* to supply a formal bid for the *News.* Powers reasoned that the Tribune Company's refusal of Murdoch's bid would strengthen the union's legal claim for salary payments beyond the severance and pension pay it would receive if the *News* closed. Murdoch agreed to at least match Allbritton's offer if it was not accepted by *News's* management. The Newspaper Guild wanted any layoffs to be determined by seniority only instead of managerial preference.

Bargainers for seven unions generated some $30 million in concessions; however, union negotiators regarded complete acceptance of Allbritton's terms as "unconditional surrender." They would not talk further on job cut allocation if they could not also propose alternatives to the wage freeze and the longer contract. George McDonald of the Allied Printing Trades Council wanted the right for unions to recommend other cost-saving alternatives after having reviewed income and revenue projections for the *News.*

Theodore Kheel, a mediator in these negotiations, urged New York Mayor Ed Koch to bring the parties back to the table. Koch declined this offer, but publicly indicated that continued bargaining was necessary because "New York would lose part of its soul" if its operations ceased.

The resolution of bargaining between the unions and a potential buyer was precluded by the Tribune Company's decision to keep the *News.*[9] Kheel suggested the company's about-face occurred because management reestimated its employee severance payment costs to be $185 million instead of the originally estimated $85 million. The additional amount mainly reflected the pay of 610 printers and stereotypers who had lifetime job guarantees, and 700 pressmen, whose jobs were guaranteed until March 30, 1984. These guarantees were legally enforced by a U.S. Court of Appeals in a related situation involving employees at the *Cincinnati Post.*[10] *Tribune* management was aware that the

Supreme Court denied review (in effect upholding the decision) at a time near its announcement to retain the *News*.

Tribune management was also impressed with the concessions given to Allbritton and thought similar bargaining with its unions would eventually make the operations profitable. Stanton Cook therefore urged the unions to reopen the contract and pledged to invest $92 million ($44 million investment in the Brooklyn plant and two new suburban printing operations) in the paper if the negotiations generated $50 million in payroll cuts. Unions were eager to return to the bargaining table but indicated that related discussions would have to include the *New York Post,* where fellow union members (also represented by the APTC) and management faced an estimated $20 million in annual losses.

Agreements were reached with five unions (printers, Guild, machinists, electricians, and garage mechanics) by August. *New York Daily News* publisher Robert Hunt indicated that the company would provide substantial termination bonuses to unions not having job guarantees in their labor agreements, expressed the company's willingness to extend the labor agreements to 1987, and promised to modernize the *News* production plant operation. Hunt also maintained that all unions needed to settle by August 6 or else financial pressures would force a reduction in the operation (eliminating an early edition of the Sunday *News,* shutting down some presses in the Manhattan plant, and curtailing circulation in some areas).

The plain fact is, these savings are necessary if the *News* is to be saved. . . . Peat, Marwick, Mitchell and Company, the nationally recognized accounting firm chosen by the unions, has seen all our financial records and forecasts. The firm verified that our figures are accurate, that we need the cost reductions we've requested, that continuation of business-as-usual will result in annual losses averaging about $30 million a year for the next three years, and that our survival plan (which included $92 million of new expenditures and the cost savings proposed to the unions) will work.[11]

Agreement with all eleven unions came in two phases. As August 1982 ended, all unions agreed to the "equivalent" reduction of 1,340 jobs (some $50 million in annual cost savings) although much of this figure consisted of reductions in part-time employees and overtime shifts. Union employees could typically receive $30,000 or more in severance payments if they left the organization.

Two unions representing pressmen and the mailers nevertheless had letters of agreement with the *News* that stated that these cost-savings programs could not be implemented unless the labor agreements were extended until 1987. On October 25, Hunt announced that all unions had agreed to the labor agreement extension and would receive weekly wage increases of $38, $35, and $37 in March of 1984, 1985, and 1986. A cost-of-living wage adjustment clause and a possible re-opener if the paper attained a profit exceeding 6 percent of net worth were also included in the settlement. Hunt further indicated that the *News* would return to profitability by 1983, and was "here to stay."

1987 Negotiations at the *Daily News*

Negotiations over the 1987 labor agreement occurred against a backdrop of financial uncertainty and loss. The paper's daily and Sunday circulation continued its decline to 1.3 million and 1.6 million respectively in 1986. The organization also lost some $13 million in advertising revenues in 1986 because three of its major advertisers, Gimbel's, Ohrbachs, and Lafayette Electronics, went out of business. A net loss of $5 million was reported for the paper for the same year, and management was predicting more than $40 million in losses for 1990 if it could not obtain contract concessions from the union. James Hoge replaced Hunt as publisher of the *Daily News* in 1984 and was given a mandate to turn the newspaper around by stemming circulation losses, facing down the *News's* unions, and bringing the paper into the black alongside the Tribune Company's other properties. Hoge maintained that the 1987 negotiations should result in a "linkage" between the *Tribune's* commitment to spend and the unions' commitment to give back what was necessary for the *News's* survival.

Bargaining activities continued past the March 1987 contract expiration date with union officials predicting that a settlement would not be reached by June or later. Much of this delay was due to interpreting detailed financial data furnished by *Tribune* management to the unions to indicate the organization's dire situation. George McDonald, president of the APTC, maintained that affected unions would implement bargaining concessions if they were assured that management had certifiable financial problems. Peat, Marwick, Mitchell and Company and Stanley Simon and Associates were retained by the unions to analyze the company's books and explain the situation to the union rank and file. Stanley Simon informed the unions that the *News* would be losing $44.4 million a year by 1990 if dramatic changes were not made.

By July, agreement had been reached on a major bargaining aspect, the Mutual Investment Plan (MIP), that called for $60 million to be invested in the newspaper and up to $50 million in buy-outs and severance pay in return for $30 million in contract concessions from the unions. This agreement contained rather complex and sometimes vague language to protect both union and management interests. For example, the agreement outlined what an "investment" could represent but gave management discretion where to invest. Related possibilities included color printing equipment, a new inking system, and front-end systems for various departments. The MIP did include a $20 million cap on how much of the $60 million could be used for buying land for a new plant site.

The MIP also gave the unions extra severance if the *News* folded or was sold before the full $60 million was invested. Unions would receive half the investment shortfall; for example, $15 million added to severance payments if the *News* invested $30 million during the terms of the labor agreement. A representative for the *News* reported "no major stumbling blocks" in reaching the agreement and further stressed that the agreement "demonstrates that both the company and unions are deadly serious about turning this newspaper around."[12]

Attention then turned to negotiating specific concessions with each union. Within a month, the Photographers Local 1-P represented the first union to reach a tentative pact with the *News*. Stanley Ashlanian, president of the union, indicated that his organization focused on present members: "Technology is such that you can't worry about taking care of people in the future. Forty years ago you would have been shot [for that logic]."[13] Earlier in the year, 30 percent of the photoengraving department either received buy-outs or were laid off, an action estimated to save the company $1.5 million annually. The contract also gave management scheduling flexibility to reduce overtime, waived union contesting of new technology, eliminated certain minimum staffing levels, and permitted members to be transferred to other departments if work was unavailable. In return, management furnished a company-purchased medical plan to replace the union's financially troubled plan. The union agreed to accept whatever wage package agreed upon by the other unions.

Management also announced that 94 members of the International Typographical Union, Local 6 (representing the printers) had accepted severance payments as much as $110,000. This agreement was estimated to save the company $5 million annually. Since the buy-out plan exceeded the *News*'s original savings target, the paper paid an additional $3.67 per employee per shift into the printers' health and welfare plan for the terms of the agreement. Gregory Thorton, the *News*'s chief management negotiator praised the printers' union for having taken a leadership role in helping management to save the newspaper by increasing its competitiveness.[14] He also hoped that the other unions would follow suit in the newspaper's cost savings negotiations.

The lithographers' and printers' settlements both focused on a three-year labor agreement, a year longer than the company's original proposal. This duration extended to all unions when the *News*'s largest union, the Newspaper and Mail Deliverers' Union of New York and vicinity, which represented the drivers, reached a settlement about a month later. Some $6 million in annual savings would occur through job buy-outs and reductions in jobs and job functions, manning requirements, and overtime. Drivers who resigned voluntarily would receive $65,000. Remaining drivers would receive no wage increase the first year and wage increases of 4 percent ($26 per week) and 5.25 percent ($36 a week) in the second and third years of the agreement.

Similar three-year agreements were reached with all of the unions by mid-December. Some $25 million (13 percent) of annual cost savings were realized, a figure largely caused by a one-time buy-out payment of $45 million for some employees.[15]

Publisher Hoge indicated that he was "pleased, really pleased" about the settlement, and expected the paper to be "profitable over the next three years" because of "an improved product and enhanced advertising and circulation services." Hoge also indicated that the *News* must operate profitably before the Tribune Company would invest in color presses that were crucial to the paper's future success. George McDonald's assessment of collective bargaining results might have been addressed at Hoge's possible omission of the labor factor. McDonald succinctly stated, "The unions saved the *Daily News.*"

Speculative tension notwithstanding, the negotiations between the Allied Printing Trade Council and the *News* in 1982 and 1987 did not reflect the peripheral bargaining approach at the *Chicago Tribune* in 1985. Most bargaining attention and efforts at the *News* were focused on measurable issues/working conditions as opposed to personalities and principles at the bargaining table. External activities (rallies, for example) and influences such as the media, political/community leaders, legal hearings, and enlisting the community's support were seldom, if ever, employed.

Management and union officials at the *News* entered the 1990 negotiations with two previously and traditionally concluded bargaining settlements. Yet, they could also have been influenced by peripheral bargaining that characterized the *News*'s sister publication, the *Chicago Tribune,* run by Charles Brumback, and owned by the *News*'s parent, the Chicago Tribune Company. Management had to at least consider two other, somewhat contrasting legal and economic pressures at this time.

LEGAL AND ECONOMIC INFLUENCES

Potential Influence of the National Labor Relations Board

On December 12, 1989, Administrative Law Judge (ALJ) Marion C. Ladwig issued a decision concerning unfair labor practices filed by the Chicago Web Printing Pressmen's Union No. 7 that arose from the 1985 *Chicago Tribune* strike. Some of Ladwig's decision related to management's proposal to modify contractual language pertaining to the "scope of bargaining unit." The expired 1979–85 collective bargaining agreement defined this issue in both sections 1(a) and 1(b):

Section 1.
(a) The Employer recognizes the Union as the exclusive collective bargaining agent for the employees *engaged in the operation of the presses.* . . . The pressroom department shall be interpreted to mean the entire pressroom . . . made up of union employees and in which the Union has been formally recognized by the Employer.

(b) It is mutually agreed that *the above is defined to mean all work* currently recognized between the parties as *embracing the operation of all printing presses* . . . and shall be interpreted to include [listed make-ready items 1–6]. (Emphasis added.)[16]

Management actively sought the addition of the following "zipper clause," which read in part:

This contract *supersedes* and replaces any and *all* agreements . . . *practices* . . . *understandings* . . . governing the relationship between the Employer and the Union, whether written, oral or implied. (Emphasis added.)[17]

It moreover contended that this clause when added to the "scope of the bargaining unit" portion of the labor agreement meant that the unions' work jurisdiction was confined to those activities specifically mentioned in 1(b). This interpretation excluded a majority of the presswork, including the part of the reel room work performed in operating the presses.

According to ALJ Ladwig, as a condition for signing the agreement, management was demanding that the union accept its interpretation that would deprive the union of contractual jurisdiction over most of the pressmen's traditional work, which could, in turn, be assigned to nonbargaining unit employees. Thus, the "zipper clause" was used to change the scope of the bargaining unit, which is a nonmandatory or permissive subject of bargaining.

Union and management officials can agree to negotiate over a permissive issue; however, one party cannot insist that the other bargain over the issue. The ALJ determined "that on November 13 the Company refused to bargain in good faith by bargaining to impasse on its demand, as a condition for consummating an agreement, that the scope of the bargaining unit be changed, violating Section 8(a)(5) and (1) of the Act." Ladwig also determined that management aggravated and prolonged the impasse thereby converting the pressmen's economic strike to an unfair labor practice strike.

There was no way that International Vice President De Vito and the other member of the [pressmen's bargaining] committee could recommend membership acceptance of the Company's November 13 "firm and final" offer as long as [the management negotiator] demanded, as a condition for signing an agreement, an interpretation of section 1(b) that would deprive the unit pressmen of contractual jurisdiction over most of their traditional pressroom work.

By including that unlawful impasse demand in the offer prevented the Union from evaluating the mandatory subjects in the offer separately, along with a reappraisal of its bargaining stance in light of its obviously poorer bargaining position. . . .

I therefore find that the Company violated Section 8(a)(3) and (1) by refusing to reinstate 74 unfair labor practice strikers on January 30, displacing the 74 replacements hired after the November 13 conversion of the strike. I find that the remaining unfair labor practice strikers, who were permanently replaced on or before November 13, have the same reinstatement rights as economic strikers.[18]

These and other considerations prompted the ALJ to order the *Tribune* to make whole (back pay and seniority rights) 74 unfair labor strikers as a result of its January 30, 1986 refusal to reinstate them. Also ordered was immediate and full reinstatement to employees on the preferential hiring list to former positions to fill full-time and part-time vacancies that had occurred since November 4, 1986. Management was further ordered to bargain with the pressmen's union.

Ladwig's decision was supported by the NLRB's General Counsel. However, the NLRB's three-member panel remanded the case to the ALJ for further proceedings to articulate the basis for the judge's finding that striker replacements hired by the respondent were permanent, rather than temporary. The NLRB panel also directed the ALJ to further consider the *Tribune*'s affirmative defenses, which contended that during the course of 59 bargaining sessions from February 1985 to November 1986 the union unlawfully engaged in coordinated bargaining, unlawfully engaged in surface bargaining, and unlawfully insisted to impasse on the permissive subject of including supervisors in the bargaining unit. *Tribune* management further contended that such conduct excused it from any statutory bargaining obligation and removed statutory protection from employees who struck or continued to strike in furtherance of the union's alleged unlawful objectives.

Thus, the NLRB's involvement in the 1985 *Tribune* strike represented a potential influence in the 1990 negotiations at the *News* and could have served as a wake-up call to both parties, particularly management, that peripheral bargaining could become intertwined with bad faith bargaining with costly consequences (strikers' reinstatement with back pay for example) for the Tribune Company. Yet one or both parties could have regarded the ALJ's decision as unsettled; indeed, the board's remanding of the decision suggested that the *Tribune* might have been justified in its bargaining actions. Perhaps the union and/or management negotiators at the *News* were not guided by the ALJ's decision, because subsequent procedures including various appeals could take several more years to resolve.

Conditions Between 1987 and 1990 at the *Daily News*

Both the *Daily News* and the Chicago Tribune Company reported financial gains in the year following the 1987 labor agreement settlements. The Chicago Tribune Company, excluding one-time charges, realized profits in 1987 of $163 million, a 15 percent increase over the previous year. An even larger increase in profits (47 percent) was realized in 1988. Much of this increase was due to more than $2 billion spent since 1980 to rebuild plants and purchase new businesses.

Even the *Daily News,* labeled the Tribune Company's "problem child" by *Forbes* magazine, looked healthier shortly after the 1987 negotiations than it did a few years before. Circulation and advertising had increased in the first six months of 1988 to 1.3 million and 8.3 percent respectively. These results were partly achieved through labor cost concessions given by unions in the 1982 and 1987 bargaining sessions. Also, the *News*'s "shabbiest" facility and "archaic" computer systems had been replaced at a cost of more than $100 million since 1982.

The *News*'s financial picture, however, while positive in 1988, was not glittering. Operating profit for the year was approximately 4 percent of revenues, compared with the average return of metropolitan papers of 18 percent to 20 percent. The *Daily News* had revenue of $420 million in 1989 and still lost several million dollars. Estimates for 1990 projected that the *News* would lose $20 million on revenues close to $400 million. From 1980 through 1989, the paper had lost $134 million on $4 billion in revenue. Average daily paid circulation had fallen by 400,000 copies since 1979; the paper's circulation was 1.2 million on September 30, 1989, which was down 7 percent from 1988.

A portion of the dire financial conditions bargaining influence was due to rather extraneous factors. For example, there had been a nationwide trend of reduced newspaper reading. Only 66 percent of Americans now read a newspaper on an average day, compared with 75 percent 20 years ago. Since the *News* had the largest circulation, a general decline in newspaper purchases would also cause a sizable reduction in the *News*'s readership. Moreover, the *News*, unlike the *New York Times*, did not enjoy a sizable proportion (20 to 25 percent) of readers who read the newspaper but did not live in the city and was unable to attract these readers in their suburban homes.

Management and union officials approached the 1990 negotiations blaming each other for the *News*'s financial troubles. Unions thought management in general, and publisher James Hoge in particular, were responsible for the newspaper's difficult situation. As George McDonald noted, "The *News* has bum management," and James Hoge is "a sociable guy, but as publisher he's a 4 on a scale of 1 to 10."[19] Jack Kennedy, president of the New York Printing Pressmen's Local, maintained that the *News*'s biggest problem was that it was "the most mismanaged paper in America."

Ever since *Esquire* had featured Hoge along with Hollywood personalities such as John Travolta and George Hamilton in a 1979 piece called "the Dangers of Being Too-Good Looking," Hoge has had to contend with a public image that tends to focus on his blue eyes, blond hair, weekends in Connecticut with the Kissingers, and a duplex on Gramercy Park. Hoge's wife wrote about this latter item in *Architectural Digest*, describing the residence's six fireplaces, ten-foot-high mahogany doors, Ionic columns, eighteenth-century engravings, and an "heirloom room." Another article stressed Hoge's "impeccable manners" and "magnetic presence" and further indicated that he was "so gifted and handsome that people would actually gape in admiration."[20]

Union leaders symbolized Hoge's public image with management's insincere, superficial bargaining and regarded Hoge as a "patrician errand boy for the Tribune Tower in Chicago." They also associated Hoge's hiring and first contract negotiations with "double crosses" in which management did not make investments in the *News* corresponding to the 1982 and 1987 labor agreement settlements and union concessions.

James Wieghart, an editor at the *News* from 1982 to 1984, noted that the Tribune Company pressured the *News* publisher Bob Hunt in the 1982 negotiations to obtain concessions. The unions did reopen and extended their contracts, which enabled the paper to make a $20 million profit in 1983 after having suffered a $12 million loss in 1982. But the company, noting that the relief was temporary and featherbedding practices still remained, became dissatisfied with Hunt's piecemeal approach regarding bargaining and technological change. Wieghart further noted:

So instead of investing in new plant and equipment, as it had promised, the company sold *Daily News* assets: the skyscraper on 42nd Street for $141 million, Newspoint in Queens, and the rotogravure plant on that site for millions more. This double cross undermined Bob Hunt's credibility with the unions and left him little choice but to resign, which he did in 1984.[21]

Unions were also upset over management's investment recalcitrance following the 1987 negotiations. They claimed that management never intended to purchase state-of-the-art presses. Indeed, George McDonald noted just before the 1987 labor agreement expired in March 1990 that it takes years to order and take delivery on new presses. The fact that the *News* had not ordered them suggested that the Tribune Company did not want to run the *News* anymore. McDonald further felt that management would not have made the investment even if the unions had given everything including "our blood and our toenails." Kennedy extended McDonald's assessment of management's motives: "They either want to provoke a strike so they can kill the paper or they want to get everything they can out of the ten unions and then sell."[22]

Tribune management countered that it had invested some $170 million since 1980 in the *News,* and Hoge pointed out that his company had spent $55 million on two proposed plant sites as proof that the Tribune Company "is anxious to make the investment" in the newspaper. He could not give a specific date when investments would be made in printing presses although Charles Brumback indicated around the 1987 contract expiration date that he would like to see "a year or two of solid profit growth" at the *News* before committing to "any major capital expenditures."

New presses would cost from $300 to $500 million, and the Tribune Company wanted to pay for them in eight to ten years. To achieve this objective, management would have to obtain major cost savings in the 1990 negotiations. Hoge realized this objective would not be easily obtained after a regular quarterly meeting with union heads in January 1989 where, Hoge recalled, they exploded—pounded tables with their fists shouting "No concessions," and claimed that Hoge had reneged on a 1987 promise to build a new $300 million printing plant for $30 million in union concessions. Hoge was shaken by this confrontation but was also convinced to start preparing for the worst. He maintained that union and management had shown "an awesome lack of imagination" about resolving the newspaper's problems, and further indicated that "now we are at the point where it really has to be done and it has to be done all at once." Hoge's perceived urgency likely prompted the hiring of the King, Ballow and Little firm some three months later (March 1989) to handle upcoming negotiations.

NOTES

1. Pete Hamill, "They Killed the News Today, Oh Boy," *Esquire,* February 1991, 34.

2. Mark Fitzgerald, "Bitterness in Chicago," *Editor and Publisher,* July 27, 1985, 36.

3. James Warren, "3 Unions Strike Tribune," *Chicago Tribune,* July 19, 1985, sec. 1, p. 5.

4. "When a Newspaper Is Struck," *Chicago Tribune,* July 21, 1985, sec. 3, p. 2.

5. James Warren, "Tribune, Pressmen Make No Headway," *Chicago Tribune*, August 7, 1985, sec. 2, p. 2.

6. Kevin Klose, "Tribune Strike Continues," *Washington Post*, May 11, 1986, F-2.

7. "Chicago Tribune Seeks to Replace Strikers," *Editor and Publisher*, August 31, 1985, 21.

8. James Barron, "Shifting Balance of Power in Labor Is Reflected in Strike at Daily News," *New York Times*, October 28, 1990, 20.

9. While Allbritton was the most likely potential purchaser of the *News*, two other possibilities were Donald Trump and Warner Communications Company. Rupert Murdoch did submit a last-minute offer, which was rejected April 29 because Tribune officials claimed the offer was "predatory" and "patently illusory, due to obvious antitrust complications." "Tribune: 'No Sale' of the News," *Christian Science Monitor*, May 3, 1982, 2.

10. "Justices Decline Review of Ruling on Lifetime Job Security Guarantee," Bureau of National Affairs Inc., *Daily Labor Report* 100 (May 24, 1982): A-7.

11. "N.Y. News Warns Unions of Cost-Cutting Measures," *Editor and Publisher*, August 7, 1982, 15.

12. Andrew Radolf, "New York Daily News Talks Make Progress," *Editor and Publisher* July 4, 1987, 38.

13. "Engravers Gain Accord with The Daily News," *New York Times*, August 13, 1987, B-3.

14. The eventual settlement approved by the Chicago Typographical Union members was reached in late November 1988 and included a company buy-out or a lifetime annuity, as well as company-paid medical insurance, to the 119 printers who continued to strike. Fifty printers who had remained at the newspaper since a 1986 unconditional offer to return could stay employed or accept a $30,000 cash buy-out. The printers also agreed to drop a lawsuit in federal court that contended the company violated a lifetime employment guarantee contained in the 1975 labor agreement. "The Chicago Tribune Agrees to Settlement in Printers' Disputes," *Wall Street Journal*, November 28, 1988, B-2.

15. For details of the union's settlements see Elizabeth Neuffer, "Daily News and a Key Union Reach Pact with No '87 Raise," *New York Times*, September 13, 1987, 50; and "Daily News Guild Contract Provides Buy-outs for Large Number of Employees," Bureau of National Affairs Inc., *Daily Labor Report* 225 (November 24, 1987): A-12.

16. *Chicago Tribune Company v. Chicago Web Printing Pressmen's Union, No. 7 Graphic Communications International Union, AFL-CIO*, National Labor Relations Board–Division of Judges, Case No. JD-292-89, (Chicago, Ill., 1989), p. 3. "Make-Ready Items" included "Changing and adjusting folder cutting knives" (but not "after they have been taken out of the press"); "changing oil filters and greasing press cylinders"; changing and adjusting angle bars, slitters, and trolleys; and "changing folders from straight to collect." Management also proposed adding another work item, platemaking, to section 1-B.

17. Ibid., p. 4.

18. Ibid., pp. 15 and 25.

19. Patrick M. Reilly, "At New York News, Threat of Strike Is Looming Larger," *Wall Street Journal*, April 2, 1990, sec. B, 7-G.

20. Thomas B. Rosenstiel, "A Giant of Journalism Faces Its Most Critical Decline," *Los Angeles Times*, March 27, 1990, D-1.

21. James G. Wieghart, "Owner Strangles Daily News," *New York Times*, November 28, 1990, A-21.

22. Rosenstiel, "A Giant of Journalism," D-1.

2

Bargaining at the *Daily News* Near Contract Expiration Time, 1990

Union and management officials approached the 1990 *Daily News* negotiations with substantial resolve reflected in their respective bargaining goals, preparation tactics, and behaviors. These collective bargaining dimensions were more aligned with the 1985 *Chicago Tribune* contract negotiations than with related efforts found at the *News* in 1982 and 1987. This peripheral emphasis is further illustrated in a discussion of bargaining activities and outside influences occurring both before and seven months after the labor agreements' expiration date, March 31, 1990.

MANAGEMENT AND UNION BARGAINING GOALS

Management's General Concerns

Publisher James Hoge apparently first announced management's general bargaining concern in a September 20, 1989 speech:

Excess manning, high compensation, and archaic work rules have combined to put the *Daily News* in a financial straitjacket. By contract, we are forced to employ more people than we need, pay overtime regardless of whether it's needed or even worked, and pay penalties that increase costs as our printing volume increases.[1]

This concern could be supported by statistics that indicated the *News*'s financial disadvantage when compared to its competitors. *News* management indicated its annual labor costs represent 48 percent of annual revenue versus 25 percent to 30 percent at other large newspapers, and that its $20 million in annual overtime payments represented 13 percent of revenue versus a 3 percent proportion for other large metropolitan dailies. Both ratios and their underlying causes (un-worked but paid overtime and excessive number of employees at the presses) have made the *News* an "extreme" within its industry.

Management's bargaining concerns and solutions were sharpened during Hoge's visits to publishing rival Rupert Murdoch's newspaper plants in early 1989. Murdoch maintained that the New York newspaper unions were the "world's worst," and that his breaking of the British printing unions in 1986 represented a "silver age for British journalism" and prosperous newspapers. Murdoch's nonunion facilities convinced Hoge that managerial control of the production and distribution operations were necessary to ensure on-time printing and delivery. Moreover, a highly paid but flexible work force that can perform any necessary task without restrictive work rules can reduce the number of em-ployees as well as overtime payments. Hoge further stated that obtaining control of the work force for efficient production and distribution of the newspapers was particularly necessary in 1990, since he claimed that *News* management cur-rently did not have the rights to hire and direct employees and determine the necessary work to be completed.

This situation suggested at least two rather specific bargaining goals for man-agement, namely, eliminating unnecessarily large salaries and costly work rules associated with bargaining unit employees. One payroll analysis concluded that the average pay of unskilled employees at the *News* was more than $50,000 a year. Pressmen received $65,000 to $75,000 a year before overtime, and drivers, at more than $20 an hour, could receive more than $100,000 in annual salary. Mike Alvino, president of the Newspapers and Mail Deliverers Union at the New York *Daily News* Brooklyn facility, countered that these salary figures pertained to very few union members, who "don't like their wives," since these individuals would have to work two or three shifts a day to earn that amount. Alvino further suggested that management, not the unions, wanted to increase the maximum salary for a few drivers up to $250,000 a year. The *News* would sell delivery routes to a few drivers who would serve as independent contractors, earn as much as $250,000 a year and, perhaps, no longer feel the need for a union.

Management also wanted to eliminate costly work rules that had been negoti-ated in previous negotiations and applied to various unions at the *News*. Manage-ment alleged, for example, that the tasks performed by 14 to 17 pressmen could be handled by as few as 6 to 8 employees. John Sloan, Vice President for Human Resources at the *News,* explained that some of this overstaffing was due to the pressmen's buddy system:

If you and I are buddies and you decide you don't want to come to work, I'll sign your name on a piece of paper and you'll get paid for the entire shift. Then after a couple of hours I decide I want to go home, and I'll leave and get paid for the entire shift.[2]

James Hoge has contended that the buddy system means that fifteen employees are assigned to a press, and ten typically show up for work with the names of the other five employees written in. Management technically has the right to take attendance but does not for fear of a work slowdown.

Drivers had also previously obtained some work rules that management wanted eliminated in the 1990 negotiations. For example, newspaper bundles could not be stacked higher than 48 inches in delivery trucks, so the vehicles hit the road half full. Also, a driver might have had four or five hours of contractual overtime built into each day, thereby receiving the equivalent of seven days' pay for five or six days' work. Hoge indicated that the *News* paid 36,000 hours of overtime a year for no work performed.

Other targeted work rule eliminations pertained to the retying of some Sunday inserts, including comics, which were delivered to the *News* facility already tied. Management estimated that this work rule resulted in an unnecessary cost of $2 million a year.

Management figured that the preceding work rules could be best eliminated through a more general, inclusive bargaining objective of regaining work force control. It proposed that the following 200-word management rights clause be included in the ten labor agreements affecting its bargaining unit employees:

The sole and exclusive rights of management shall include but not be limited to the right to: hire, assign, schedule, lay off, recall, transfer, suspend, discharge, or otherwise discipline employees; determine, establish and implement terms and conditions of employment; establish or continue policies, practices, and procedures for the conduct of the business and, from time to time, to change or abolish such policies, practices, or procedures in order to prevent any redundancy or duplication of work or for any other reason; determine and select the equipment to be used in the Publisher's operations and, from time to time, to change or to discontinue the use of any equipment and to select new equipment for its operations, including equipment for new operations.[3]

Unions' Reactive Objectives

The *News*'s unions approached the 1990 negotiations from a defensive posture. Union negotiators spent much of their time refuting or modifying management's bargaining goals described in the preceding section. They also attempted to stem any reduction of the status quo with management assurances that additional funds would be invested in the *News*'s operations.

Jack Kennedy, president of the pressmen's union, indicated that management's claim of a "phantom" work force (those who sign in and go home or have a co-worker sign in for him) was baseless since the practice had not happened for years. He also stressed that the "excessive" overtime was due to the working conditions that required his members to stay after their six-and-a-half-hour shift until the newspaper was finished. According to Kennedy, the pressmen's staffing level for the *News* is similar to that found at the *New York Times* and *New York Post* and is further necessitated by half-hour or longer work breaks taken by his members because of harsh working conditions at the *News;* more specifically, because of dangerous high-speed presses that are also dirty and noisy. Kennedy said that his members could not stay "chained" to the presses 60 minutes an hour; instead they would have to go to the quiet smoking room "to get your head back on straight."

The safety problems of noise, slippery puddles, ink mist, and others were also recognized by the Department of Labor, which cited the *News* six times during 1985-90 for violations of the Occupational Safety and Health Act (OSHA) that included exposing employees to excessive noise and dangerous dust; failing to supply respiratory protection; noncompliance with the Hazard Communication standard; and failing to keep fire exits clear and adequately worked.

The other two dailies in New York had not received any such citations during this time period, and George McDonald indicated that health and safety would "certainly be a big issue" during the 1990 negotiations. Pressmen did file a lot of grievances over safety issues about six months before the labor agreement expired. Although this practice helped create a "paper trail," little publicity and/or related movement over safety issues apparently occurred in labor–management negotiations. Drivers union president Mike Alvino indicated that his workers had also experienced poor working conditions since he had begun delivering the *News* in 1954; more specifically, he cited drivers being on streets where drugs are rampant at 3 o'clock in the morning with malfunctioning heaters in their trucks.

Kennedy's accusations of poor working conditions were supported by fellow union members, the author of the *Vanity Fair* article that was widely considered a "puff piece" on *News* management, and the Department of Labor. One paperhandler noted that all employees working around the presses had hearing disabilities and also had to blow black ink out of their noses after their work shift. The worker's comments were backed by the author of the *Vanity Fair* article, who praised *News* management in general and publisher James Hoge in particular. An exception was the author's description of "Dickensian working conditions" found at the *News*'s main printing plant in Brooklyn as a "grimy, noisy, miserable place . . . soaked in the inky smell of carbon black and oil."

Many of the poor working conditions were, and remain, due to the age and disrepair of the printing room equipment. For example, a most serious safety hazard at the *News,* ink mist, is a product of deteriorating technology:

All high-speed presses create some ink mist—an aerosol of droplets flung into the air by centrifugal force—but several factors contribute to excessive misting at the *News.* The heaviest mist comes from units that are running less than a full sheet of newsprint. Normally a pressman could shut down the flow of ink to parts of the press that aren't running paper. But on the *News*'s thirty-year-old presses, many of the keys will not close all the way, allowing unneeded ink to flow to the cylinders, where it is thrown into the air as they spin.[4]

Some union officials and members further argued that management's specific featherbedding charges could not be acknowledged, let alone considered because management did not raise these items at the bargaining table. Indeed, the general 200-word management rights clause proposed by management represented a clear dimension of peripheral bargaining since it precluded union and management negotiations over specific working conditions. Tangible bargaining success stories/symbols were also denied, thereby discouraging further union–management negotiations on other issues.

Some observers thought that management's insistence on this labor agreement provision might also have legal implications for the 1990 labor-management negotiations, wanted management's promise in writing that the *Daily News* would bargaining over specific management rights issues. If this reasoning were correct, then management could not legally bargain over the general management rights clause to impasse, and then unilaterally implement related work rules concerning staffing levels and job duties.

George McDonald indicated that unions would continue to bargain over specific work rules and make possible concessions to "keep the paper competitive." Yet, the unions, believing management "double-crossed" them after the 1987 negotiations, wanted management's promise in writing that the *Daily News* would build two new printing plants in exchange for work rule concessions.

News management indicated that long-term investment could not be made regardless of union agreement on general or specific work rule corrections. Hoge indicated management had lived up to its 1987 MIP pledge (discussed in Chapter 1) to invest $2 for each $1 in concessions by the unions, a figure that totaled around $30 million. He further noted that management promised a two-stage approach in the 1986–1987 negotiations, which resulted in $26 million in savings over the three-year labor agreement. The second stage would consider programs for new presses and facilities by 1990 when the labor agreement came up for renegotiation. The Tribune Company did indicate in December 1989 and in January 1990 that it had spent $55 million on two proposed production facilities that would print color pages, but that staffing issues needed to be addressed before additional investment considerations could be undertaken. Management contended that new facilities and presses would cost $300 to $500 million. The debt service of $30 to $50 million a year would, at best, equal management's estimated work rule "abuses," costs of $50 million to $70 million a year. One financial analyst for the newspaper industry assessed this situation:

It would be absolute lunacy to invest that money without understanding that at least now you have opened up a significant gap between costs and revenues. . . . And even then it is a chancy investment.[5]

Theodore W. Kheel, who had mediated most of the newspaper strikes in New York since the 1950s and served as an unpaid advisor to labor, admitted in the 1990 negotiations that the Tribune Company's aggressive bargaining stance was due to the organization being in a very good position, which Kheel, McDonald, and Kennedy attributed to the Tribune Company not desiring to remain in New York. McDonald suggested that these conditions forced unions to recognize and counter management's "win-win" situation. The *News* could beat up or even break the union with wage concessions or a smaller nonunion payroll, situations that would make the paper attractive to a potential buyer. Or management could blame the union for costly work rules and/or a strike, and close operations with relatively low shutdown costs. A rival publisher agreed with McDonald's assessment and further noted that either alternative would increase the price of Tribune Company's stock.

This scenario was also supported by a *News* editor who labeled the approach the "SS" or "Sell-it-or-shut-it" strategy, and who noted further, "There's an accountant somewhere in Chicago adding up the numbers, and it has nothing to do with putting out a newspaper."[6]

Union officials thought that management could obtain at least one major advantage through its hard-line bargaining approach and goals of selling or closing the newspaper, namely, avoiding $150 million in employee severance payments and unfunded pensions. Kheel admitted that unions would contest this loss if the facility were sold or shut down even through a strike, yet he felt that the risk of losing the severance payments through litigation was less than that of continuing to run the paper.

Some financial analysts of the newspaper industry agreed with Kheel that a second advantage of management's sell-it-or-shut-it goal would be a reduced financial burden. The *News's* losses were reduced to less than $10 million annually so that the *Tribune's* $433 million operating profit on sales of $2.5 billion in 1989 would not receive a quick lift if union work rule concessions were granted.

In addition, if management did obtain work rule concessions, it would likely have to make more investment in news operations, which could mean bad news since the *Tribune's* profits were projected to be weakened through 1991 by the continuing cyclical downturn in its large Canadian newsprint business. One analyst's best-case scenario is that the *Tribune's* commitment to new color printing facilities would generate an anemic 10 percent return on investment. Another analyst noted that management's promised investment could not be justified to stockholders, especially with the *New York Times* and *Newsday* having "deep-pocket owners."

Management denied that it had a collective bargaining goal of jettisoning the *News*. James Hoge thought the paper added to the richness of New York, while Charles Brumback stressed the Tribune Company's determination to keep publishing the paper.

There's no question that the *News* can make a return on investment. . . . That's one of the greatest newspaper franchises in the world. . . . We're not going to let one of the family jewels go down the sewer.[7]

Some financial analysts agreed that management would not want to sell the *News*, a situation reflecting bargaining complexities as well as the lack of consensus among financial experts in predicting collective bargaining goals of union and management officials. One analyst observed that the Tribune would not surrender New York's biggest media market in the United States if it could obtain "even a mediocre profit from that huge base of revenues." Another brokerage firm, while conceding that closing the paper's operations would improve Tribune Company stock, projected even better possibilities of the *News* remained after negotiations with revamped wage scales and work rules; it also noted that operating margins at the *Chicago Tribune* more than tripled in the years after its strike in 1985.

Common Goal: Sharing the Public's Support

In short, there was little if any common ground between management and union bargaining goals in the 1990 negotiations. Instead of seeking even minor common denominators on which to build some bargaining success, both parties compounded this peripheral bargaining dimension with another—attempting to formulate and control public opinion even in the early stages of collective bargaining.

Both management and union negotiators had a goal of having the public understand their bargaining concerns and objectives. One *News* executive, for example, commented, "We're fighting for the hearts and minds of New York. . . . There's a lot of disinformation out there."[8]

Management fired its first public opinion salvo in the previously mentioned October 1989 issue of *Vanity Fair.* The contributing editor/author of the article was encouraged to present a managerial perspective of the *News* by John P. Scanlon, a public relations specialist at Daniel J. Edelman whom James Hoge had hired in June 1989 for the upcoming labor agreement negotiations.

Two of the article's themes were the *News's* role as a victim of union featherbedding/labor cost abuses mostly by the pressmen and drivers, and James Hoge's multifaceted accomplishments and competence to "save the *News.*" Hoge agreed not to discuss labor negotiations with any of the magazine's competitors until the issue was processed. He also ordered 5,000 copies of the magazine before publication to be sent to advertisers and those considered to be influential New Yorkers. This effort could justify management's position if a strike occurred and could also effectively counter potential union advertising and circulation boycotts.

The *Vanity Fair* article was also sent to labor unions in an attempt to break union solidarity—to show the pressmen and drivers as irresponsible and undeserving of other unions' support. A second mass mailing to union members' homes occurred approximately a week before the labor agreements expired and contained an 18-minute videotape titled "A Paper for the '90s." The tape stressed the poor economic situation of the *Daily News* with bold financial charts full of red ink. Lou Carnesecca, the revered coach at St. Johns University, also gave a "pep talk" to the viewers.

The *News* management also knew that the newspaper had a 40 percent African-

American readership and wanted their readers and other New York residents to realize that regaining control of the work force would enable the organization to hire more minorities and/or females. *News* spokesperson John Sloan indicated that the newspaper was forced to hire pressmen from a union list that only contained the names of white males, a situation he found to be "socially unjust, morally and ethically wrong." This dimension of managerial work force control had also been raised in the 1985 negotiations at the *Chicago Tribune.*

Unions sought to defuse possible negative public opinion over this issue on both occasions. In 1985 Theodore Kheel had noted that management and the unions agreed to create this employment situation at a time management was totally disinterested in this issue. Kennedy of the pressmen's union reacted similarly in 1990 and indicated the seniority lists were derived from a 1960's consent decree: "I can't hire anybody" or "send a soul over there for a job." A spokesman for the AFL-CIO further indicated that neither minorities nor women were interested in "dying jobs" that had no future; moreover, the civil rights community in New York did not have disagreements with the union over this issue.

George McDonald of the Allied Printing Trades Council also reminded the press about a month before the contract expiration date of the *News's* decision to move the production of the Sunday color sections out of New York City to Allentown, Pennsylvania. This action, taken in 1987, resulted in the firing of 100 women and minorities who were members of the Mailers' Union Local 6. McDonald also stressed that management had always controlled the hiring process; therefore, any discriminatory practices would be conducted under James Hoge's direction.

The Kamber Group was hired to implement the unions' public relations efforts during the 1990 negotiations. In some cases, this organization attempted to counter the specific public relations efforts initiated by management. One related example is found in the following excerpted press release by Jack Kennedy through the Kamber Group on January 25, 1990:

In yet another attempt to deceive the people of New York and divert attention from their dismal failures as managers, the *Daily News* yesterday planted an erroneous and misleading film clip with "Eyewitness News."

In the same vein as the lottery hoax several weeks ago, James Hoge sent a video crew into the *News* Brooklyn plant in November allegedly to film footage of a running press, for internal purposes. The crew told my members who were working at the time to please step aside for a few moments so they could get a clean shot of a press in action. My members agreed, not realizing that this was just another in a long line of carefully orchestrated dirty tricks planned by Hoge to deceive and distort the truth.

The Chicago Hoaxsters have taken news simulation to new heights. Perhaps Jim Hoge should change his name to Joe Isuzu. . . . Why we would have thought the fabrication of news would have stopped after the *Vanity Fair* article, I don't know.

The folder is the heart of the press and is always monitored continuously. To be any distance from the folder is a very dangerous practice. What the viewers of Channel 7 were not aware of is that while the *News* was filming the press, my members were just out of camera shot monitoring the folder as they always do. I invite "Eyewitness News" and all the press to visit the *News* plant in Brooklyn to see how things really work and to witness the draconian working conditions that my members work in day after day.[9]

This organization also transmitted general themes such as that unions and management both agreed to various "costly and outmoded" work practices in the 1960s, and that it was unreasonable to expect the unions to give these practices up in one sitting, particularly to a management that could not be trusted to keep its commitments to the union.

Union officials also wanted the public to know that they strongly preferred to save the newspaper at the bargaining table, whereas *News* management wanted a show of force. For example, George McDonald sent a letter to New York City's Police Commissioner Lee Brown, requesting police protection for the union presidents who were negotiating with *News* management. The accompanying news release stated, in part:

The only person who is planning and anticipating a strike is Jim Hoge. The unions only want to sit down at the bargaining table like civilized human beings and negotiate a fair agreement. Our number one priority is to insure that the *Daily News* stays in business. Now we read in the papers that Hoge has settled into a siege mentality, he has two former FBI agents as his 24-hour bodyguards, and he himself has created an atmosphere of fear and intimidation that now has us scared.

Jim Hoge has fashioned himself a modern-day robber baron, right out of the pages of Upton Sinclair's *The Jungle,* and we demand that the city of New York protect us.[10]

Another news release by George McDonald stated that Hoge employed a hardline nonconstructive negotiating strategy so that he could become a member of the Tribune Company's Board of Directors. "The brass ring is in sight, if he can destroy the lives of the working people at the *News*."[11] Many of the unions' press releases were directed at various management preparations before the labor agreement expired.

Bargaining Preparations

Management initially approached the 1990 bargaining negotiations in late March 1989 when it hired Robert Ballow of King, Ballow and Little, a law firm that represented more than 300 daily newspapers throughout 42 states and that had a specialty in employment relations. Ballow himself was known variously as "Cat Ballow," "Brumback's hired gun," or "the cracker" (due to his having earned a law degree at the YMCA night school in Nashville, Tennessee).

Ballow's hiring represented an immediate symbol of management's bargaining stance in several respects. McDonald, for example, noted that he learned of Ballow's hiring through a newspaper article. "Hoge didn't have the decency to call me." Deborah Friedman, an employee of the Kamber Group and the union's spokesperson, further reacted that Ballow's hiring sent a clear antiunion message because they knew what he would say "before he opens his mouth." Don Singleton, a member of the Newspaper Guild's negotiating committee, described his reactions to Ballow's behavior at the first collective bargaining session:

He came on cocky, all Southern drawl and home-turf confidence, like some cracker sheriff who had just caught a New York driver doing five miles over the speed limit through some jerkwater town. Ballow plopped his contract proposal on the table and invited us to sign it right then and spare ourselves the pain he implied would certainly ensue if we tried to get around him.[12]

Ballow issued few public comments about collective bargaining at the *News* although he did indicate that his first responsibility was examining and understanding the distribution system. More general comments previously made by Ballow reflected the minor, unnecessary role of unions. He had noted that unions represent only 17 percent of the work force, about the same percentage that is "susceptible to television evangelism." He further contended that unions did not provide employees with any new legal rights and that educated people usually found unions unnecessary. Ballow's actions had no doubt outstripped his words as he and/or his law firm were associated with a series of union decertification elections (in places such as Wilkes Barre, Pa.; Austin, Tex.; and Danville, Va.), and two of the most bitter strikes in the last decade at *Wilkes-Barre Times-Leader* in 1978 and the *Chicago Tribune* in 1985.

As noted in Chapter 1, Charles Brumback (then president of the *Chicago Tribune*) hired Ballow's firm to handle the 1985 negotiations and strike. In 1989 three months after his promotion to CEO of the Tribune Company, Brumback personally hired Ballow for a similar assignment with the 1990 *News* negotiations.

Thus, Ballow's appointment also symbolized the shift of managerial influence from Hoge and others based in New York City to Brumback and other officials located in the *Chicago Tribune* corporate headquarters and elsewhere. Brumback at least suggested to some that he neither knew nor cared about *Daily News* operations. When Brumback met with Wall Street analysts in the spring of 1990 and was asked which boroughs represented the *News*'s major support, he was unable to name them.

Newspaper operations at the *News* had been overseen by an executive group of vice presidents. One former member of the group noted that its membership had "rolled over" at least twice since 1985, losing some 13 members including the finance officer and executives in human resources and production. Nearly all of these individuals were replaced by *Tribune* people with zero New York experience. For example, the *News*'s new vice president for circulation came from the Tribune Company's Fort Lauderdale paper, which had 64 percent of its daily circulation home-delivered in a nonunion town.

Author Pete Hamill, who had once worked for the *News,* noted that this experience gap also included attitudinal differences:

As union contracts began to run out last spring, bad faith became the ruling emotion of the negotiations. Once, intelligent men from both sides would have sat down over steaks at the Palm, explained what each needed, and worked out compromises. But the Tribune Company wouldn't do it the old way anymore. It wouldn't open the books to union scrutiny and ask for help. It acted as if the unions were run by people who were socially, ethically, and morally inferior. The unions could do it the way Brumback and Company wanted to do it or they could go to hell.[13]

This situation may have encouraged peripheral bargaining instead of resolving differences between the parties.

Management reinforced its bargaining stance with activities that occurred before the 1990 negotiations and cost the *News* an estimated $25 to 50 million. Some of these efforts were directed toward securing the *News* operations while negotiations were occurring and union members were at the facilities. Armed guards in uniforms were stationed at the paper's four printing plants. Many of these individuals also had cameras to videotape "incidents," and build a case.

Employees accused the guards of taunting them and hurling racial epithets. Union officials further indicated that management intentionally used these tactics as psychological warfare as they conjured past images of repression of a helpless population. Drivers' union president Michael Alvino complained of "guys in paramilitary-type uniforms, goose-stepping through the plant." George Mc-Donald indicated that employees were uneasy and disappointed with management's tactics, and, further, that "Hoge's actions harken back to the days of Pinkertons in the early 1900s when mine company owners brought in goons from out of town to intimidate workers and bust heads."[14] Management's inclusion of German shepherd dogs in its parking lots further exacerbated tensions. Mc-Donald also contended that the *News* hired other new employees during this period, supervisors who were expected quickly and frequently to "write up" and suspend members for violating company rules.

Management's negotiation preparation activities were also directed toward producing a newspaper should a strike occur. For example, in the fall of 1989, more than 100 editors and managers were flown to the *Fort Lauderdale News* and *Sun-Sentinel* (another Tribune Company operation) to learn how to make printing presses:

They each spent two weeks learning how to operate presses in the event of a strike. It was odd work for them. Some of the men training them were missing fingers. When the trainees returned, they would jokingly wave to each other in the halls using three fingers, as if they were missing the rest.[15]

The Tribune Company also allegedly recruited reporters from its papers in Orlando, Newport News, and Fort Lauderdale to serve as replacements in *New York Daily News* operations should a strike occur. Those individuals accepting the offer would receive room and board in New York hotels in addition to their salaries for the duration of a strike. They also received from *News* management the following out-of-town living instructions:

- Don't stop to talk to anyone who approaches you.
- Don't make eye contact with passersby.
- Don't frequent restaurants in close proximity to the office or hangouts traditionally populated by journalists.

Trained and available strike replacements were introduced to alternative production operations, such as a Sears warehouse in North Bergen, New Jersey, that was converted into a phantom newsroom a few months before formal bargaining began.

Inside a football-field-sized room, management installed a plethora of personal computers, photo equipment, and computerized page-layout gear. Outside, the warehouse was surrounded by a chain-link fence topped with barbed wire. As workers moved equipment in and out, security guards patrolled the grounds in boots, dark glasses and wide-brimmed hats, with German shepherds in tow.[16]

Union officials' bargaining preparations, like their previously discussed bargaining goals, were defensive in nature. As John Kennedy of the pressmen's union, for example, noted, "You play the hand you're dealt. . . . If they go after me, we go after them." Mike Alvino claimed to be a faithful churchgoer who abhorred violence and did not want his drivers' union members to become uncontrollable.

A major step in union bargaining preparations was taken in June 1990 when the Allied Printing Trades Council of Greater New York announced the hiring of Samuel C. McKnight, a partner in the Southfield, Michigan firm of Klimist, McKnight, Sale, and McClow. Tom Donahue, Secretary-Treaurer of the AFL-CIO, recommended that McKnight be hired to serve as a necessary counterweight to the philosophies and actions of Charles Brumback and Robert Ballow. Theodore Kheel said the addition of this external, possibly peripheral bargaining dimension was needed because the dispute had far-reaching national implications.

Like the *News*'s unions, McKnight believed that a strike would largely serve management's interests; therefore, any such job action should reflect a deliberate, disciplined decision by union leaders and members instead of a "momentary statement." He also wanted the public, particularly *News* readers and advertisers, to become educated in negotiation issues and urge the parties to settle their differences at the bargaining table.

What I hope to do here is to develop a dialogue with customers and advertisers of the *Daily News* and the Tribune Company, to help them understand our situation, our needs, our relationship to them, and our members' relationship to them. . . . Whether or not we'll ask them to suspend advertising remains to be seen.[17]

BARGAINING ACTIVITIES BEFORE MARCH 31, 1990

Formal bargaining between the parties began in January 1990, when management presented the unions with a list of concession requests. One union official noted that management's action confirmed that the Tribune Company under Charles Brumback's leadership had never been committed to the bargaining process. A member of the Newspaper Guild maintained that from day one of collective "bargaining," management wanted to test its belief that the newspaper could be published without any of its unions.

Indeed, the ten unions representing *News* employees voted in February 1990 to look for a buyer willing to share ownership with employees. John Sloan, management's chief negotiator, countered that the company was not antiunion, just antiabuses; moreover, he asserted that management wanted to eliminate featherbedding, overmanning, and unworked overtime, and wrest control of the employment and supervision process from the union.

Management's bargaining efforts, however, were neither intensive nor directly tied to the preceding bargaining issues. For example, one active member of the Newspaper Guild said that management did not mention specific, "archaic" staffing and overtime compensation rules in any bargaining session held with his union in 1990. George McDonald further explained in a subsequent Senate hearing how management officials wanted to frustrate the bargaining process, thereby baiting union members into a strike:

From the beginning, the negotiations at the *Daily News* were a charade. First, the company's negotiating team was unlike any that had ever negotiated in the New York newspaper industry before. The team did not include any long-time *Daily News* officials, anyone who had ever before engaged in negotiations in the New York newspaper industry, or anyone who had any responsibilities or expertise in the actual day-to-day operations of the newspaper. Although the *Daily News* was publicly stating that its goal was to eliminate inefficient work practices, no one on the company's negotiating team understood the company's work practices. Although the *News* was stating that the newspaper sought union cooperation, no one with any prior relationship with the unions served on the company's negotiating team.

Second, the contract proposals made by the *Daily News* to each union did not even focus on any particular work practices at the company, and they certainly did not make any constructive suggestions regarding any such practices. Instead the proposals sought in substance to eliminate the union from the workplace and to free the company from virtually all the requirements of a typical collective bargaining agreement. The proposals eliminated the jointly administered pension and welfare funds, the use of union hiring lists, and the union dues checkoff. The proposals restricted the powers of arbitrators in discipline cases and declared that no past practices or prior understandings in any area would bind the company. Most important, the proposals included an all-but-limitless management-rights clause that would permit the publisher to change virtually any aspect of the paper's operations at his whim, without any further negotiations with the unions.

These proposals were obviously designed to prevent agreement, provoke a strike, and thus create a situation for using permanent replacements. As negotiations progressed, this design became even clearer. Although Mr. Ballow repeatedly stated that he was motivated only by the newspaper's financial needs, he admitted that no cost studies of particular proposals had been made. Although Mr. Ballow insisted that existing work practices were grossly inefficient, he rejected the unions' repeated offers to discuss specific changes in those practices. Let me underline the last point. The unions repeatedly insisted that we were willing to negotiate for changes in any inefficient practices, but Mr. Ballow insisted that the *Daily News* would only be satisfied with the right to make any changes the *News* wanted at any time the company wanted to do so and without having to negotiate further with the unions.[18]

McDonald also indicated that Ballow, the company's chief negotiator, taunted him:

At one meeting Bob Ballow said to me, "You're the union official that doesn't like to strike; you're not representing your people very well by not striking. . . . What kind of union leader are you that you don't want to strike?"[19]

At least two general management activities, however intentional, could have provoked a strike. Management created at least some union members' strike apprehension by retaining negotiation preparation tactics aimed at producing a newspaper with a nonunion work force should a strike occur. Throughout the winter of 1990, management kept a "preparedness pool." Editors would form car pools complete with "captains," who were given access to rental cars and assigned to pick up members along designated routes if the need should arise.

This preparedness mentality intensified in the spring of 1990. All editors had to wear beepers at work and remain on call at home so that management could assemble quickly if a wildcat strike occurred. In early March, some management officials assembled in the phantom newsroom for a dry run at producing a newspaper. They successfully put out a mock-up of a 32-page paper, performing every operation except actually printing it. Union leaders were no doubt aware of this development since they monitored this location, dubbed "Fort Hoge," on a daily basis.

Management also negotiated with only a few of the ten unions, thereby dividing and isolating the other unions most likely to strike. George McDonald suggested that management's "better offer" to some unions would be quickly recognized as a "charade" by all affected union members.

No bargaining progress was evidenced during the first three months of 1990 although management did present offers to the electricians, machinists, and the Newspaper Guild during this time period. About a week before the contract expiration date, management suddenly offered the electricians 15 percent wage increases over three years and 18 percent to the machinists in exchange for large benefit concessions.

The unions' nonacceptance of these offers were likely eclipsed by a March 25 "solidarity rally" attended by several thousand individuals. This event occurred approximately a week after Bertram Powers, head of the International Typographers Union, said that he would advise his union not to strike to protect lifetime employment guarantees given the printers in 1974 in exchange for allowing *News* management to introduce automated typesetting equipment. Leaders of other *News* unions expressed disappointment with this decision but did not appear to adjust their bargaining plans accordingly.

Management also gave the Newspaper Guild members a proposed three-year labor agreement on March 26, 1990. It differentiated the Guild from four other unions (pressmen, deliverers, paperhandlers, and mailers) that represented over half of the newspaper's 2,500 employees, and, according to management, engaged in "abusive labor practices." One source at the Tribune Company indicated that management would never offer a contract to the drivers that they would deem acceptable.

Another observer contended that management's disparate contract proposals were intended to drive a class/status wedge between the white-collar Newspaper Guild's reporters and the other unions' blue-collar employees. At least two reporters suggested serious bargaining differences, and the possibility that a strike by blue-collar unions would not be honored by Guild members:

I don't feel even remote solidarity with those guys. . . . My contract is fine. I don't want to be out of a job. I have no desire to go on strike and exhaust my savings. . . . I don't know whether I would cross the picket lines. It's a scary thought.

It's kind of hard to feel sympathy for them when you see the gross overmanning. . . . They make a lot of money, more than most reporters at the paper. I work 12 hours almost every day; I love this paper. It knows what it is and does what it does better than any other tabloid. It would be a terrible tragedy for the *Daily News* to go under because of 200 jobs.[20]

Under management's 60-plus-page package proposal, all of the items had to be accepted by the union. Newspaper Guild members would receive an approximate wage increase of 30 percent over three years. Reporters with five years' experience would have their weekly salaries increased from $929 to $1,110 in the first year; to $1,221 in the second year; and to $1,343 in the third year (an annual salary of nearly $70,000 by 1993). Also proposed were extending bereavement benefits, adding one-half day to the holiday schedule, and increasing mileage for personal car allowance from 22 cents to 26 cents a mile.

Guild officials contended that the raises amounted to 6, 9, and 9 percent when adjusted to reflect a company request for an increase in the work week to 37½ hours from 34½. Union calculations were based on the extra three hours being paid at a straight rather than overtime rate, which was paid for hours exceeding 34½.

Management also requested the elimination of severance pay, which had been calculated at two weeks' pay for each year served, as well as a potentially large cut in paid sick days. These conditions prompted Newspaper Guild president Barry Lipton to label management's wage proposal "a cruel hoax," since the *News* would save $23 million by eliminating members' accumulated severance pay and additional money by reduced contributions to pension and health and welfare funds. Lipton said management wanted to "put money in one pocket" while, at the same time removing it from "all the rest of our pockets."

This proposal also sought concessions from the reporters such as an increase in the workweek hours from 34½ to 37½, the right to hire temporary editorial employees for $5 an hour, and a "zipper clause" that would eliminate several of the practices not included in the labor agreement that had evolved over the years. Management wanted to include a general, all-encompassing management rights clause in the labor agreement, one, according to a reporter, that would give management power over benefits, job security, and severance, thereby converting the other labor agreement provisions into an "irrelevant footnote." Management further sought the elimination of the previously agreed-upon automatic collection of members' dues, an inflammatory concession as one Guild official explained:

It's not only ridiculous, it's an affront to any relationship between management and a labor organization. . . . It's tearing a contract to shreds. . . . If we don't get the dues checkoff, fuhgeddaboudit! It's like breaking the union.[21]

A day after management's proposal, the Guild voted 267–19 to authorize a strike if the union leadership could not obtain an adequate agreement at the bargaining table. Union and management officials did meet on March 30; however, management recessed talks shortly after 1 P.M. and indicated that "other commitments" precluded further talks on the day before the labor agreement was scheduled to expire. Lipton indicated that his Newspaper Guild was ready to engage in serious discussions, dialogue, and continued negotiations, and was stunned by management's refusal to meet and receive a new contract proposal from the union.

Other Guild negotiators and members also expressed frustration, anger, and doubt over management's bargaining style as the contract expiration date approached. One negotiator said Ballow tried to sound ominous during these sessions by making statements like, "I feel sorry for you guys." Some *News* reporters, once sympathetic to management, became more militant as negotiations floundered.

News unions and management focused their attention on outside sources instead of the bargaining table approximately two days before the labor agreements were about to expire.[22] The unions warned advertisers in a letter that their messages would not be read if the *News* was created, produced, and distributed with "scab" employees. They also planned an informational picket line April 2, 1990, at a Tribune Company reception for members of Congress at the Library of Congress. George McDonald was "jubilant" when *News* management canceled this reception and thanked AFL-CIO president Lane Kirkland as well as the presidents of several national unions, such as the Communications Workers of America, Newspaper Guild, and the Graphic Communications Union, for influencing the intended guests not to attend; McDonald maintained that union solidarity could defeat the "Goliaths" of Jim Hoge and the Tribune Company.

Management ran help-wanted ads in the classified sections of some New York City newspapers for 116 mailer jobs in the event of a strike, an action that indicated that the mailers union was the first to conduct a strike vote. *News* Vice President John Sloan indicated that jobs held by members of four other unions, including the Newspaper Guild, that authorized a strike might also be jeopardized because management regarded these actions as blatant threats and would respond by permanently replacing any employee who struck the *News*.

The advertisements for potential mailers' vacancies generated a large response from an estimated 2,000 to 4,000 applicants who showed up at the *News*'s 42d Street headquarters, an unmistakable message for union members if the labor agreements expired at midnight, March 30. Deborah Friedman, of the Kamber Group and the unions' spokesperson, described this event as a pathetic soup line out of the 1930s, where poor, unskilled, and unemployed applicants were recruited for management's bargaining power game.

This tactic also introduced another outside influence, the *News*'s competitors, through the use of collective bargaining advertisements for strike replacements, which were run in the *Daily News* and *New York Times,* as well as the *Amsterdam News,* an African-American weekly. Two major competitors, however, the *New York Post* and *Newsday,* did not run the ads. *Newsday*'s Senior Vice President of Marketing reasoned that his paper was "neutral" in the *News*'s labor dispute, and therefore could not print the *New*'s advertisement. John Sloan of the *News* angrily retorted that acceptance of the *News*'s advertisement did not equal endorsement of the *News*'s bargaining position and also suggested that any newspaper who refused this advertisement "should reexamine their so-called commitment to free speech and the First Amendment."

BARGAINING ACTIVITIES AFTER THE LABOR AGREEMENT EXPIRED

Peripheral bargaining continued after the March 31 labor agreement's expiration date. On April 9, *News* management withdrew its previous bargaining proposal with the News Guild, and notified its ten unions that their labor agreements were terminated. Charles Brumback also indicated during March that union bargaining concessions would not automatically translate into management's "major capital expenditure" of color printing presses, a decision that only would be made after one or "two years of significant profit growth."

George McDonald retorted that Brumback's remarks reflected a rare display of honesty and that James Hoge was nothing more than a slick figurehead whose buttons were pushed in Chicago. McDonald further contended that Brumback's remarks reflected management's broken promises in the 1987 labor-management negotiations at the *News* and an incredulous approach toward future technological investments:

Brumback took the profits meant to renovate the *Daily News* [in the 1987 negotiations] operations and distributed them among the other Tribune papers, which now boast state-of-the-art equipment and technology and modern, safe working environments. . . . The *News* is more than ever the abused stepchild of the Tribune Company.

Two years? [For management to determine interest in color presses] . . . It's not like you can shop for modern presses in a supermarket and pay for them at the express counter. With the time it takes to order new presses, it would probably be the next century before those presses could come on-line. The *Daily News* would be closed by then, and Brumback knows it.[23]

Union officials preferred to keep their members working instead of striking the *News.* Yet, they also planned a multifaceted boycott that would be first aimed at display advertisers, then at those who could advertise in the classified section, and finally at a campaign to persuade readers to boycott the paper. John Sloan countered that unions failed to realize that advertisers are "behind us 110 percent" because they identified with *News* management's right to run the business without union interference.

In May, union officials and members attempted two meetings with management officials away from the bargaining table. One Sunday morning, about 500 pressmen and drivers gathered outside what was thought to be Hoge's apartment building, waved banners, shouted slogans and tried to ring his doorbell (police stopped this latter effort). Finding themselves in the well-heeled Gramercy Park section of New York, some shouted, "We want brunch." All of these efforts were thwarted, however, when the visitors eventually realized that Hoge had moved.

New York and Chicago unionists converged on the Tribune Company shareholders' meeting May 3. In addition to union demonstrations outside the building, the meeting featured the announcement that Stanton R. Cook would step down in August as the Tribune Company's chief executive officer and publisher of the *Chicago Tribune.* George McDonald charged in the meeting that the company had reneged on Cook's 1987 "pledge" to build new printing facilities in exchange for union concessions and asserted that the two sides were "again in mortal conflict." Cook denied ever making the 1987 pledge and stressed the company's total commitment to the collective bargaining process.

Another development external to the bargaining table that occurred in May was the reactivation of the AFL-CIO Strategic Approaches Committee, which was chaired by Lynn Williams, president of the Steelworkers, and coordinated by AFL-CIO Secretary-Treasurer Tom Donahue. Committee members included union presidents Rich Trumka of the Mine Workers, William H. Wynn of the Food and Commercial Workers, John Sweeney of the Service Employees, Gerald W. McEntee of American Federation of State, County, and Municipal Employees, and George Korpias of the Machinists.

AFL-CIO head Lane Kirkland had formed this committee in 1986 and it had been since called into action nine times. In 1989, this committee coordinated efforts of all 90 AFL-CIO unions in support of employees at Pittston Coal, Eastern Airlines, and Musicians. The ten local unions involved in negotiations at the

News included units of five AFL-CIO affiliates – Graphic Communications, Newspaper Guild, Communication Workers, Electrical Workers, Machinists – and an unaffiliated local of drivers.

After strategy meetings, Lynn Williams held a press conference during which he stressed that the unions very much desired a settlement. He maintained that management was working from a familiar "script" that had never included good faith bargaining. The committee did announce, however, that employee input ("Save the *Daily News* Action Meetings") would be obtained through meetings held at four locations in New York within the week.

June witnessed virtually no union–management negotiation efforts at, or away from, the bargaining table. One possibly related event was an announcement by British media mogul Robert Maxwell that he intended to buy a U.S. newspaper valued "in the mid-hundreds of millions of dollars." Maxwell would not identify the newspaper, or even say that it was a daily.

Union officials turned their attention toward extending negotiations or at least preventing an impasse declarations/strike situation in the month of July. They thought that *News* management would declare a bargaining impasse and impose new work rules (reduced staffing levels, for example) no later than June 25. This management strategy would save money if employees continued to work without an agreement. A better scenario could occur for management if new working conditions were posted for traditionally militant unions like the pressmen or deliverers. Then the *News* could continue publishing with replacement employees while eliminating what it called "financially ruinous" labor agreements. Yet, John Sloan countered that the unions had a "miserable track record" in predicting an impasse since they had previously thought this event would occur on March 31, then sometime in April, then Memorial Day, then Father's Day.

The unions were wrong again as management declared no bargaining impasse in July 1990. This situation was partly due to an AFL-CIO advisement to the union negotiators to slow the negotiations on the ground that Robert Ballow was purportedly at the table "for the express purpose of not negotiating." Sloan agreed that the union's footdragging strategy had begun long ago. He cited detailed statistics that demonstrated numerous times the union negotiators had arrived late, took long lunch hours, or otherwise moved bargaining sessions at a glacial pace.

Management's deferred impasse resolution may have also been affected by two outside influences: the National Labor Relations Board's decision pertaining to Greyhound Lines, and involvement by state officials and agencies. Greyhound had ceased negotiating with its drivers and hired strike replacements. In May 1990, the NLRB filed a complaint that the company's actions constituted an unfair labor practice that, if upheld by the courts, could make Greyhound liable for $13 million in back pay for every month the strike continued.

Theodore Kheel noted how the Greyhound case could influence *News* management:

It's their duty under Federal labor law to bargain on wages, hours, and working conditions. . . . If they say starting tomorrow we're changing the delivery routes, so we'll have

68 fewer drivers, without having first bargained in good faith to impasse, then I think they would be committing an unfair labor practice. . . . The Tribune Company has to be concerned, principally in light of the Greyhound experience, that the NLRB might hold that any such action came without bargaining in good faith on specific items.[24]

Kheel's comments were likely more credible given the unfair labor practice charge pending against the Tribune Company (previously discussed in Chapter 1) in which management unlawfully bargained to impasse over a "zipper clause" with the pressmen's union.

A state board, mandated under a seldom-involved statute (Section 8805 of the New York Labor Law), could also become involved in the labor dispute, thereby thwarting possible management and/or union bargaining initiatives at the bargaining table. Under this procedure, a 60-day cooling-off period could be invoked that would make it difficult, if not impossible, for *News* management to declare a bargaining impasse over the summer, when low advertising revenues would make a strike strategically beneficial for management or at least less costly to disagree with the unions. City Labor Relations Commissioner Eric Schmertz strongly supported a board of inquiry because the potential dispute could adversely affect a legendary newspaper's existence, thousands of jobs, and New York City's economy.

Thomas Hartnett, Labor Commissioner for the State of New York, agreed with Schmertz, particularly after the chairman of the State Mediation Board certified that despite more than 100 negotiating sessions over six months, efforts toward a voluntary settlement were not successful. Hartnett appointed three "impartials"[25] to the board of inquiry, which had no legal authority to compel actions by either side. The chairman of the board hoped that management would be "full participants" because the panel's members were "assistors," not "intruders." Hartnett charged the board with investigating such issues as balancing management rights against employee rights in economic cutbacks, staffing levels, benefits, use of independent delivery contractors, and grievance procedures. Another issue to be investigated was whether the "denial of management's overall proposals (would) lead to the inevitable shutdown" of the newspaper.

Hartnett maintained that the board might be one of the only tools to preserve the future of the *Daily News* and could not imagine why any one would oppose this action. His attitude was reflected by union leaders, Governor Mario Cuomo, and Mayor David Dinkins, who said a board of inquiry was "a sensible way to help resolve this dispute."

News management did not share enthusiasm for this initiative, and their reaction no doubt reflected a Tribune Company statement made two days before Hartnett's announcement that quarterly operating profits from its newspaper division had plunged $27.1 million, "primarily due to operating losses at the *Daily News.*" John Sloan, moreover, dismissed the board as "a blatant intrusion on the collective bargaining process" and stressed that *News*'s management wanted to solve unresolved collective bargaining issues through face-to-face negotiations with the ten unions instead of involving an outside party. Sloan indicated that the company would likely appeal the board's creation to State Attorney General Robert Abrams, the National Labor Relations Board, and possibly the federal courts. Sloan also suggested that the union leaders' encouragement of board activity signaled their realization that a bargaining impasse had occurred. Therefore, management could legally impose unilateral working conditions. Sloan's remarks were countered by Michael Alvino, who maintained that an impasse could not be reached if previous negotiations had not occurred.

Controversy continued even before the board established an informal meeting on July 30. The *News* had run an editorial in its paper on the previous day protesting Governor Mario Cuomo's role in establishing an unnecessary board. The editorial charged that the appointment of the board was "wired from the top" as a "cynical political move by a potential presidential candidate to curry favor with national labor leaders." Cuomo responded that the "hysterical" editorial was a management ploy to avoid looking objectively at the issues.

Theodore Kheel also reacted to the editorial when he requested editorial space to counter management's editorial; however, Sloan suggested that Kheel, along with other *News* readers, were invited to comment on editorials in letters to the editor. Kheel responded that he would file an unfair labor practice charge with the National Labor Relations Board if unions were not given suitable newspaper space for their response.

The State Mediation Board's first formal hearing session date, scheduled for August 6, was precluded by a suit filed by the *News* management that contended that the board's activity was in direct conflict with national labor policy favoring free and voluntary negotiations and was also preempted by the National Labor Relations Act. Management contended, moreover, that a final report issued by the board of inquiry would "exert governmental and public pressure on the *Daily News* and the unions in an undue and unwarranted attempt to coerce or otherwise improperly influence a resolution of the labor disputes and negotiations."

George McDonald of the Allied Printing Trades Council indicated that he was not surprised by the lawsuit, which he thought represented an attempt by management to avoid accountability for improprieties committed against the people of New York and their own employees. Hartnett responded to management's lawsuit by directing the board to delay the session a week pending the outcome of an August 10 hearing in U.S. District Court.

During the hearing, a lawyer for the *News* stressed that the board

destroys the entire process of collective bargaining. . . . It is like a power game. All of a sudden we are having to lay our cards on the table. There is no negotiation anymore.[26]

A representative for New York state countered that the board could not threaten negotiations as neither side was obliged to act on its recommendations, which were made to encourage a settlement instead of mandating a change.

Judge Kenneth Conboy delivered an 18-page decision that enjoined the New

York State Board of Inquiry from continuing its operations. Conboy's rationale also stressed the dangers of peripheral bargaining on the negotiations process. He said an inquiry, even though separate from negotiations, would "destroy any atmosphere of frank and open discussions" and force the *News* to reveal its bargaining "goals and strategies, tactics, and settlement points." In fact, Conboy said, "This kind of public truth-finding process will lead to assessment of blame," as a final report by the board would "put broad public pressure on the parties to reach the particular agreement advocated by the board."[27]

Conboy's decision was echoed by the National Labor Relations Board, which sought to enjoin the State of New York and the State Labor Department permanently from investigating the current collective bargaining situation at the *News*. The NLRB maintained in its motion that such scrutiny of labor negotiations was the "exclusive jurisdiction of the National Labor Relations Board."

Two other collective bargaining developments also occurred in July. Alvino and the drivers' union wrestled with management's insistence that it had the right to sell some 1,354 delivery routes. Management wanted to give its 700 drivers the first chance to buy "lucrative" routes before they were sold to outsiders. Alvino resisted this divide and conquer tactic because he was not interested in making a few drivers rich at the expense of the majority. Adding to the drivers' uncertain, tense situation was the addition of more than 40 potential replacement employees, mostly drivers who had been hired in June.

On July 24, labor leaders announced an "all-fronts boycott" against the *News*. McDonald stressed this action was necessary because the *Daily News* and the Tribune Company represented the "enemy." The announcement came less than a week after unions had begun mailing thousands of "informational" letters to advertisers that suggested a boycott possibility: "Because you support the *Daily News* with your advertising, you are directly involved in the bitter labor dispute that now exists at the paper."[28] However, no specific details regarding how or when the boycott would emerge were given at this announcement. Sloan maintained that the *News* management was confident that New Yorkers would overwhelmingly reject the "misguided" attempt to harm the operations of their hometown newspaper.

At least one union advisor was also concerned about community reaction and feared that a boycott or a badly timed one could hurt the unions' cause by alienating readers. Some union leaders thought the *News* would either not be harmed by a summer boycott or be encouraged to take a strike during this time period when advertising was normally slack and they could most easily weather the potential advertising losses. There was also some union sentiment that a "successful" boycott could backfire — play into the paper's already shaky economic base and alleged strategy of closing or selling the newspaper.

NOTES

1. James Warren, "Daily News, Unions Near A Showdown," *Chicago Tribune,* March 26, 1990, sec. 4, p. 4.

2. Howard Kurtz, "Showdown at the Daily News," *Washington Post,* February 24, 1990, C-1 and C-5.

3. David E. Pitt, "200 Contract Words Stall News Talk," *New York Times,* December 4, 1990, B-6.

4. Jonathan A. Bennett, "Daily Dangers at The Daily News," *Business and Society Review* 73 (Spring 1990): 61.

5. Thomas B. Rosenstiel, "Woes of N.Y. Daily News Go Way Beyond Current Strike," *Los Angeles Times,* November 14, 1990, D-1 and D-5.

6. "Right To Bargain Is Focus of New York Daily News Fight," Bureau of National Affairs, Inc., *Daily Labor Report* 198 (October 12, 1990): C-4.

7. Edward Klein, "Front-Page Drama," *Vanity Fair,* October 1989, 265.

8. Edwin Diamond, "The Incredible Shrinking Newspaper," *New York,* December 3, 1990, 41.

9. "Printing Pressmen's President Issues Statement," PR Newswire, January 25, 1990. Dialog File 613, item 0237334–NY077.

10. "Daily News Unions Ask Police Commissioner Brown for Protection from Chicago Goon Squads," PR Newswire, February 8, 1990. Dialog File 613, item 0241149–NYTH004.

11. "Allied Printing Trades Union Issues Statement," PR Newswire, March 1, 1990. Dialog File 613, item 0247261–NY080.

12. Don Singleton, "New York Forum About the News-II. The Strikers Won Weeks Ago," *Newsday,* March 15, 1991. Dialog File 638, item 060787228.

13. Pete Hamill, "They Killed the News Today, Oh Boy," *Esquire,* February 1991, 34.

14. "Daily News Unions."

15. Patrick M. Reilly, "EXTRA! EXTRA!: How Daily News Spent Months and $24 Million Preparing for A Strike," *Wall Street Journal,* November 2, 1990, A-8.

16. Ibid.

17. "Union Group Retains Detroit Labor Lawyer to Coordinate Strategies in Daily News Dispute," Bureau of National Affairs, Inc., *Daily Labor Report* 121 (June 22, 1990): A-11.

18. Congress, Senate Committee on Labor and Human Resources, *New York Daily News Strike and Permanent Replacements:* Hearing Before the Subcommittee on Labor, One Hundred First Cong., December 11, 1990, 20.

19. Ibid., 21.

20. Kurtz, "Showdown at the Daily News," C-1.

21. Ibid.

22. The *News's* unions did hold a joint membership meeting on March 25, 1990, so that employees could ask questions and hear updates from the ten presidents of the Allied Printing Trades Council (APTC) of Greater New York. While not focusing on a completely "outside" source, this action nonetheless conforms to the peripheral bargaining model as it diverted earnest bargaining efforts between the union and management negotiators. "Allied Printing Trades Members Attend Membership Meeting," PR Newswire, March 23, 1990. Dialog File 613, item 0253891–NY062.

23. "Union President Thanks Tribune CEO for 'Finally Speaking the Truth,' " PR Newswire, April 27, 1990. Dialog File 613, item 0263675–NY053.

24. David E. Pitt, "Unions Loath to Strike Daily News," *New York Times,* July 10, 1990, B-4.

25. The creation of the board of inquiry had occurred only eight times in the past 49 years, most recently during a 1973 cemetery workers' strike. The members of the board

were Martin F. Schinman, chairman and a lawyer/arbitrator; Fred L. Denson, also a lawyer/arbitrator; and Thomas F. Carey, a professor emeritus of collective bargaining at the City College of New York.

26. "Judge Cites Doubts on Panel Examining Talks at Daily News," *New York Times,* August 11, 1990, 28; see also "Federal District Court Hears Arguments on Petition to Halt Daily News Inquiry," Bureau of National Affairs, Inc., *Daily Labor Report* 156 (August 13, 1990): A-7 and A-8.

27. Robert D. McFadden, "Judge Bars Inquiry in Daily News Labor Tally," *New York Times,* August 12, 1990, 35.

28. David E. Pitt, "Unions Prepare Boycott Against the Daily News," *New York Times,* July 25, 1990, B-2.

3

"The Battle of Wounded Knee": Antecedents and Aftermath

Two peripheral bargaining developments occurred in September 1990: (1) a rather quickly formulated and implemented labor agreement negotiated with the *New York Post* that featured substantial union concessions; and (2) a National Labor Relations Board unfair labor practice decision pertaining to the 1985 *Chicago Tribune* strike. Both of these situations should have influenced the parties at the *Daily News* to resolve their differences at the bargaining table; no related efforts were forthcoming, however, which likely prompted the unions to engage the larger community in a consumer boycott.

The initial absence of traditional bargaining assumptions and behavior extended into October was heightened by a confrontation between a supervisor and a union employee. This incident, labeled the "Battle of Wounded Knee," precipitated a strike of nine unions at the *News*.

PERIPHERAL BARGAINING BEFORE OCTOBER 25

Concession Discussions at the *New York Post*

In early September, Peter Kalikow, owner of the *New York Post,* indicated that he needed $18.5 million in wage and benefit concessions from its nine unions by September 14 or the paper would cease publication. Kalikow expected that management could reduce its overhead costs by $7 million for the year, an estimate punctuated by his arranging the resignation of Valerie Salembier, who was president of the *Post.*[1] Kalikow further maintained that these combined savings would enable the paper to reach his firmly insisted-upon goal of breaking even since the 1990 estimated *Post* revenues of $180 million were about $27 million below expenses. Kalikow indicated a willingness to operate the paper indefinitely without a profit; however, he would no longer subsidize the operation. The $27 million gap must be filled, or the paper would be closed as Kalikow did not regard movement from losing $20 million to $5 million a "victory." Unions would receive a stake in the paper's ownership and a seat on the board if they agreed to the concessions.

Unions were basically receptive to Kalikow's concerns, although some members noted that Kalikow's threat to close the *Post* came quickly after the Board of Estimate enabled him to build an apartment complex on his office site, which had previously been designated as a landmark. Union members' lukewarm to positive reaction was somewhat surprising given the hostility that characterized labor–management negotiations at the *News*. They did not regard Mr. Kalikow's request as a bluff. Some, if not all of them, knew that New York City could not support more than two daily newspapers and realized that the *Post*'s continued existence "was due to a wealthy individual's whim." Kalikow was regarded as a "White Knight" after spending some $120 million (and out-of-pocket costs of $93 million) on the financially troubled *Post* since having acquired it from Rupert Murdoch in 1988.[2] A spokesperson for the unions noted:

We don't think they are fooling; they're in trouble. . . . They are upfront management; they are not blaming the unions but are saying it's because of recession and bad newspaper industry conditions generally. . . . The *Post* has good relations with the unions in contrast to management at the *News,* which is out to kill the unions, period.[3]

Kalikow reinforced this attitude by opening the paper's ledger books to the union's accounting firm, Peat, Marwick, and Mitchell. The accountants found that the owner's claims were "substantially true," according to George McDonald; moreover, documents provided to the unions by Kalikow estimated 1990's advertising revenues at $13 million less than the comparable 1988 total.

Union leaders also realized that negotiations at the *Post* could have both a positive and negative impact on similar activities at the *News*. A successfully attained labor agreement at the *Post* might generate public opinion to pressure *News* management to drop an insistence on a general management-rights clause, which was not a consideration at the *Post*.

If the unions were unable to agree on bargaining concessions, however, the *News* would most likely exploit this lack of solidarity at its negotiations. This situation would be even more explosive if one union effectively threw all other union members out of work because it rejected *Post* management's requested bargaining concessions.

McDonald and the other unions entered negotiations at the *Post* with these realizations and the top priority of saving jobs for their members and families. He noted that the unions would be negotiating separately on whether to focus more on reducing wages or eliminating jobs, but there would be cross-checking between the unions to keep everybody informed and help each other. Round-the-clock negotiations were scheduled for September 11, three days before management's imposed deadline. The mailers' union, headed by McDonald, reached a settlement with management two days after negotiations had begun, and some of the smaller unions were close to an agreement at this time, but rather serious obstacles remained for two employee groups:

1. drivers who were primarily concerned about the large amount ($8.5 million) of concessions requested of them; and
2. pressmen who were concerned that reductions in staffing for the presses to achieve $2.7 million in savings would change future negotiations with the *News* and *Times,* which have similar presses.

These unions held out to the last minute but eventually agreed to losses of overtime and shortened work weeks in addition to layoffs (95 of the 263 drivers and 40 of the 80 pressmen). The *Post* gave these and other unions settling with the paper 20 percent equity (employee stock ownership plan) in its operations including its building and the land underneath it. Also included was a representative seat on the board of directors.

News advertising and clerical employees were also concerned about *Post* management's insistence that most of the requested $5 million in concessions come from significant wage reductions instead of layoffs. Management contended that efficient operations depend on retaining the younger and lower-paid employees, whom a layoff would remove. The Newspaper Guild was asked to accept a four-day week (in effect a 20 percent pay cut) and layoffs of 43 of 452 members. This proposal raised potential Newspaper Guild membership differences due to members' varied jobs classifications and related working conditions preferences. Editors and reporters, unlike secretaries and clerks also represented by the union, could more likely recover the lost wages through other work options.

Tensions among Guild members were further increased through two actions taken by the *Daily News* during the *Post's* bargaining sessions. The *News* ran a story on September 16 under the headline "Drivers Post Sweet Deal," which indicated that members of the drivers' union at the *Post* would receive "$100-a-week raises" instead of a pay cut. Both Kalikow and Michael Alvino of the Newspaper and Mail Deliverers' Union of New York characterized the article as inflammatory and misleading. They indicated that from 90 to 96 of the paper's 263 drivers would be laid off; moreover, those remaining would no longer receive guaranteed overtime, which averaged ten hours a week, and other benefits. The $100-a-week increase in base pay would, in view of these concessions unmentioned by the *News,* represent a decrease in take-home pay for the drivers. *News* management responded that the paper was reporting what information it had available; moreover, it ran an editorial in the same edition expressing hope that the *Post* would carry on.

The *News* also notified the Newspaper Guild that it would seek any concessions granted to the *Post* through a portion of the Guild contract known as a "me-too" or "most-favored-nation" clause. The *New York Times* did not have this labor agreement provision but also announced that it would also seek any concessions granted to the *Post* to the extent they were created by overall economic conditions. Kalikow sharply responded to these efforts, contending that the *News* and the *Times* were trying to "ride on the back" of the *Post's* negotiations and may have broken the law with their efforts. Union advisor Theodore Kheel agreed with Kalikow, because the two newspapers appeared to have acted in concert to scuttle the *Post's* negotiations, thereby incurring possible criminal and civil liabilities under the Sherman Antitrust Act. Newspaper Guild President Barry Lipton also maintained that *News* management terminated its labor agreements with the union, thereby making any "me-too" claim irrelevant.

Lipton noted the *Post's* layoff/wage offer posed a hardship to the members but also realized that the newspaper would shut down and its 900 employees would lose their jobs if the contract were rejected. Lipton's qualified approval of the labor agreement was not shared by the Newspaper Guild's negotiating committee, which rejected the proposal by a 7–3 vote.

After this vote, Kalikow headed to a makeshift press room at the negotiations site to indicate the paper's closure. But union leaders persuaded Kalikow to defer his announcement and continue negotiations, particularly since New York Mayor David Dinkins had arrived to lend his efforts. Dinkins was credited with getting the final decision delayed until the membership was able to vote three days later. Severance pay, an issue not featured in the concession discussions, represented a major impediment in the members' acceptance decision. Long-term Guild members would receive several years severance pay if the *Post* ceased operations; however, that contractual arrangement expired in March 1991. The *Post* was also required to pay its employees 60 days' pay plus other severance arrangements specified in the labor agreement if it closed its operations. Conversely, these arrangements might have been reduced, even eliminated, if the *Post* continued operations, a feat many members thought would be short-lived. Kalikow made a last-minute proposal that any employee could receive the 60 days termination fee if he or she resigned within a 24-hour period and would receive their contractual severance pay arrangements regardless of their resignation intention. This condition swung a predicted close union vote on concessions to 242 votes in favor and 45 against. It also resulted in roughly one third or 79 of the *Post* news staff resigning from the paper.

News management was not publicly impressed with the *Post's* settlement. Charles Brumback, CEO of the Tribune Company, for example, indicated that he consistently refused to participate in a joint operating agreement (JOA) having similar, even identical, work rules for unions at both newspapers because he found it antiquated. Brumback thought the solutions to labor–management problems were modifications in current work practices. Another *News* executive indicated the *Post's* labor–management approach represented the traditional Band-Aid method where unions gave some concessions but still retained control, and that management would return in a few months for more concessions. James Hoge, publisher of the *News,* noted that the *Post* is much smaller than the *News* and that its settlement would not be applicable to the *News* because it generated no profits for the company to invest in itself; therefore, it offered no future.

Another NLRB Decision Against The Tribune Company

On September 21, 1990, an Administrative Law Judge (ALJ) issued a decision against the Chicago Tribune Company for actions taken against the Chicago Mailers' Union Local No. 2 pertaining to the 1985 strike. Management's violations of the National Labor Relations Act did not completely parallel circumstances in the 1990 negotiations; therefore, a summary of these efforts and excerpts from the ALJ's remedy will suffice.

Management was found guilty of (1) refusing to sign the collective bargaining agreement it reached with the union; (2) not providing names of permanent strike replacements to the union; (3) withdrawing recognition from Local 2; (4) refusing to give proper offers of reinstatement to strikers for vacancies that arose in December 1989; (5) withholding payroll information (employee names) from the union; and (6) paying replacement employees less than the rate provided in the July 27, 1989 contract ($10.31 an hour instead of the $14.89 rate specified in the labor agreement). The ALJ's decision in part ordered the company to sign and implement the terms of the July 27, 1987 collective bargaining agreement and reinstate strikers with back pay from December 1989.

Union officials of Mailers Local 2 figured the Tribune Company would have to pay at least $10 million or more under the ALJ's decision (upheld by the National Labor Relations Board, July 15, 1991) although the Tribune Company indicated that it would appeal the ruling. A settlement was eventually negotiated between Tribune Company management on this NLRB decision, another NLRB decision involving the pressmen (discussed in Chapter 1) and a federal lawsuit filed by the printers. Management agreed to rehire 63 of 250 union printers and paid $8.6 million to the rest of the union members who lost their jobs.

Therefore, management should have realized the economic costs of peripheral bargaining–NLRB remedies and the attendant legal/administrative costs that could approach, if not exceed, those contained in a collective bargaining settlement. Instead management continued their previously formulated bargaining approach in the 1990 labor–management dispute at the *News*. Also, around the time of the NLRB's decision, *News* management demoted all driver-foremen, giving them the option of taking a pay cut and returning to the driver ranks or leaving the bargaining unit to become management. None elected to join management.

Perhaps management viewed its continued bargaining efforts to obtain concessions from the unions worth risking a subsequent unfair labor practice charge because of urgent financial pressures. The Tribune Company's third-quarter net income dropped 39 percent ($38.2 million in 1990 compared to $62.7 million in 1989). Though the *Chicago Tribune*'s results were said to have been positive, operating profits for the newspaper group were down 15 percent, a situation blamed in large part on higher operating losses at the *Daily News*.

Around the time of this disclosure, management announced the hiring of Lisa Robinson, a former news reporter and public relations professional who had previously worked for GPU Nuclear Corporation, owners of the Three Mile Island nuclear power plant, site of the nation's worst nuclear power accident.

Operationalizing Boycott Activity

In the first week of September, nine out of the ten unions at the *Daily News* sent letters to 350 display advertisers and advertising agencies indicating that the 1.3 million union members in New York City would decline to buy from stores that continued to fund the *News's* antilabor actions through their advertising dollars. Unions also indicated they would target selected letter recipients who continued their advertising in the *News* and start handbilling their potential customers with "Do not patronize" leaflets.

The boycott was not endorsed by the New York Typographical Union No. 6; also, some 90 members of the Newspaper Guild opposed the boycott, contending it represented a mistaken bargaining tactic. Barry Lipton encouraged the boycott because he believed it would put immediate economic pressure on management to negotiate while not hurting the paper irreparably. Mike Alvino, president of the Mail Deliverers' Union, indicated that the unions would continue to press for compromise settlements with management, who were responsible for the newspaper's future. John Sloan predictably maintained the unions' boycott would have no effect on labor–management negotiations at the *News* and be "destined for failure." He noted that the unions did not realize that their boycott would be aimed at business executives, who have the same objectives as *News* management; namely, "to run our business ourselves."

The boycott had ineffective results for the next two weeks when the campaign was officially announced in a September 25 news conference. Also announced at this time was the formation of a Committee to Boycott for Justice at the *Daily News,* a group comprised of state and national union officers, which was in turn staffed in part by three AFL-CIO field representatives provided by the AFL-CIO Strategic Approaches Committee. A publicity campaign was also implemented at the time of the boycott. It included 200 bus signs and 16 billboards emblazoned: "The Daily News Is Bad News for Its Workers."

"THE BATTLE OF WOUNDED KNEE"

The nonproductive bargaining goals and preparation tactics that have been previously discussed and the attendant tensions between unions and *News* management crystallized at 2:00 A.M. on Thursday, October 25, 1990 in a much-disputed incident. Dominic Proce, a nonunion supervisor at the *News* Brooklyn printing plant, told employee Gary Kalinich to stand as he was working at a machine that bundled newspapers. Kalinich had worked as a driver at the *News* for 23 years and, by his account, had undergone a rather significant shift in his workplace attitudes. Initially he had been deeply concerned about the months of tense peripheral bargaining tactics employed by management–union officials:

Then, I came to terms with it. . . . I can walk around working myself up into an ulcer, getting gray hair and high blood pressure over it, or I can just not care anymore. That's the hard part about it: I used to care.[4]

Kalinich was then responsible for slapping a cover sheet every 15 seconds or so on a stack of newspapers that rolled to the bailer. These sheets were coded to inform drivers where the bundles should be delivered. Kalinich had been given this assignment because of torn knee ligaments injured when he tripped over some plastic bailing wire in the back of his truck the previous June. He had returned to work in September with a doctor's note recommending light duty, such as attending the conveyor belt. Kalinich informed the supervisor that the work he did could only be performed while sitting down and that his injury prevented him from standing.

Most of the other details concerning this event remained contested. Management, for example, later contended that Kalinich was sitting with his back toward the bailing machine and/or sitting at a lunch table reading a newspaper. Moreover, claimed management, the employee was not paying attention to the operation where the cover sheets were going awry (falling off the belt or getting crumpled) because the machine was jamming up with newspaper bundles. Therefore Kalinich was twice ordered to resolve the problem — to stand up, place the covers correctly, and remove the jammed bundles. A *News* spokesperson also indicated that the employee had been repeatedly warned by management months before this incident to stand at his work station.

Kalinich later stated that the supervisor, Proce, had created shop floor incidents in the past and had also provoked this one. Moreover, according to one union official, Kalinich had never been previously disciplined for his work performance. Kalinich then sought advice from Seymour Goldstein, a business agent for the drivers. Goldstein had no authority in this matter but told Kalinich to remain seated at his workplace.

Supervisor Proce then suspended Kalinich for insubordination because he had not been authorized to sit on the job and had rejected previous warnings. Goldstein was then ordered out of the plant for countermanding the supervisor's orders. What happened next was also disputed. Union officials and Kalinich contend that some 30 to 34 nearby drivers quickly followed Goldstein out of the plant to discuss the incident further and were denied reentry because management feared possible sabotage of machines. The officials later said *News* supervisors told the other 230 drivers to leave the building. Management contended that 230 drivers walked off the job with Goldstein in an illegal work stoppage and were followed by the other 30 drivers soon afterward. Kalinich was surprised that other employees supported his job action since he claimed that three quarters of the unions' membership did not know who he was even though he had worked at the operation for more than two decades. He was, however, pleased that the impasse had "finally come to a head," since he thought management's previous bargaining approach amounted to "union busting."

When all of the drivers were out of the plant, *News* management asked another business agent, Mike Diana, if he could provide individuals to replace those not on the job. This question was necessary under law and under the expired labor agreements. Diana said that he could not furnish the number of individuals required, thereby enabling the *News* to call in replacements.

Some union leaders were unhappy with Goldstein and Diana for their contributions to this predicament. George McDonald criticized Goldstein for not filing a grievance protesting Kalinich's suspension and then insuring that Kalinich and the other employees remain in the facility. Others said that Diana should have agreed to provide substitutes, thereby keeping nonunion employees out of the plant. Another union official contended that the drivers "screwed up twice," by walking out in the first place, then using "their muscle instead of their brains when they threw up picket lines rather than fight the firings in court." One observer further contends that the sudden, imprecise nature of the strike reflected heated disagreement within the drivers' union over whether to strike or to continue working as negotiations lagged. Alvino was part of a moderate wing in the drivers' union that discouraged strikes and was willing to make major concessions on drivers' staffing.

Within an hour after the discussion with Diana, a bus carrying 14 strike replacements arrived at the plant. The suddenness of this action led many unionized employees to believe that management provoked the incident to achieve its long-denied goal of publishing with a nonunion work force. One union official commented that "If I had a topless dancer, I couldn't get twenty guys together in twenty minutes."[5] Angry drivers threw rocks at the bus, which broke the windshield. They also smashed the side-view mirrors and dented the bus's sides and doors with trash cans and baseball bats. The bus did not get through although management made some videotapes of some of the violence that included the firebombing of four delivery trucks and slashed tires and/or punctured radiators on 40 more vehicles. Police surrounded the plant by 5:00 A.M. so that a second bus carrying replacements could enter the facility by 7:30 A.M., and the first truckloads of papers could leave with a police escort an hour later. *News* spokesperson Lisa Robinson indicated that the company was legally justified in hiring replacements and that police were needed to stop the "horrifying" violence and protect the employees' safety. John Sloan, the *News* vice president for labor relations, moreover found it unfortunate that the union-provoked strike occurred at a time "when we were involved in the collective bargaining process to resolve our differences."

George McDonald tried a twofold approach toward resolving the situation. He first tried contacting Charles Brumback, CEO of the Tribune Company, to offer him a settlement similar to that reached at the *New York Post* to settle the dispute, but Brumback did not return the call. Second, McDonald and other union leaders also requested a meeting with *News* management, which was held Thursday at midafternoon. McDonald, Alvino, and Kheel represented the unions at this meeting, which was also attended by Edward Gold, director of labor relations for the *News,* and Bud Johnson of the King and Ballow law firm.

Gold informed the union participants that 60 employees had been offered and had accepted permanent replacement jobs. These individuals would replace the 60 drivers with the lowest seniority. Moreover, 200 of the drivers who walked out in Brooklyn would return to work their Friday night shift although the other 60 would not be reinstated.

McDonald indicated that this situation was the most "devastating" of his 34 years of experience in labor relations but that the only alternative was to "pull the plug" — that is, have all ten unions strike the *News:*

I pleaded with them to let the people go back. I said go to grievance, go to arbitration, file for damages for what happened last night. But please don't let this thing spread. All we wanted to do is get the genie back in the bottle.

But they were adamant. They refused to say anything but that these guys were fired and permanently replaced. That's a declaration of war. When you say that there's no way they can get their jobs back. There's no way the unions can reach a collective bargaining agreement. That's the end of the game. There's no way out.[6]

McDonald further indicated that in this "war" the union had to shut down the *News* so that Chicago Tribune executives would realize that the newspaper could not operate with current *News* management and that other management participants needed to return to the bargaining table. Kheel agreed with McDonald that Gold's summary of management's actions made this dispute "unsettleable" and noted that the new permanent replacements would acquire a superior employment status over the strikers, who included some 40-year veterans, and that no union leader could urge members to return to work when 60 or more of them would be "executed."

Michael Alvino, the remaining union participant at the meeting, suggested that the union did not call a strike over the Kalinich/Proce dispute. He charged management with orchestrating the "wounded knee" incident and then locking out employees because no one could come up with buses and strike replacements within an hour without a previously established objective and strategy. A rival publisher agreed with Alvino at least to the extent that this situation placed Charles Brumback's Tribune Company in a "win-win" situation — either publishing a nonunion paper with a smaller payroll or folding operations with few related expenses. Either scenario should result in increased prices for Tribune stock.

In a letter to Mayor David Dinkins, James Hoge indicated that the drivers' job action was caused by "an internal struggle within the drivers' union," not by management's desire to provoke the confrontation. Hoge maintained that an out-of-power faction within the union "manipulated a minor incident to precipitate a strike by 2,400 union workers." Hoge further alleged the feud was between Douglas LaChance, who was president of the drivers' union during the 1978 strike at the *News,* and Alvino, who had won a close election to become president some 16 months before the current job action. Alvino had testified under immunity at a federal trial of LaChance and indicated he was a conduit for payoffs to LaChance from *News* wholesalers who wanted to lay off drivers. LaChance had later been sentenced for corruption and was subsequently employed as a driver at the time of the incident. Hoge at least implied that Seymour Goldstein, who had been involved in the "wounded knee" incident and another altercation six weeks prior at the *News's* Garden City, New Jersey facility, was working on behalf of LaChance's rumored political comeback in the drivers' union. Alvino countered that no current bad blood existed between himself and LaChance and that the strike was "premeditated by the *News,* pure and simple."

Allocation of blame notwithstanding, unions held the faint hope that management's threat to permanently replace 60 employees would evaporate if all the drivers reported to work at 9:00 P.M. Thursday, October 25. Theodore Kheel also attempted to enlist external support from Governor Cuomo and Mayor Dinkins for this situation, but neither political figure returned his call in time. Management held firm to its position, and Alvino responded 47 minutes later—nearly 20 hours after the "wounded knee" incident—that his union was officially involved in an unfair labor practice strike. Alvino brought external considerations into his strike decision: "This is New York City. . . . It's a union town—and the *Daily News* right now is attacking our union, bringing in these hired guns from out of town to take jobs away from my men."[7]

Instead of urging resolution of labor–management differences at the bargaining table, *News* management responded in a similar peripheral fashion. John Sloan regarded the strike as "unfortunate" but indicated that New Yorkers believed in the *News,* thereby enabling the newspaper to survive, prosper, and grow.

THE STRIKE'S FIRST DAYS

Involvement of Other *News* Unions in the Strike

Soon after the drivers' strike decision, Jack Kennedy, president of the pressmen's union, announced that *News* management had caused his organization to join the drivers in an unfair labor practice strike. Six more unions joined the strike Thursday night, reflecting a most dire, irreversible situation according to George McDonald:

This isn't something that can heal. . . . New York will have to lose another paper. We have bent over backwards but management doesn't want to try.[8]

Picket lines were established at the paper's Manhattan building and outside its three printing plants. This development's suddenness did surprise some; for example, one craft union official found his organization on the picket line; "and I'm not even sure how we got there." However, one veteran reporter, who had worked on four New York dailies, maintained that management's quick and firm decision to permanently replace some of the drivers with strike replacements ensured this coordinated effort by *News* unions:

It was this death sentence that brought the reluctant unions into the street. New York has seen many strikes, some long and bitter, but no one could recall an oath by management never to rehire the strikers.[9]

Composing room employees, represented by the International Typographical Union, Local 6, crossed the picket lines because of lifetime employment contracts guaranteed by a 1973 labor agreement when the unions agreed to let newspapers switch from hot-lead type to computer typesetting. Newspaper Guild of New York Local 3 was the last union to make a strike decision, although it indicated it would honor the picket lines of other unions, which were established Thursday, October 25. The Newspaper Guild, unlike the other unions, had not been accused by management of protecting unneeded jobs although the union in April gave union leaders the right to authorize a strike.

After a raucous two-hour meeting, midafternoon Friday, October 26, the 775-member Newspaper Guild, representing editorial, advertising, and circulation employees, voted to join the other eight unions in strike. Barry Lipton, president of the Guild since 1985, indicated this action was due to management's illegal raising of the permanent replacement of an unspecified number of his members and contended the strike would bring the newspaper "to its knees." This decision was no doubt reinforced when editorial employees arriving at the paper's headquarters Friday morning were surprised to discover that card-keys they had used to enter their offices were no longer valid. But replacement editorial employees — with the correct card-keys — were already performing assignments in the city room.

Barry Lipton might have differed from previous Newspaper Guild presidents when he encouraged cooperation instead of rivalry with other union leaders in the delivery and production departments. He viewed the addition of some new nonunion editorial employees as well as the changed locks on Guild members' workplaces as evidence that *News* management, along with its "union-busting" attorneys, had engineered the strike, and he thought that most of his members were too intelligent to comply with management's return-to-work ploy designed to divide the union. Lipton's attitude was seconded by one union member, who indicated that *News* management had declared an all-out war on the unions, seeking total capitulation instead of negotiation.

Some other Guild members expressed grudging support of the strike. Their beliefs, sampled below, suggest that Guild members' strike support might be indecisive and ephemeral:

I hate the way we are being treated . . . But the idea of going to bed knowing that I lost my job because some guy wouldn't stand up just seems ridiculous.

[Unions and management] are both scum. . . . Both my parents are Democrats; we listened to Pete Seeger. [Crossing the picket line is] . . . just a terrible thing to do.

My whole adult life I have worked for this newspaper, and I really loved it. The *Daily News* is dead. It's just a matter of time. People at the Guild meeting had this "We'll get them" attitude. They don't seem to see that the only ones who will get hurt are themselves. . . . Watching them run to the picket line, it just seemed ironic, like seeing people march to the gallows.[10]

On one hand, I think crossing the picket line is a completely reprehensible thing to do. . . . On the other hand, I think the unions have made a major mistake. We've walked into the hands of management.[11]

This is a little like Vietnam. . . . You wonder why we're here and what we're fighting for and can we win. But to me there is no question I have to be here picketing. Life is more than about a paycheck. I have a moral responsibility to be here, to do the right thing.[12]

Most of us in there [the strike vote meeting] are thinking the *News* is dead in the water whether we go back or not. That's almost irrelevant; what matters now is some dignity.[13]

Concerns During the Strike's First Weekend

News management dismissed most of its 2,400 unionized employees Friday, October 26, and then struggled to publish and distribute the newspaper with mostly untrained and edgy replacements. An employee during this time period was surprised that the months of prestrike preparations still produced an "amateurish managerial organization," one where there "were more chiefs than Indians." Some of these individuals had been already hired at the time of the strike while others were being flown in from all over the country. Many of these individuals, particularly replacement pressmen and drivers, were not told the duration of their assignments. They were also not permitted to leave the facility and instead were offered three-hour naps on mattresses and cots provided, as well as sandwiches and junk food. Supervisors also distributed a quickly dwindling supply of fresh underwear, disposable razors, and cigarettes.

As the weekend progressed, many of the replacements were experiencing both "cabin fever" and the fear that the strikers shouting threats and obscenities outside would eventually storm the building.[14] One interview with a replacement pressman explained why he and possibly others accepted these working conditions:

There are a lot of hungry boys out here, including me. If they don't want to work for a thousand dollars a week, I will. . . . They are killing the goose that laid the golden egg.[15]

This employee knew that his decision could result in physical harm, but he already regarded his life at the *News* or elsewhere as a daily gamble because he lived in Brooklyn, New York.

Strike replacements drove trucks containing newspapers out of the Brooklyn and Kearny, New Jersey plants at 1:15 A.M. Saturday. The trucks were escorted by a dozen automobiles and were pursued by striking employees. During this time, four strikers had been arrested for reckless endangerment and criminal possession of either dangerous instruments (rocks, baseball bats, and bottles, for example), or explosive devices such as M80 firecrackers. Some strikers were involved in other disruptions such as throwing rocks and eggs at buses transporting strike replacements to the Brooklyn plant at the start of Friday's night shift, shouting such epithets as "scab, scab," and "your wife should get cancer." John Sloan, *News* vice president for labor relations, said that many of these violent, vandalistic occurrences were "deplorable" and "purposeful criminal acts."

Also, 75 strikers snarled traffic when they sat down in the middle of a busy thoroughfare at Atlantic and Flatbush Avenues. Hundreds of Guild and pressmen union members gathered at *News* headquarters in Manhattan and chanted "the *Daily News* is bad news" and "stop union busting." The members were further encouraged when passing commuters and trucks responded noisily to signs reading "Honk if you support the unions." One striker entered the Winner's Circle, a coffee shop next to the Brooklyn printing plant, and showered customer-strikers with a large bundle of the morning *News* that he had taken from a newsstand and urged his fellow strikers to engage in similar actions.

News management claimed that 611,000 copies of an abbreviated newspaper (48 pages—less than half its normal size) were printed October 26, compared to a normal press run of 1.18 million for the day. Police cars had escorted the delivery trucks out of the Brooklyn complex and into the streets for about half a mile. However, distribution of Friday's newspaper was curtailed and concentrated in Manhattan, possibly no more than five miles from the printing plant. According to one management estimate, some 500,000 Friday newspapers were actually delivered; union officials placed this figure at 200,000.

Even the *Chicago Tribune's* coverage of this time period realized that this strike differed from most labor–management disputes because no negotiations were in progress, nor were any planned. The *News* sought continued publishing with newly hired replacement employees; however, the publication performance on Saturday, October 27, prompted *News* management to consider hiring striking employees even if they were not dealing with their union representatives.

Saturday's newspaper, the first to hit the street prepared and delivered without union employees, was 64 pages, 16 pages more than that published the previous week. John Sloan noted the "outstanding" performance of replacement employees, which had exceeded management's original expectations for the strike's second day. He did, however, acknowledge that the newspaper's quality was not that of prestrike issues and that its delivery of 710,000 copies was about 200,000 short of a normal Saturday run. Some of this reduction was no doubt due to increasing violence. Between Friday night and Saturday morning, 12 strikers, who were said to be mostly drivers or pressmen, were arrested, most on charges of stoning delivery trucks and buses carrying replacement workers.

On Saturday, a bus taking seven strike replacements from a printing plant was attacked while stopped at a traffic light. A van and a jeep pulled alongside the bus; one man jumped from the jeep and fired two shots into the air while seven men wearing ski masks jumped out of the van and started banging on the bus with baseball bats. Another incident concerned a substitute driver, who was attacked and beaten with a baseball bat when his truck was waylaid near an exit of the Brooklyn-Queens Expressway. Management maintained that since the strike had begun, eight delivery trucks, each worth about $35,000, had been destroyed by firebombs and that 60 others had been damaged by slashed tires, punctured radiators, and smashed windows and windshields.

Management responded to the strike's first 24 hours in its Saturday newspaper. The front-page headline, "The Fight For The News," was placed above a photograph of strikers vandalizing a bus carrying replacement workers. Advertisements for job vacancies formerly occupied by strikers in all departments were featured inside the newspaper.

It also urged striking employees to return to work Monday (October 29) at their old jobs and old salaries. Details of this announcement were somewhat confusing, even contradictory, a situation possibly due to two management officials relaying the announcement and/or different media coverage of the announcement. John Sloan indicated the *News* had not fired anyone; therefore, any employee could return to work. Yet *News* spokesperson Lisa Robinson indicated that employees could return to work if they had not been permanently replaced. She further indicated that employees could cross the picket line and ask management if they can work or if their jobs have been permanently replaced.

According to management, there were about 40 to 50 managers/professionals working 16-hour shifts in various departments, including the newsroom. There were 24 reporters and editors imported from the *Chicago Tribune* and from Tribune-owned papers in Fort Lauderdale, Orlando, and Newport News. Also, 100 of the 2,200 job slots had been permanently filled so far, mostly with nonwhite and female employees. John Sloan justified the company's release of the permanent replacement's sexual and racial backgrounds because "six of our ten unions are composed of all white males." One union account refuted Sloan's racial advancement motives, contending that 29 of the 60 employees fired by management on October 25 were minority members.

Management indicated that no Newspaper Guild members had been permanently replaced. Indeed, one description of the normally bustling city room was a "sea of empty desks" dotted with editors "long out of practice as reporters." As soon as the strike began, *News* management tested the extent the Newspaper Guild's white-collar members would support the drivers and the pressmen. Senior editors and management personnel urged Guild members to return to work.

A message received by one reporter the first week of the strike read, "You are welcome back to your job and to a future here. . . . The window is open now; we can't guarantee how long we will keep it open."[16]

Managerial behaviors surrounding this announcement might have brushed the acceptable limits of labor law. Unionized employees have the legal right to strike and to return to work if job vacancies have not been filled by permanent replacements. Legally, management cannot impose deadlines; however, supervisors can speak of "windows" and replacements; thus, management could inform reporters that they could return to work on a certain day and be employed but if they waited a day longer their jobs would be filled. Then they "could stay at the paper only by replacing one of his old coworkers (and most likely, a friend) who was still out on strike."[17]

Barry Lipton, president of the Newspaper Guild, indicated that each member could determine how he or she would respond to management's offer, but he thought his organization would continue this fight because most if not all union members realized their only hope was to remain unified and "not let this vile management split them."

The Newspaper Guild represented rather diverse employee classifications; reporters, editors, photographers, clerks, and business department personnel. On Sunday, October 28, a committee of nine reporters met with Lipton to discuss whether the Guild's previous strike vote should be rescinded. In addition to the previously mentioned membership divisions (those who did not empathize with some of the other involved unions, particularly the drivers, for example), some reporters maintained the strike was called on a faulty basis—they took this job action because they thought their jobs had been permanently taken by replacements. Lipton said that he was informed of this situation by the paper's director of labor relations, Edward Gold. Management's announcement Saturday that all reporters could return to work on Monday, October 29, enabled some Guild members to have second thoughts.

The meeting generated a decision by reporters to remain on the picket line. Lipton said the unhappy union members had come to the conclusion that there was at least some union momentum that might eventually pressure management to return to the bargaining table. However, this reaction did not reflect a firm, consensual resolve. One reporter said that he was "scared" because management "can win and most of us know it. . . . We know that, if some reporters start to go back inside, then we'll all lose because they will be able to produce a decent product."[18]

Meanwhile, *News* management was attempting to resolve production/distribution difficulties associated with the Sunday paper whose news section was 96 pages more than the previous week's prestrike publication. Yet this edition's production did not start until 8:45 P.M. Saturday, compared to a normal 4:45 P.M. start-up time in prestrike production. The delivery of 1.2 million Sunday editions (compared to a 1.4 million prestrike run) produced by 100 nonunion drivers and 54 trucks (each accompanied by a security guard) began later than normal. Much of this situation was no doubt due to production problems, although management did suggest that drivers would be safer if deliveries were made in the daylight hours.

John Sloan stressed that "each day our performance gets better"; however, a spokesperson for the *New York Post* indicated that the *News* management must be printing the newspaper in "invisible ink" because very few were found on the newsstands. The *Post* published 800,000 copies of its own Sunday edition, 200,000 more than usual, and there were 28 pages or so of advertisements more than usual.

Many of the *News's* delivery problems were caused by the new drivers not knowing all of the stops. Many vendors complained that they received too many or too few newspapers, or none at all. Some of these individuals were also intimidated, a situation that further curtailed newspaper sales. For example, one vendor in Brooklyn noted that club-wielding men had seized all 300 copies of the Sunday *News* and scattered them in the gutter. At about the same time, a convenience store employee noted windows at his workplace had been smashed after the strike began, and that three individuals with masks came in the middle of the night and warned him that if *News* copies were again sold, his store would be burned down.

PERIPHERAL BARGAINING THROUGH THE STRIKE'S INITIAL WEEK

Potential Return to the Bargaining Table

Both management and union negotiators had some incentives to return to the bargaining table during the first week of the strike. Management continued to have distribution problems. It maintained that it was printing more than 900,000 copies a day, which represented 75 percent of its normal distribution of 1.2 million papers. Union negotiators did not dispute management's publication figure although they likely agreed with an assessment made by a former Newspaper Guild official who contended that "getting ink on paper" is less important than surviving as a profitable company and having a normal relationship with the community.

The unions estimated moreover that only 200,000 newspapers (less than 17 percent of its normal run) were getting into the reader's hands. Management was aware that 80 percent of its circulation was in single-copy sales and acknowledged that copies at newsstands were hard to find. At least one spokesperson blamed union members for stealing, burning, and destroying the newspapers.

The *News's* competitors attempted to take quick advantage of this situation. The *New York Times* was reportedly distributing more of its newspapers to newsstands; *Newsday* delivered an additional 100,000 copies of its *New York Newsday* a day. The *New York Post* increased its daily distribution by 200,000 copies and indicated that it was considering the start-up of a Sunday edition to be published during the strike.

George McDonald stressed that the unions were trying everything possible to return to the bargaining table, end the strike, and get the members back to work. The unions also had a tangible issue to discuss at the bargaining table, namely, strike replacements. Union advisor Theodore Kheel alleged that *News* management used the "Battle of Wounded Knee" incident with its wildcat strike as an excuse for hiring permanent replacements. Further, this incident, if resolved through the National Labor Relations Board and/or the courts, could involve an unfair labor practice with job reinstatement and back pay given to *News* strikers. This process could involve the following complicated issues: Did management prompt the incident, either directly or as part of a calculated strategy that assured the incident would occur? Was the incident a strike, or a temporary job action caused by management's escorting a union representative out of the facility? And, did the union president make an unconditional offer to return to work? The hiring of strike replacements represented a clear and measurable bargaining issue, which Kheel contended should be resolved at the bargaining table since the strike's first week hurt management, unions, and employees alike.

Management and union negotiators may have been prompted to return to the bargaining table during the strike's first week; however, there were several peripheral bargaining conditions involving unions that prevented this occurrence. For example, dissension within at least one union, the Newspaper Guild, diverted attention away from the bargaining table. There were also strike-related activities, boycotts and violence that involved the broader community. Finally unions sought the involvement of other individuals and organizations who were not at the bargaining table.

Dissension Within the Newspaper Guild

Barry Lipton told dozens of reporters attending Sunday's meeting (October 28) that two major advertisers were about to withdraw their advertising from the *News*. One major advertiser, however, Alexander's department stores, indicated shortly after the meeting that it expected "to advertise in the *Daily News,* as long as it prints."

Many Guild members expressed anger and frustration toward management and the union for being "somehow maneuvered onto the street," according to one reporter. One librarian–Guild member explained this situation:

If I go back, management owes me. If I stay out, I become another unemployment statistic in the city. [The decision to cross the picket line or remain on strike is like suicide as] I'm on the chair, with the rope around my neck . . . trying to decide whether or not to jump.[19]

Several reporters wanted to cross the picket line on Monday, October 29, the day *News* management wanted them to return. They believed that the *News* could afford a long strike, an assessment reinforced when management said on October 29 that it had hired some permanent replacements for striking Guild members in the editorial department. These individuals joined the 24 "on-loan" editorial personnel mentioned earlier. One reporter, for example, indicated little sympathy for the pressmen, deliverymen, or the "FOWGs (Fat Old White Guys)" who have been phoning in their crime stories for decades.

According to the *News*, 45 of more than 350 Guild members in the editorial department, including many photographers, accepted management's invitation to return to work on Monday. About 50 to 80 reporters discussed this turn of events at the second strike meeting the following day. Many reporters hoped this session would urge most members to return to work, but, after some soul searching, the group decided to remain on strike a bit longer.

The meeting also reflected differences among Newspaper Guild members along occupational lines. Reporters had repeatedly met to question the strike decision but other Guild members had no such meetings, and few publicly questioned the Guild's leadership. A rare exception came from a nonjournalist member who attended Tuesday's meeting when she publicly advocated a strike and rebuked the reporters' faction, who, she claimed, mistakenly thought they were elite within the union.

Membership unity was further weakened one day after the meeting when almost half of the *News*'s 25 sportswriters and all but one of its 30 unionized photographers, along with an assortment of copy editors, librarians, advertising employees, and others, crossed picket lines. Pete Hamill, a former reporter for the *News*, summarily blasted the first of these two employee groups for their decision:

In normal times, the photographers were the most vehement in demanding strict adherence to the Newspaper Guild contract: every dime of overtime, every cent in expenses. Virtually all of them crossed the picket line. "Fuck the Guild," one of them said. "I gotta eat." Most of the sportswriters crossed, too, all those men and women who so glibly stand in icy public judgment of the moral and physical courage of athletes.[20]

The total number of Guild members who had crossed the picket lines the first week of the dispute was in dispute. The union said the figure was less than 100; however, management insisted that some 300 of the Guild's 750 members returned to work. Management estimated that more than 200 Guild members were again working in the advertising, circulation, and classified departments, while more than 80 others were working in the newsroom.

Traffic through the picket lines was not one way, however, as several returning union members walked back out of *News* facilities in August. Jack Newfield, a columnist and supervisor of a *News* investigative team, was classified as management and thereby exempt from Guild representation. Newfield acknowledged that "real abuses" existed in some of the unions but nonetheless tendered his resignation to publisher Hoge within the first week of the strike because

my conscience and self-respect just can't allow me to ratify the breaking of unions with my labor and my name. . . . I would be just miserable working for a paper that locked out its unions and sitting next to scabs at desks once occupied by my friends.[21]

After his resignation, Newfield accepted a position with the weekly *New York Observer* at about half his former pay.

STRIKE-RELATED ACTIVITIES AFFECTING THE LARGER COMMUNITY: BOYCOTTS AND VIOLENCE

Unions at the *News* claimed responsibility for boycotts as their attorney, Samuel McKnight (technically working for the APTC but receiving his salary from the AFL-CIO), indicated the boycott would begin on October 30 with hand-billing of advertisers and dealers listed in the *News* to begin the next day. (At the request of one of the striking unions, the Communication Workers, the *Daily News* was also added to the AFL-CIO national boycott list during this time period.) Strikers would distribute "Boycott the Daily News" leaflets outside department stores and other outlets, which stressed the following:

With your help and support of this boycott, the Chicago-based management of the *Daily News* will realize New Yorkers are aware that *what is on the newsstands is NOT your newspaper.* With your help, we can go back to the bargaining table and back to our jobs so you can again enjoy the paper we love and New York deserves.

Customers were encouraged to take four boycott actions: (1) not to buy the *News;* (2) to encourage news dealers not to sell the *News;* (3) to report any dealer who did sell the newspaper to a telephone hot line; and (4) to refuse to shop in stores having items advertised in the *News.* They were also encouraged to inform their Congressional representative to support any bill that banned strike replacements and to make a $5 contribution to help support strikers and their families through a 900 telephone number.

In accordance with federal law, the leaflets would only criticize the *News,* not the advertisers; also the distributors of the leaflets would not try to block customers. On October 31, strikers fanned out outside of Alexander's at 58th and Lexington Avenues. They distributed leaflets to potential customers of the *News's* single biggest advertiser that read, "Don't Advertise or Buy the News." The boycott's organizers claimed that members of all unions in the New York area, plus their families, represented 4.5 million consumers.

News officials were unaware of any major advertiser canceling its ad schedule in the few days after the boycott announcement, although some advertisers canceled their Sunday inserts because of perceived distribution problems. At least one advertiser, Bernadette Castro, head of Castro Convertibles stores, gave the *News* reason to think the boycott would fail since she refused to pull her advertisements because of her long-standing relationship with "a great newspaper," her belief that Jim Hoge could successfully operate the *News,* and her concern about union strike violence.

There were some indicators, however, that suggested the boycott could have a potential, if not immediate, adverse impact, on the *News.* For example, Lord & Taylor had scheduled its first advertisement to be run in three years with the

Daily News. The advertisement, aimed at a cosmetics' line for African-American women, was pulled because of perceived distribution problems at the newspaper. Lord & Taylor remained on the union's boycott list even though the advertisement never ran.

The following *Editor and Publisher* account of the *News*'s advertising situation in its October 31 edition also suggested the boycott's effectiveness:

The number of pages with advertising in the Oct. 31 *Daily News* — nearly one week into the strike — was counted as 29, whereas the previous Wednesday papers carried about 41. Classified advertising pages were down from eight pages to four.

Advertisers such as Newmark & Lewis, Bloomingdale's, CVS pharmacies, Chemical Bank, Manufacturer's Hanover, Chase Manhattan Bank and Caldor's were not found in the Oct. 31 newspaper, but were frequent advertisers in weeks prior to the strike.[22]

One advertising agency executive indicated that none of his clients' advertisements would be run in the *News* until the strike was over because he could not rely on the *News*'s circulation figures as an accurate indicator of sales and could not determine the extent to which his clients' messages were reaching the audience.

News management charged unions with violent acts since the strike began. An official of the Teamsters Union (one not directly involved in the dispute) joined the picket line soon after the strike was called, and maintained that the national scope of this strike would escalate tensions and inevitable violence:

This isn't just a J. P. Stevens affair somewhere down South. . . . This is the *Daily News* in New York, a highly visible employer, and this is going to attract a lot of attention from all over the country. Labor is going to have to fight this one. They can't afford to lose or to let the *Daily News* win without making it suffer.

They didn't fight when Reagan broke the air traffic controllers' union and look what happened. They will have to go to the mat on this one. There is going to be a lot of violence, and down the line someone is going to get shot. Some of the people in the drivers' union were the tough guys the papers hired years ago to make sure their papers got to the newsstands first. These people aren't mild-mannered reporters.[23]

On October 29, the *News* said it would increase protection for news dealers, asserting that union strikers, having failed to block delivery trucks from leaving its printing plants in Garden City and Brooklyn, New York, and Kearny, New Jersey, focused on "dealer intimidation and the outright thievery of bundled papers on the streets."

Several dealers reported visits by groups of four to six individuals who threatened to burn down the store if the *News* were sold at their locations. In some cases, groups took hundreds of *Daily News* copies off the stands. Dealers associated these threats with economic and possibly physical destruction. One dealer in Queens noted he was informed by a group that something would happen to him if he sold the *News*. Another dealer, who normally sold 160 copies of the *News* daily, left papers sitting by the curb since the strike had begun because he did not want to face strikers' hostility.

Some strikers privately indicated that they were trying to intercept trucks carrying the *News* and/or grabbing up or scattering bundles of newspapers left for dealers. One striking driver even admitted to taking three-quarters of the available newspapers from a distribution point in Flushing, even though the location was near a police station.

These acts were assailed by then-current and previous *News* officials. John Sloan maintained that strikers would lose public sympathy if their violence continued, while a former editor of the *News* commented:

Everyone has the right to strike, to protest. But attacking innocent newsstand operators—who are not even a party to a labor dispute—that's terrorism, the kind we condemn in Northern Ireland and Iraq, but about which our elected officials and labor statesmen seem strangely quiet.[24]

A *News* editorial called on community leaders to speak up so that New York would not be turned into Dodge City:

As one company is victimized by undaunted mob terror, every New Yorker is terrorized. Every business and business person stands under this threat: Capitulate to the brutes or your business will be trashed or burned. You will be beaten—or worse.

Think about that. Hard and long.[25]

Union leaders involved in the dispute stressed they were unaware of specific violent episodes involving union members and did not condone violence in any form; moreover, they thought the causes and/or results of violence should be attributed to management. George McDonald indicated that despite *News* management's blame to the contrary, union leaders neither encouraged nor condoned violence. He further commented that each union in the Allied Council would inform its membership "to cool it," even though he maintained that management caused this situation through "mental violence" committed on employees before and during the strike, particularly when members were replaced from jobs they had held for three or four decades.

Michael Alvino, head of the drivers' union, said that he was not aware of violence and that he had informed neighborhood dealers "in a nice way, please do not buy the *News*." Alvino further remarked that he had renounced violence and had urged his members not to engage in these efforts at the beginning of the strike. He suggested that management claimed union violence to suppress his members' picket line behavior and obtained police protection of *News* trucks and drivers to strengthen its bargaining position:

We are not free to picket any more like we used to. . . . We're penned up like cattle. I don't know what free collective bargaining is anymore when management uses taxpayers' money to stop the unions.[26]

Union leaders' nonviolent appeals to the contrary, violence continued during the strike's first week as evidenced by 41 related arrests in this time period.

Union-Requested Involvement of External Parties

The Allied Printing Trades Council (APTC) sought the help of other unions in its dispute with the *News*. It had hoped, for example, that the Teamsters would not cross the picket lines, thereby not delivering essential printing supplies to the *News* production facilities. Local 1199, Drug, Hospital Care Employees Union furnished perhaps the most assistance to the *News*'s unions with its 200-line telephone bank for boycott activities. This local's support was somewhat ironic because the organization was formed and to some extent sustained by appealing to members' racial/ethnic pride. Evidently, *News* officials' efforts to emphasize the "lily-white" nature of many unions at the *News* were not successful. Dennis Rivera, president of Local 1199, urged his 100,000 members to "adopt a newsstand in your neighborhood and visit vendors and gift shops in the hospital and/or nursing home where you work" to persuade them not to sell the *News*. Rivera regarded a union's social/ethnic composition less significant than clearly establishing that New York City would not be a "haven for union-busting employers," who attempted to remove basic collective bargaining rights that employees "sweated and fought for."

Many Local 1199 union members agreed with Rivera. On October 30, for example, some 500 members of 1199 joined pickets at the *News* mid-Manhattan office building and marched to chants of "The People United Shall Never Be Defeated." They also carried picket signs that read "Your Fight Is Our Fight" and "Down With The Bosses, Up With The Unions."

Unions throughout New York City also asked each member to contribute $1 to the APTC. The anticipated goal of $2 million would be partially spent to help striking employees with living expenses until they started receiving their unemployment checks. Additional funds would pay for newspaper, radio, and television advertisements that would explain to the public the issues and the history of the unions' strike and lockout. Also, the New York City Central Labor Council was asked to send letters to each of its members asking them to boycott the *Daily News* and its advertisers. George McDonald maintained that minimal financial and moral support from each union member in New York City would either return *News* management to the bargaining table "or bring it to its knees."

Mayor Dinkins, who wanted to serve as a "catalyst" in the dispute resolution, had sent both union and management negotiators telegrams offering his assistance a few hours after the strike started. Union leaders quickly accepted the offer but publisher James Hoge offered no immediate response, an action that surprised Dinkins, who thought Hoge would be willing to sit down and talk. Hoge had earlier attempted to persuade his editorial board to endorse Ed Koch instead of David Dinkins for mayor. He was unsuccessful in his efforts, and the *News* ended up endorsing Richard Ravitch, who in turn received 4 percent of the mayoral vote. Eric Schmertz, the city's Director of Labor Relations, indicated that Hoge's nonresponse precluded Mayor Dinkins from mediating the dispute since he needed acceptance from both sides before he could become effective. Dinkins symbolically straddled employer and union interests during this time period. For example, he indicated that he would not refuse to answer any questions posed by replacement reporters in their various work assignments at City Hall. Yet, he also refused to cross picket lines at *News* headquarters to discuss city employee layoffs as one of a regular series of scheduled visits before newspaper editorial boards.

Hoge did meet with Mayor Dinkins on October 31, to discuss alleged violence by strikers against news dealers, replacement employees, and their families. Suggestions about resolving the dispute were also discussed although *News* management stressed that no consideration of the mayor's suggestions for resolving the dispute would be considered until the violence ceased. An aide to Mayor Dinkins indicated allegations of violence were being dealt with by the police department and were not yet a matter of mayoral policy; however, the city's involvement of police protection in *News* operations riled union leaders as representing unfair interference. Barry Lipton was disturbed that the city could spend money on publishing a newspaper with "scab" employees while claiming insufficient funds to run the city properly.

Unions also met with John J. Cardinal O'Connor, who had intervened in the *New York Post* negotiations concluded about a month earlier. Hoge was not invited to this meeting but publicly hoped that Cardinal O'Connor could

persuade the union leaders to denounce the violence and vandalism their members are inflicting on newsstand dealers, other small business people, and *Daily News* employees.

I also hope the Cardinal will encourage the unions to return to the bargaining table and, for the first time during these protracted negotiations, make a sincere and good faith effort to reach new collective bargaining agreements. The *Daily News* is prepared to meet with the unions with that objective in mind.[27]

O'Connor indicated that allegations of violence and intimidation by strikers against news vendors were discussed at the meeting; moreover, he was convinced that union leaders wanted to "do the right thing" and have no involvement with violence. "All of us know that when tempers get heated and that when people are terribly frustrated and are worried about their jobs and their families, violence can flare up."[28]

Unions also involved federal government organizers in their labor dispute. Theodore Kheel indicated that the unions were updating unfair labor practice charges already filed with the National Labor Relations Board; also, the NLRB was taking depositions on the "wounded knee" incident.

Several scheduled bargaining sessions conducted by individual unions under the auspices of a federal mediator were not canceled during the strike's first week although the results of these sessions were not publicized. On November 1, the director of the Federal Mediation and Conciliation Service appointed federal mediator John Sweeny as his special assistant in the *News* dispute and also indicated that Kathleen Murray-Cannon would continue her mediation efforts in this situation.

NOTES

1. Salembier subsequently sued for the balance ($261,500) of the year's severance pay ($400,000) she claimed was in her contract. Her forced resignation appears unusual in that seven months earlier she had informed *USA Today,* "We are so close (to breaking even) that we can taste it." She was so optimistic about the newspaper's future that she informed the New York City's Deadline Club that she would return in ten years to talk about the *Post's* role in the twenty-first century. Pat Guy, "Exec Sees Rosy Future at N.Y. *Post,*" *USA Today,* February 7, 1990, 2-B.

2. Unions at the *Post* also gave nearly $24 million in concessions to Murdoch to make this sale possible.

3. "New York Post Threatens to Close; Advertisers Asked to Boycott News," Bureau of National Affairs, Inc., *Daily Labor Report* 175 (September 9, 1990): A-13.

4. Alex Martin, "Driver's Bad Knee Started Strike," *Newsday,* October 27, 1990. Dialog File 638, item 05806051.

5. William Bunch, "This Time The Buses Did Come: After Months of Anxiety, The Explosion," *Newsday,* October 28, 1990. Dialog File 638, item 05807406.

6. Robert D. McFadden, "The News Strike: From Job Dispute to Maelstrom," *New York Times,* October 30, 1990, B-4.

7. "Daily News at War: The Combatants," *New York Times,* October 27, 1990, 26.

8. Michael Specter, "N.Y. Daily News Strike May be Final Showdown," *Washington Post,* October 27, 1990, A-3.

9. John L. Hess, "A Fight to Salvage 2,800 Good Jobs," *Los Angeles Times,* November 11, 1990, M-7.

10. Alessandra Stanley, "Some Guild Workers Rush to Picket, Some Mourn," *New York Times,* October 27, 1990, 26.

11. Joseph W. Queen, "News Invites Strikers Back; Wary Unions See Move to Divide Ranks," *Newsday,* October 28, 1990. Dialog File 638, item 05807347.

12. Dennis Duggan, "News New York Diary. Firebrands of '60s, Wimps of the '90s: Labor's Love Lost," *Newsday,* October 30, 1990. Dialog File 638, item 05809172.

13. "Nine Unions Strike New York Daily News, Claiming That Management Provoked Walkout," Bureau of National Affairs, Inc., *Daily Labor Report* 209 (October 29, 1990): A-11 and A-12.

14. Scott Ladd, "Scoop from Inside The News. Worker Tells of Harried Conditions," *Newsday,* November 12, 1990. Dialog File 638, item 05822127.

15. Scott Ladd, "Replacement Workers Settle in for Long Stay," *Newsday,* October 28, 1990. Dialog File 638, item 05807356.

16. "Replacements Start to Fill Strikers Posts at N.Y. Daily News," *Chicago Tribune,* October 28, 1990, sec. 1, p. 12.

17. Edwin Diamond, "The 'News' at War," *New York,* November 12, 1990, 40.

18. Howard Kurtz, "Daily News Strike Illustrates Decline of Newspaper Unions' *Washington Post,* October 31, A-3.

19. Alessandra Stanley, "Among Striking Reporters, Fears and Misgivings Grow," *New York Times,* October 31, 1990, B-2.

20. Pete Hamill, "They Killed the News Today, Oh Boy," *Esquire,* February 1991, 32.

21. George Garneau, "Daily News Shifts Strategy," *Editor and Publisher,* November 10, 1990, 40.

22. George Garneau, "Strike Gets Nasty in New York," *Editor and Publisher,* November 3, 1990, 13.

23. Duggan, "News New York Diary."

24. Michael J. O'Neill, "36,000 Hours of Overtime," *New York Times,* November 8, 1990, A-35.

25. Garneau, "Strike Gets Nasty," 13.

26. Thomas B. Rosenstiel, "Daily News Strike Goes According to Plan," *Los Angeles Times,* October 30, 1990, D-1 and D-9.

27. "Daily News Union Pursuing Ways to Get Paper Back to Bargaining Table," Bureau of National Affairs, Inc., *Daily Labor Report* 211 (October 31, 1990): A-8.

28. David E. Pitt, "Strikers Strive to Block Ads in Daily News," *New York Times,* October 31, 1990, B-1 and B-2.

4

The Strike's Next Month

Appointing mediators in the *Daily News* dispute suggested at least some hope that union and management officials might resolve their differences at the bargaining table. As will be discussed in this chapter's first section, however, the smallest portion of November's labor–management activities at the *News* involved bargaining table behavior or issues.

Both *News* union and management officials remained away from the bargaining table to resolve and/or enhance peripheral bargaining considerations. Union officials were primarily concerned about presenting a unified front both within their sometimes diverse membership (particularly the case with the Newspaper Guild) and with other unions not directly involved in the strike. Two general activities, rallies and a consumer boycott, were employed by unions during the strike's next month to produce a united organized labor–community stance against management's bargaining approach. Management likely eschewed bargaining-table efforts to concentrate on advertising and distribution problems that were, in part, due to the unions' external activities as well as to three managerial strike miscalculations.

Violence—activities, atmosphere, and allegations—pervaded, if not suffocated, traditional bargaining assumptions and behavior. Union and management negotiators focused on the degree and attribution of these acts instead of measurable bargaining issues and labor–management relationships should an agreement be reached.

ABSENCE OF BARGAINING TABLE ACTIVITIES

John Sweeney's federal mediation assignment at the *News* was likely eclipsed the same day by Theodore Kheel, who reinforced the continued avoidance of bargaining table issues and behavior when he urged management to sell the *Daily News* to a group of investors headed by himself. Kheel did not name the proposed investors but said they were Americans (thereby excluding international press barons Rupert Murdoch and Robert Maxwell) who would offer Tribune Company management "an honorable way out." In a November 1 letter sent to Charles Brumback, Kheel suggested that he could negotiate fair and equitable labor agreements with union members, who would, in turn, receive 20 percent of the purchasing entity's stock and, possibly, other working conditions previously negotiated with the *New York Post*.

A Tribune Company spokesperson dismissed Kheel's offer as an insincere, diversionary ploy to distract management from bargaining table issues. James Hoge reacted in an even stronger fashion, claiming that Kheel's offer was an outrageous joke: "First, they try to ruin our business; then they say they want to buy us."[1]

Collective bargaining continued to be conducted in the streets and through press conferences rather than at the bargaining table. One report estimated that only five bargaining sessions had been held from the start of the strike through the month of November with little result. George McDonald was asked in an early November press conference to comment on James Hoge's assertion that the unions had made minimal concessions in the ten months of bargaining talks that preceded the strike. McDonald angrily placed the *News*'s bargaining issues and resolution in the perspective of a major competitor, the *New York Post*, where a labor agreement had been reached about a month earlier:

Go back and say to Hoge that McDonald said at a press conference: "We'll match what we gave the *Post*."

[Management officials at the *Post*] came to us very honestly and said, "Look, we've lost some $29 million this year, we'll show it to you." We saw their books. We believed them. We said, "We'll help you." We put together a $19 million package in 10 days—in all areas, with great sacrifice to the workers.

Now the same people who are members of our unions would do the same thing at The *Daily News* if they had the opportunity. Do you think they like to be out on strike?[2]

A *News* spokesperson informed reporters that McDonald's remarks were inappropriate because he should realize that negotiations should take place at the bargaining table, and that *News* management has been continually willing to have more frequent and longer meetings with the unions.

Hoge was again informed in late November that the unions sought a concessionary bargaining settlement like the one the *New York Post* had received. Hoge responded that publicized union givebacks were illusionary, moreover, unlike Peter Kalikow, owner of the *New York Post*, he had accountability to stockholders and could not fund a newspaper with personal wealth. Hoge also maintained that management had to regain control of such things as press staffing and that Kalikow's break-even labor agreements constituted a "slow suicide."

Unions regarded the *Post* settlement as a necessary, joint approach to one general collective bargaining issue, labor cost reductions. George McDonald further indicated that management could immediately end the strike with these additional activities:

1. reinstating the strikers and dismissing strike replacements; and
2. eliminating its all-inclusive management rights proposal, which no union leader could accept because it would render the unions irrelevant in the bargaining process.

Each side seemed to focus on the other's bargaining wrongs rather than on issues, however small, that could provide a symbolic if not substantial settlement. Unions channeled their potential bargaining efforts through appeals to public officials to mediate the dispute. In late November, for example, the unions urged that a "super board of mediation" be appointed by Governor Mario M. Cuomo, New York City Mayor David N. Dinkins, and John J. Cardinal O'Connor to address the unresolved collective bargaining issues.

Management was charged with not opening its financial records, an action that the *New York Post* took and that prompted a union–management problem identification and subsequent labor agreement. Some also thought that management's extensive, hard-line strike preparations precluded its good-faith bargaining intention. John Scanlon, the *News'*s public relations representative, suggested this situation was still consistent with good-faith bargaining.

The fact that The *News* was prepared for a strike is well known. The fact that they have people organized and they have security shouldn't come as a shock to anybody.

Look . . . this is not about a subcommittee of the College of Cardinals debating in some stygian cave at the bottom of the Vatican about the tense of a verb in some papal encyclical. You're talking about a fight to save the newspaper. So you prepare. And if you don't prepare, you're a sissy.[3]

Hoge further informed Mayor Dinkins[4] that management had bargained in good faith as it offered wage increases for those employees for whom there were productive work, a "solid" benefits and grievance procedures package, and "fair severance for those who must be let go." Hoge further asserted that the unions stalled bargaining through "meager counter proposals" and the raising of "diversionary issues."

John Sloan of the *News* also encouraged the unions to join federal mediators already at the bargaining table for round-the-clock negotiations and asserted that unions were "doing members a disservice" if they failed to "heed the call." To be sure, strike funds did not match the strikers' salaries during this time period. The Newspaper Guild, for example, received $150 weekly in strike funds compared to the top Guild minimum of $928 before the strike.

Some thought that unions were more concerned with keeping the *News* all but invisible on the newsstands than with prolonged efforts at the bargaining table.

Holders of this attitude suggest that the unions never thought management was interested in a bargaining settlement and that, therefore, lost revenues would pressure management into selling the *News* to another organization where a subsequent bargaining settlement could be reached. In late November, unions were reportedly interested in the efforts of Patrick A. Flanagan, who was managing director of the Fidelis Group, an investment company that specialized in arranging buy-outs of troubled companies by using employee stock option plans. Flanagan declined to name "three very real" potential buyers for the *News* in late November although he said each buyer expected the unions to make major work rule concessions in exchange for stock if the newspaper's purchase were realized.

Accusations notwithstanding, both union and management representatives remained away from the bargaining table in November because each side focused on shoring up its organization's objectives while weakening the other. Compounding these diversions was the atmosphere of violence that pervaded the strike in November.

PRIMARY UNION CONCERN: SECURING SUPPORT

Membership Differences Within the Newspaper Guild

On November 2, the *Daily News* hired its first permanent replacement for a striking reporter, a situation that escalated tensions and uncertainties among Guild members. This individual and subsequent replacement reporters were required to sign a proviso that they could be released immediately. Many nonreporter Guild members had crossed the picket lines before this action, as had reporters in the sports and features departments. Few of the 75 metropolitan reporters, however, who were regarded by some as "the heart of the newspaper," crossed the picket line. As previously noted, since the strike had begun, the metro section had been staffed with 30 probationary employees who would eventually become union employees under terms specified in the labor agreement, and temporary employees such as editors, editorial writers, and employees from other Tribune locations. The Guild informed probationary employees to continue working "under protest" at the *News*.

The union, of course, did not urge temporary employees to pursue the same course of action. At least one temporary employee did not fully understand why striking Guild members would view him as a threat to their livelihoods; indeed, he thought he was doing the strikers a favor by holding their jobs so that permanent replacements would not take them.

There were three major categories of Newspaper Guild members in the dispute: those who crossed the picket line, those who did not cross the line but were wavering ("fence sitters"), and those strikers who rather strongly believed in this job action's necessity ("hard-liners"). Betty Liu Ebron, author of the "Apple Sauce" gossip column and a Guild member who crossed the picket line, described the strike's impact on newsroom operations and the Newspaper Guild's membership, while Frank McKeown, a 33-year reporter for the *News* close to receiving his pension, explained his strike return:

It's been like "Invasion of the Body Snatchers." . . . One day, before the strike, I'm leaving a newsroom full of really wild, larger-than-life journalists. I came back to a room with new faces I don't know. Every day there are more and more new faces. The old familiar faces get more and more tired, more drained, more overworked.

Whether you're inside or outside, everybody feels the same. . . . Everybody's hurt, battered, angry, and confused. The unions are trying to save their families, and management is trapped between profit and loss. It's a tragedy in which nobody wins.[5]

I am scabbing. . . . I just don't like what is going on. To be honest, I shouldn't be here. With the economy the way it is—and I have two years to go before I retire—it scared me too much. I am not sure if it is in my self-interest to walk.[6]

Their assessments were at least acknowledged by some Newspaper Guild members who had not crossed the picket line. Paul La Rosa believed James Hoge had helped him receive the assignment of covering the labor–management situation at the *News*. La Rosa was also proud that the newspaper published one of his articles in which Barry Lipton called Hoge "an awful bastard." Yet, two days after the *New*'s October 29 return-to-work invitation, La Rosa called his wife and indicated he was about to cross the picket line. He informed her a half-hour later that he had changed his mind because "it would feel like I was betraying people more than anything." However, La Rosa's resolve was not firm. He contended that the leaders of the Guild mishandled the strike situation, misleading the members in the process; moreover, he reasoned,

There's no place else I can get a job like this. . . . Psychologically, I just can't hold out much longer. . . . And frankly, I really believe that the more of us who go back, the more it will be like the old *Daily News*.[7]

La Rosa's wavering remarks were faulted by striking Guild members on two grounds: expediency and principle. Jerry Capeci, author of an organized crime column, indicated that those crossing the line did not have financial problems rougher than he was experiencing; moreover, they were trying to rationalize the fact that they were afraid for their jobs by not considering themselves union workers. Capeci did realize degrees of economic difficulties experienced by Guild members, but concluded, "a scab is a scab." Annette Bolinsky, a Guild official, further indicated that some members had trouble personalizing the strike because they bought Hoge's "propaganda" that he regarded Guild members as more significant than other unionized employees.

A reporter in the "hard-liner" category acknowledged that management's announcement of replacements at the onset of the strike caused each reporter to ask "What will happen to me?" However she also maintained that this initial "ripple of fear" had dissipated, and many reporters maintained that the unions would go to court and sue the company to get members' jobs back after the strike was over.

Another striking reporter emphasized that principle rather than economic con-

siderations had caused this dispute and a hard-liner stance among some reporters:

We are bitter at the way management has taken away our ability to do our jobs; bitter that
Tribune Company (which owns the *News*) doesn't have any understanding about the credi-
bility of reporters, the importance of sources, or that 40 percent of the work force in New
York City is unionized.[8]

By mid-November, management likely affected Guild members' dissension in
two respects. At a news conference, New York Newspaper Guild president Barry
Lipton accused management of "surface" bargaining with no intention of settlement. Lipton claimed that management in a 15-minute bargaining session rejected a "comprehensive" Guild contract proposal that had been on the bargaining
table since August 22.

Also, during this time period, *News* editor James Willse urged three organizations representing minority member reporters to furnish some 50 strike newsroom replacements. Willse informed the Asian-American Journalists Association
(AAJA), the National Association of Hispanic Journalists (NAHJA), and the National Association of Black Journalists (NABJ):

The idea of replacing a striking worker is not an appetizing one for any of us. . . . But it is
also a rare chance to build an editorial staff that truly mirrors the community we serve, an
evolution that otherwise would take years to complete.[9]

Some union officials maintained that this message reflected management's cynical, deliberate use of affirmative action principles to generate minority discord
within their striking unions. David Louie, president of the AAJA, refused the
News's request because his organization had never before made its membership
list public. Louie also noted that the newspaper had never contracted the AAJA's
hot-line service or "jobs coordinator" for job vacancies before the strike. Don
Flores, president of the NAHJA, also rejected Willse's request because he did not
want to condone the dismissal of some of his association's members who were
striking the *News*.

Thomas Morgan, president of the black journalists group (NABJ), however,
agreed to supply its membership roster for a standard, nominal fee of $400. Mor-
gan's decision reflected the NABJ's consistent goal of promoting African-American hiring, but he stated that this action did not sanction management's position in
the labor dispute. This initiative, regardless of intent, did not set well with black
strikers. David Hardy, a reporter, and Joan Shepard, an editor, expressed their
reactions:

[The *News*] wants to break the unions and create a subclass of workers who will be paid a
lot less than the people who are on strike. . . . The name of the game here isn't affirmative
action — it's corporate greed.[10]

This is a historic strike. If we go down it's like dominoes. Since Ronald Reagan, there has been an attempt to crush the labor unions in America. The unions are saying "No, you're not going to crush us."[11]

It is a violation of the very essence of unions for a union member to help in any way for management to recruit scabs during a strike. I never heard of this in my life.

It was absolutely vile . . . not only was he helping to recruit scabs, he was helping to recruit scabs to replace some of the NABJ members walking the line.[12]

Hardy's and Shepard's remarks punctuated the *News's* ironic solicitation of black reporters, since they and two other black employees of the *News* had been successful plaintiffs in an employment discrimination suit filed in 1987. The jury had found that all four plaintiffs were denied promotions on the basis of race, and a settlement estimated at $3.1 million was subsequently reached. It was likely that Morgan was influenced by Hardy and Shepard since he reversed his position and denied the management's request for a membership roster because he felt his organization, despite attempts to remain neutral, was being drawn into the union–management dispute.

Another symbolic, if not significant, event for the Guild occurred in November when columnist Mike McAlary left the *News* to join the *New York Post*. McAlary was regarded as the premier street-savvy writer, who connected the *News* to its claimed audience, "working people of New York." He indicated that he was on strike not because management wanted some employees' jobs—unions had in the past agreed to job reductions and would likely agree to them if current negotiations were conducted at the table. McAlary's strike decision was based on management's untenable desire to "have the unions." He probably provided the most humorous picket line exchange with the controversial preacher and civil rights advocate the Reverend Al Sharpton. When Sharpton urged McAlary to get the strike settled because he was tired of breaking in replacement reporters, McAlary replied, "Al, we need your support (pause), come out in favor of management."[13]

McAlary subsequently resigned from the *News* because of their harmful treatment of employees during the strike and his notion that his best revenge for managerial actions would be writing for the *New York Post*. Another reporter, Harvey Araton, had crossed the picket lines early into the strike, but left the *News,* and rejoined his striking colleagues. Araton maintained that he could not simply close his eyes to the *News* strike, and that his work during this period was neither good for his conscience nor his career. Araton's actions and attitudes were echoed by six sportswriters who had earlier crossed the picket line, leaving the *News* building in support of the Newspaper Guild. One of these individuals, Sam Marchiano, indicated that his crossover decision was made because he felt like a "scab" instead of a sportswriter, and thought the real *Daily News* was outside the building.

Management countered these defections, indicating that 410 Guild members had returned to work by November 17; however, the Guild disputed this figure. There were no defectors reported by striking craft unions.

Appeals to Outside Unions and the Community

Rallies

There were at least six rallies held in November with some 10,000 to 15,000 employees and others initiating this activity from 5:30 to 6:30 P.M. on November 1 in front of the newspaper's midtown office tower on 42d Street between Second and Third Avenues. A press release by the Allied Printing Trades Council stated that strikers and other New Yorkers would demonstrate a solidarity that would overcome the "blatant union-busting tactics used by *Daily News* management." There were several scuffles before the start of the rally. Some *Daily News* employees trying to leave the building were spat upon by demonstrators, and police in riot gear moved in to protect them. There were neither injuries nor arrests reported, however. Thomas R. Donahue, Secretary-Treasurer of the AFL-CIO, indicated that his national organization would give full backing until just labor agreements were attained. He further stressed that New York City represented a union town that would never tolerate the destruction of its hometown newspaper, particularly when the Tennessee law firm of King and Ballow represented management.

The next day, some 4,000 people were involved in a second rally, far less than expected, particularly in view of the first rally's attendance. This occasion featured the Reverend Jesse Jackson, who optimistically informed the public that both *News* management and the unions had indicated to him that they wanted Hoge to be at the bargaining table more frequently and longer. Publisher Hoge was incredulous when informed that Jackson would speak on this occasion, and publicly informed him:

You've got to be kidding. . . . It isn't conceivable that the founder and driving force behind the Rainbow Coalition would choose to endorse or align himself with six lily-white craft unions whose membership rolls are strictly closed to blacks and females.[14]

Hoge noted that the union-involved hiring situation before the strike resulted in only 2 percent female and/or minority employees, a figure that contrasted sharply with 80 percent of the permanent strike replacements. Moreover, Hoge said that Jackson would be subsequently embarrassed for discovering too late that he had chosen the wrong side of this dispute.

Jackson met with Hoge and publicly retorted "There are racial sins on both sides." At the rally, Jackson said that the *News* was using the race issue as bait, a technique that must be rejected. "When they lock you out, close the doors, and pull the blinds, you can't use color for a crutch."[15] Jackson also reminded replacement employees that if they took a $10 job, an $8 crowd would wait the next day.

At least some union representatives hoped that Jackson would serve as mediator on a key strike issue: the strikers' rights to return to their jobs. Hoge did not categorically reject this suggestion; however, he urged Jackson to encourage the unions' end of discriminatory hiring practices and their return to the bargaining table for serious negotiations.

A November 7 rally drew more than 1,500 building-trades employees and later that day thousands of printing-trades and city employees also demonstrated their support for the striking unions. A fourth rally occurred a week later and involved a crowd estimated at 2,700. Lane Kirkland, president of the AFL-CIO, informed the strikers that they had the full support of the entire labor movement for "as long as it takes." Kirkland indicated that management would not get away with its calculated decision to destroy the union. He further charged management with provoking physical violence by hiring "thugs," and economic violence by stealing employees' jobs. Owen Bieber, president of the United Automobile Workers, also spoke at the rally. He indicated that solidarity was needed to achieve the unions' major bargaining objective of preventing management's union-busting tactics.

Two more rallies occurred before the end of the month. One, sponsored by the AFL-CIO and the Amalgamated Transit Union to support strikers at the *Daily News* and Greyhound Bus Lines, featured a march of more than 2,500 people from the Port Authority bus terminal on the West Side of Manhattan to the *News* office tower on East 42d Street. Another rally, billed as "family day" by the unions, featured 75 striking employees and their children.

Other Examples of Union Support

The *News* dispute continued to draw widespread interest from both local and national unions from officials and members since it was maintained that it represented the first major attempt by an employer in heavily unionized New York City to break unions. The Allied Printing Trades Council (APTC) initiated at least two efforts in November to enlist the support of other unions in their strike efforts. The first attempt was the publication of one million copies of the *Real News,* an 8-page graphic twin of the *Daily News,* which, along with traditional news features and subjects, included information on the "what and why" of the labor–management dispute. These newspapers were given to many city unions representing teachers, Teamsters, hospital workers, and firefighters to distribute free of charge.

The APTC also announced the formation of a $2 million strike fund for a media campaign run by the Kamber Group public relations firm to spread the strikers' message. Half of the fund represented a loan guarantee from local units of the Transport Workers Union, Local 1199, the Teamsters, the United Federation of Teachers, the Communications Workers of America, the United Automobile Workers, and the Retail, Wholesale, and Department Store Workers Union (RWDSU). The remainder was to come from weekly collections of one dollar per member from those belonging to the city Central Labor Council and the state AFL-CIO. The November 14 rally generated additional funds of nearly $300,000.

Several unions offered more than financial support to the striking unions during November. For example, some 200 members representing 23 unions canvassed neighborhoods in Queens to ask subscribers of the *News* to cancel home delivery. Dennis Hughes, a state AFL-CIO employee who coordinated the campaign, said that this geographic area represented the most important portion of the *News*'s home delivery system, the only facet of the *News* operation not affected by the strike. One union official indicated this one-on-one tactic enabled unions to present their positions to individual customers and answer any related questions. *News* management claimed that unidentified unions/union members also attempted to reduce the paper's home delivery when a leaflet, said to have been released by the newspaper, was sent to parents of paperboys and papergirls living in Staten Island, warning them that their children's safety had become jeopardized by strike events and that the children should not deliver newspapers until the strike was over. The RWDSU provided sandwiches and drinks daily at all picket locations, and the Service Employees International Union reported that volunteers had made a computerized list of names and addresses of some 8,800 outlets where the *News* was being sold. (There had been some 25,000 outlets selling the *News* before the strike.)

The Transport Workers Union (TWU) also provided nonfinancial support to the Allied Printing Trades Council when TWU president Sonny Hall said the newspaper would be banned from the subways, as any sellers of the *News* in this area would have "their ass belong to us." Many dealers had declined to sell the newspaper in the subway system during the strike; however, the management's hawker-homeless program (discussed later in this chapter) introduced additional sellers into these areas. The Metropolitan Transit Authority (MTA) then rescinded its agreement with *Daily News* management, which had allowed the newspaper to be sold by hawkers in the subway. One "well-placed source" indicated the MTA took this action after Governor Cuomo's administration contacted the organization to express its concern "about potentially harmful effects of drawing commuters and subway riders into the dispute."[16] *News* management sought and received a temporary restraining order to enforce its subway newspaper sales agreement with the MTA.

Many unions did not approve of this decision, which enabled the *News* to be sold in the subway system. Barry Fernstein, president of the teamsters in New York, said:

We are not going to let a scab newspaper survive in the subways. . . . The strikers are going to be down in the subways with the hawkers, and if that screws up service, you can thank the *Daily News* for that.[17]

Some of the United Transportation Union locals that represent conductors and train and track workers on the Long Island Railroad (LIRR) and Metro-North cited safety problems as a reason for refusing to work during rush hours. James Phelan of the UTU referred to *News* management's estimate of 861 violent incidents caused by strike confrontations and expressed the view that his members as well as the traveling public should not be subject to "great personal risk" because of the hawkers.

The Transit Patrolmen's Benevolent Association (TPBA), whose members provide security in the subways, also did not want to be placed in the middle of a labor dispute and requested Judge Miriam Cedarbaum to lift the restraining order. Judge Cedarbaum had previously presided in the racial discrimination suit won by four *News* employees and had been criticized by *News* lawyers for not allowing crucial evidence to be introduced at the trial. She denied TPBA's request in the subway situation. A representative of the MTA indicated that an appeal of Judge Cedarbaum's decision "does not seem likely" since he was informed by counsel that it was strictly based on the First Amendment Right of Free Speech. At least one account suggested that the MTA's reluctance to appeal the restraining order was due to the friendship between James Hoge and Robert Kiley, chairman of the MTA.

John Sloan, the vice-president for Human Resources at the *News,* indicated that he was pleased that the court enabled the *News* to exercise its first amendment right to sell newspapers, and hoped that the transit police would enforce the decision. Sloan also indicated that the *News* would send 534 hawkers to 178 locations because the arrangement allowed three hawkers at each location, who could approach within ten feet of a newsstand that was not selling the newspaper.

There were no reported incidents during the first morning rush hour that hawkers were in the subway although *News* management reported that hawkers were physically abused and harassed at four of the seventeen locations on the Long Island Railroad for the first day of the federal court order. Management also contended that law officers who ignored these incidents had been identified and that appropriate legal actions would be taken to insure adequate law enforcement. In a related move, James Hoge sent the head of the MTA a strongly worded letter warning him that strikes by any transit employees would be illegal under the Taylor Law. Phelan of the UTU criticized the judge's decision and maintained that *News* management's intended response would result in "pure anarchy":

I think service is going to be interrupted. I think it's going to be chaotic. I think someone's going to be hurt. . . . The *Daily News* isn't doing these hawkers any favors by putting them on the platforms.[18]

Boycott

Management and the unions differed on the early impact of the advertiser boycott announced on October 30. The day before, Tom Van Arsdale, president of the Central Trades Council, had sent a letter to the top 100 *Daily News* advertisers, warning them that continued advertising in a "scab newspaper" would result in a boycott by unions who represented 1.3 million employees. A *News* spokesperson claimed the boycott was not effective as advertisements were holding steady; however, union representatives claimed that more than 70 retailers had pulled their advertisements. There was some evidence suggesting that the boycott exerted an early, adverse impact on the organization. *News* sales people began offering huge discounts for potential advertisers; an advertisement that normally cost $8,500, for example, was supposedly offered for $1,500. Many advertisers such as Macy's, Kiddie City Toys, Herman's World of Sporting Goods, Radio Shack, and Alexander's eliminated or considered eliminating advertisements from the *News* and/or placed advertisements in other New York newspapers. Advertisers' reluctance was due to uncertain and likely low circulation figures, and the fact that many of their employees and/or customers were union members. Alexander's decision might have been also influenced by a planned "shop in" involving one thousand union members. A union spokesperson indicated how this tactic would work:

People are going to go in like normal shoppers; they are going to the check-out counter and ask, "Are you advertising in the *Daily News?*". . . If they (cashiers) say yes, then they will say "I can't shop in this store" and dump their purchases on the counter and walk out.[19]

On Sunday, November 4, *New York Newsday* carried 115 ad pages, up from 40 before the strike. The *Post* had no Sunday paper but it carried 74 ad pages Friday, November 2 versus 46 the day after the strike began. Both *Newsday* and the *Post* had substantially increased their daily circulation since the *News* strike (from 714,000 copies to 870,000 copies and from 510,000 copies to 750,000 copies, respectively). The *New York Times,* however, had seen only a slight increase in circulation since the strike, and its 56 pages in advertising in its November 1 paper were identical to the total advertising pages a week before. A spokesperson for the *New York Times* indicated there was very little duplication in the advertising bases of the *News* and the *Times.*

Some radio stations pursued a different strategy than the *New York Times* by intentionally setting aside some inventory of time slots in case of a strike. One New York advertising agency president noted that many radio stations had special commercial packages targeted to *Daily News* advertisers.

One Tribune Company vice president indicated the *News,* while in a *"jihad"* with the unions, needed to continue its commitment to the New York advertisers to put the *Daily News* on a profitable basis. Yet, an editorial in *Advertising Age* during this time period noted that both management and union negotiators might have surrendered the fate of the *Daily News* to a peripheral third party, its advertisers, who, at the crucial Christmas holiday traffic period, would turn to other sources if the newspaper's messages could not be delivered soon.

By November 13, the *News* had become almost completely devoid of advertising. Its Veteran's Day issue had only four full-page ads — for a new brand of cigarettes; an airline; the city advertising its foster care program; and the *News* seeking newspaper vendors. These results were in spite of reported rebates of more than 80 percent made by the company. Adding insult to injury, *New York Newsday* published a 176-page newspaper on November 9, a near record for a weekday, filled with many advertisements traditionally placed in the *News.*

Unions also realized that they could lose if their advertising boycott were too successful. This action could prompt the *News* to close operations, thereby requiring the unions to have lengthy and expensive litigation to receive lost severance and wages.

Despite the eventual impact of the advertising boycott on union and management negotiators, more advertisers (Alexander's and Abraham and Strauss, for example) had pulled out of the *News* by November's final week. Macy's, which had been spending $8 to $10 million a year on advertisements in the *News,* ended its relationship with the *News* immediately before its most public event of the year, its Thanksgiving Day parade. John Sloan did not indicate the precise magnitude of the advertising boycott in November:

Due to the pattern of intimidation and threats against our advertisers, we are not going to confirm or deny any specific advertisers either leaving or staying in the *News.* We consider this continued intimidation and these threats grounds for criminal conspiracy charges, and when these issues are resolved and the strike is concluded, any advertisers that have temporarily left the paper will come quickly back to the *News,* since both large and small advertisers have told us that we are a large part of their advertising, marketing and promotional strategies.[20]

Samuel McKnight, the union lawyer who engineered the boycott, said that the *News* had lost all but 40 of its 615 prestrike advertisers.

MANAGEMENT'S DIFFICULTIES DURING THE STRIKE

Circulation Setbacks and Financial Losses

Management had to regard the strike's early days with optimism. One insider estimated that 175 replacement drivers were doing the work although they were only reaching just over half of the *News's* individual drop points. James Hoge further noted that 19 employees operated the mailroom with no overtime after the strike, compared with 179 employees performing these tasks before the strike occurred. John Sloan reported that 1,300 management, union, and replacement employees were producing the *News* since the strike began, and that operating costs had declined "dramatically" since the strike.

These statistics reinforced the notion previously discussed in Chapter 3 that management could convert the strike into a win-win situation. Reduced, if not eliminated, employee severance payments would result if the organization's operations were closed by a strike. Lower operating costs could also be realized if the *News* continued to be run with strike replacements and other nonunion employees. An executive at a rival newspaper indicated that in either situation, management would indicate that unions would not be tolerated at other Tribune operations. Wall Street reflected, if not acted, upon management's win-win situation:

Tribune's stock price has hardly moved in reaction to the strike, a fact that several analysts take as a sign that the most cold-blooded barometer of all, the stock market, sees the paper's death as no worse than its survival.[21]

Yet, management's situation was altered, if not reversed, as the strike extended beyond the first week. Theodore Kheel claimed the strike cost management $1 million a day, but Hoge refused to give a specific strike cost because "the figures are changing all the time." One rival newspaper executive familiar with the *News*'s bookkeeping procedures estimated that the newspaper's daily strike losses were substantial, but less than Kheel's figures. His estimate used the newspaper's 1989 revenue of $420 million as a baseline, split 50–50 between advertising and circulation revenues ($4 million a week in each category):

If the *News* is now selling papers at about one quarter of prestrike level, that brings in $1 million weekly. If the *News* has lost half of its ad revenues, it is left with $2 million, for a total of $3 million a week. On the expense side, *News* prestrike costs were around $9 million weekly. . . . Now the *News* truncated press runs and smaller work force produce savings of perhaps $3.5 million a week—$1 million on newsprint, $2.5 million on staff. This cuts expenses to $5.5 million—for a net weekly loss of $2.5 million.[22]

Other estimates figured the *News* was losing between $12 and $24 million a month during the strike compared to its prestrike losses of about $2 million a month.[23]

Much of this situation was due to declining circulation figures during the strike that eventually all but eliminated advertising revenues. Management's claims that it was distributing 600,000 to 1 million newspapers a day immediately after the strike occurred were ridiculed by circulation officials at rival newspapers who thought that a figure of 300,000 copies a day or fewer was more realistic. Eight days into the strike, management stopped issuing any circulation figures at all; Charles Brumback publicly acknowledged that the *News* had not expected such severe circulation problems. About two weeks into the strike, Hoge acknowledged that deliveries were being made to only 2,000 of the *News*'s more than 12,000 outlets.[24]

Management's Strike Miscalculations

Management had made at least four miscalculations that turned its win-win situation at the strike's start into a no-win "dance of death." First, it underestimated union solidarity found in the Allied Printing Trades Council and in New York City that reinforced the strikers' resolve. Second, management also erroneously assumed that *News* advertisers would continue participation and related funding because of an ideological identification with management in this dispute. Yet, one advertising agency representative suggested that decisions to advertise in the *News* were based on specific business considerations of where to spend

"precious money" instead of supporting the *News*'s quest to receive more managerial discretion over its employees. This situation was intensified by a factor also
not anticipated in management's strike preparations—the skidding local economy,
which made *Daily News* advertisers especially nervous.

Management's third miscalculation pertained to the sales outlets, particularly
newsstands. One executive, who was involved in strike preparations, likened the
dispute to a "war" and assumed that the dealers "would be on our side and
wouldn't be intimidated." Even John Scanlon, ardent *News* management backer
and spokesperson, agreed that management failed to consider the ethnic corporation of newsstand dealers:

The people selling papers at the newsstands today are the new immigrants and they are
easily intimidated. . . . The old-timers would have told the unions to shove it and continued to sell papers.[25]

Finally, perhaps no one could have foreseen the atmosphere of violence (described at the end of this chapter) that caused this intimidation, but in its strike
preparations, management appeared to be too narrowly focused on avoiding a
repetition of its failure during a 1978 strike to load trucks with newspapers. This
focus gravely obscured or discounted other considerations, such as the fact that
other members of the drivers' union visited almost all of the sales outlets every
day to deliver the *New York Times,* the *New York Post,* and magazines.

The *News* had accused many of these nonstriking drivers with threatening
newsstand operators. These individuals at a minimum provided daily reminders
to dealers of their own vulnerability should they decide to sell the *News.*

Perhaps management made its biggest miscalculation when it employed others,
including the homeless, to sell its newspaper. Jerry Nachman, editor of the *New
York Post,* expressed amazement at this recruiting development, "The homeless
are so repulsive to New Yorkers . . . that in many minds, the *Daily News* has
replaced the empty, stretched-out hand as an object of aversion."[26]

Many angry verbal exchanges took place between the hawkers and New York
City residents, particularly those who were union members. A Teamster official
described his rather vivid exchange with a homeless hawker selling the newspaper on an uptown Seventh Avenue express train:

I saw him coming and shouted out to the passengers "Don't buy that scab paper." . . . The
next thing I know he is shouting at me and pointing his fingers at me in gun style, saying
that "I would kill you except I am on parole."[27]

At least some newsstand dealers also thought that homeless hawkers were "bad
news," since they could keep all revenues from the sales of the paper. Dealers
only received 7 cents for every paper sold; however, they thought that their competitors would quickly diminish as winter arrived. One dealer commented that he
sometimes froze even under a newsstand with a heater at his feet.

The *News* first recruited homeless men at the Greenpoint Men's Shelter in Brooklyn on November 7, gave them subway tokens, and told them to report to the newspaper's headquarters the next morning. Nineteen individuals who showed up were then given bundles of newspapers to hawk to passersby. There seemed to be several potential financial arrangements between the *News* and the hawkers. Some of the homeless said the *News* would charge them 5 cents a copy but they had not received a bill. Others said they had been promised an initial cash payment of $24, plus a percentage of the money they took in, while others said they were told to keep the money from their newspaper sales on street corners and in subways.

This action brought rather sharp responses from unions and representatives of the homeless. George McDonald issued the following public statement two days after the homeless started selling the newspapers:

Hoge wants New Yorkers to think he is a humanitarian, but the truth is that in desperation to get his scab paper out, he is using the most desperate group of people in our city to do his dirty work for him. . . . As soon as Hoge gets what he wants, he'll discard the poor homeless just as he ruthlessly discarded 2,600 of his loyal long-time employees last month. People mean nothing to him.

The next thing you know, Hoge will be using poor children to peddle his scab rag. Obviously, his greed knows no bounds, and human life is cheap to him.[28]

McDonald's remarks were somewhat echoed by two advocates for the homeless. Peter Smith, president of the Partnership for the Homeless, which oversees 140 shelters in religious institutions, accused the *News* of targeting "the most vulnerable and the cheapest labor." As Mary Brosnahan, the executive director of the Coalition for the Homeless, contended:

It is unconscionable to be using the poorest of the poor as strike-breakers. What the homeless need is real jobs, and the *Daily News* is not interested in really helping these people.[29]

A management spokesperson denied that the organization was recruiting the homeless or at homeless shelters; however, the newspaper could not deny the related advertisement for "hawker programs" that read:

OWN AND OPERATE YOUR OWN BUSINESS

NEWSPAPER STREET SALES

UNLIMITED INCOME

The Daily News has immediate need for individuals who want to OWN, OPERATE, and DIRECT THEIR OWN WORK FORCE selling newspapers.

If you can organize and manage people and know the "streets" of New York, we want you to run a "Hawkers" program, which, in return, will provide you unlimited earnings.

We will assist you in starting your business and will advise you on how to set up and manage your operations.

Apply in Person:
Daily News
Patterson Room
220 East 42d Street
New York, New York 10017

DAILY NEWS
New York's Home Town Paper

The *Wall Street Journal* blasted specific homeless "advocates" on its editorial page. It contended that Mary Brosnahan and others sharing her attitude should have been demanding better police protection for the homeless, who had been given an alternative to panhandling:

Free enterprise may not be a panacea for the homeless. Many need treatment for mental disorders or drug addiction before they can be expected to work productively. But it is the best hope of those who are homeless simply because they're down on their luck. Siding with the unions and other supporters of economic regulation may establish the liberal credentials of homeless advocates. But it's disastrous for the homeless, who can compete in the work force only if the market is free.[30]

Controversy over the proper role for homeless advocates notwithstanding, several hawkers reported they made between $20 and $150 a day and experienced very little harassment. One hawker indicated that he did not mind being called a "scab" and "union buster" so long as he did not suffer physical violence. Another commented that this represented the only decent job he had in two years. While he felt sorry about the strikers, he thought his troubles at least equaled theirs.

Little evidence exists, however, to suggest that employing 800 homeless hawkers, while increasing circulation (according to Sloan, 150,000 copies a day), resulted in any significant advertising or newspaper revenues for the *News*. Indeed, this action likely galvanized union solidarity and related public support, which ignored if not condoned strike-related violence in the city.

STRIKE VIOLENCE

Police had recorded about 180 strike-related incidents and made at least 89 arrests by November 18. Management had indicated that 130 arrests had occurred by November 30 and that a total of 722 serious incidents had impeded or obstructed the distribution and publication of the newspaper. They further contended that 51 people were injured (10 of them hospitalized) and 112 *Daily News* trucks and buses had been damaged. Most of these incidents occurred in the first two weeks of the strike. For example, management reported that 655 serious incidents had occurred by November 8. The incidents also did not directly apply to a large proportion of the vendors, since the prestrike *News* had been sold in some 25,000 retail outlets, including about 300 newsstands.

The continuation of these incidents through November, however, exerted a far larger impact on distribution than that directly derived from their specific occurrence. Newspaper delivery was hindered by such violent acts as rock throwing, the attack on a driver's vehicle with golf clubs, and the beating of a driver with a pipe. One of the more violent strike incidents occurred on November 14 when 12 men pulled two nonunion *News* drivers out of their truck, beat them with baseball bats, and bombed the truck. The driver was treated for minor injuries while his assistant was hospitalized with a broken arm. Police labeled the event a "guerilla attack" because the attacker's van had blocked the truck, enabling the attackers to let air out of the truck's tires. No arrests were made, however. Mike Alvino, president of the drivers' union, contended that his members were not involved in this episode that could have been committed by many angry, unemployed people in New York City, even members of *News* management whose strike handbook urged them to do everything to make the unions look bad. Some members of the drivers' union did admit, however, that they either stole or scattered bundled copies of the *News* from delivery points. There was also some evidence that union drivers of rival newspapers engaged in these activities and blocked *News* delivery trucks with their vans.

Violence was also directed at newsstands and other retail outlets that sold the *News*. One of the earlier and more publicized incidents (in the *Daily News*) involved a Queens news dealer's store:

The enforcers had visited him several times, explaining how it worked: On Queens Blvd., you don't sell the *Daily News*. On Thursday, Nooruddin Kurji decided that he didn't work for anyone but himself and that he would sell whatever newspaper he liked.

Yesterday, before dawn, Kurji's Rego Park News Inc. was visited again. A flammable liquid was splashed over the bundles of newspapers that had been dropped outside during the night—and set afire. The blaze spread to the 15-foot storefront.

"We sold the *Daily News*," Kurji explained to customers yesterday as he cleaned up the fire and water damage. "We got punished."

Daily News officials said they will provide Kurji, who is about 5-feet-5 and 120 pounds, with 24-hour security and will offer him $5,000 for his loss.[31]

The article also indicated that many of Kurji's neighbors expressed outrage over this event. But a related article in the *New York Times* indicated that the *News* offer fell far short of the $15,000 that had been suffered in store/inventory damage. Also, Kurji blamed *News* management for the fire, charging that he had resumed selling the newspaper only after being assured that it was safe because the delivery trucks had security guards with them.

Blame notwithstanding, other dealers quickly received the message, which was reinforced by visits from employees working at the *Post, New York Times,* and *Newsday,* and did not attempt to sell the *News*. Although vandalism such as broken windows, glue in locks, and the occasional use of M80 firecrackers, continued to occur after this incident, there were no reported injuries from individuals who sold the newspaper through November 18. Two days later, however, a fire-bomb thrown at a Bronx bodega slightly injured two owners. Vendors' fears of violence remained widespread. Michael Alvino conceded that a few of his drivers' union members might have issued threats in the emotional heat of the strike, but that the large majority of his members politely, albeit persistently, asked dealers not to sell the *News*. Theodore Kheel agreed with Alvino and suggested that subtler factors than violence were behind the dealers' decisions not to sell the *News:*

When a great big, strapping *Daily News* driver comes and politely pleads with you not to sell the paper, that is intimidating in itself. . . . Also, the vendors' sympathies may be with the striking drivers because they know them and because they figure they may have to deal with them once the strike ends.[32]

Kheel's comments were supported by a top executive of a competing newspaper who indicated that dealers had "no brand loyalty," particularly if they could obtain the same revenues selling another product. Dealers seemed to be able to pick up the slack with selling copies of other newspapers. For example, a dealer along 42d Street typically sold 700 copies of the *Daily News,* 100 of *Newsday,* and 600 of the *Post*. During the strike he sold no *Daily News,* 300 to 400 *Newsdays* and 1,200 copies of the *Post*.

Dealers no doubt maintained their sales of other items (tobacco, candy, and so forth) associated with similar or higher newspaper sales. One observer also maintained that dealers could maintain another source of income by cooperating with the drivers.

Neither the *News* nor its competitors have touched on the real street story. The drivers and the newsstand operators have a good deal going; intimidation is hardly needed in a relationship based on mutual advantage. "There's not a newspaper or magazine doing business in this town that doesn't have a category called 'unaccountables,' " explains the circulation director at one of the city's papers. A driver can make an off-the-books delivery – say, an extra bundle of skin magazines – and split the cash proceeds with the newsstand operator. The operator needs no physical threat to forego the loose change from his *News* sales: Why should he offend his driver–business partner?[33]

Dealers' reluctance to sell the *News* may have also been prompted by fears of violence by union sympathizers. This situation was evidenced in early November when a driver of a *Daily News* delivery truck heaved more than 100 bundles of inside sections of the next day's edition onto the sidewalk in front of a branch of Alexander's (a major *News* advertiser). As a description of the subsequent events indicated:

Passersby fell on the bundles, tearing them open and rooting through the comics and color advertising inserts – including one touting a sale at Alexanders – scattering newsprint into the air.

"We ain't buying it" . . . as [a participant in the event] put a rolled-up newspaper under her arm. It's free, that's why I took it. I'm a union person and I won't buy it until they let the union back in.[34]

Management's Charges

Management never seemed to have much of the public's sympathy during this time period. There was little public indignation expressed over the violent incidents and no demand that the *News* be sold. One observer noted that the newspaper had actually "disappeared" in certain sections of the city and "no one asks for it."

A *Chicago Tribune* editorial acknowledged its company's self interest in the strike's outcome. However, it further indicated that sellers of the *News* ended this relationship, not because they disagreed with *News* management, but because they feared retaliatory violence, which, "tolerated to an unbelievable degree by the authorities, puts [New York City] outside the system of free expression. . . . New York is a labor town, they say, as if this excuses behavior that, if done by any other group in society, would be considered an insult to the liberal values of which New York likes to think it is the stoutest guardian."[35]

Management also criticized Mayor Dinkins for not insisting that the police give more protection to *News* vendors and drivers during the month. Albert Scardino, Mayor Dinkins's press secretary, responded to one such criticism, "The Mayor has been very forceful in his instructions to the Police Department to keep the public order and the streets clear. . . . There are not enough police in the city to guard every newsstand."[36] Scardino's comments might have been correct; however, they ignored attitudes of some police officers charged with regulating labor–management behaviors during the strike. As one spokesperson for the Patrolmen's Benevolent Association suggested:

The cops are treading a thin line between being union members and doing their jobs . . . [and] are in the middle of a bad situation. They have to protect the scabs.[37]

James Hoge also publicly berated New York City's residents for not having the moral sense to support management in its fight against the striking unions' violent actions; moreover, he blamed rival newspapers for not aggressively investigating and reporting the management's claims of serious violence:

We have provided tons of information. . . . the list of violent incidents is [some six inches] high. . . .
But reporters for competing newspapers don't take the trouble to check out the story. The violence on the streets has been unreported.
If they bothered to look, they would find of course there's a conspiracy out there.[38]

Hoge had promulgated the "conspiracy" consideration in early November when he accused the striking unions of "an organized, systematic, centrally controlled conspiracy of crime" whose goal was to "cripple delivery of the paper." He further claimed that hundreds, maybe thousands, of small businessmen received threats to their lives and property by striking union members, who behaved like "hoodlums." He moreover likened the "outrageous" tactics employed by unions to the "protectionist racket of organized crime."

Management's first legal processing of its "conspiracy" charges featured three civil suits against 11 people who had already been arrested and charged in three incidents during the strike's first week. Each action sought punitive damages of $100,000 and unspecified compensatory damages. One suit alleged that a member of the drivers' union set fire to a delivery truck outside the Brooklyn plant on October 25; moreover, this action and others so frightened news dealers that they stopped selling the newspaper.

Another named two nonstriking *Wall Street Journal* drivers, who were charged with engaging in a conspiracy to hurt the newspaper when they allegedly stole bundles of the *News* that had been left at a drop-off point by nonunion drivers. The eight other defendants (four paper handlers and four pressmen) were charged with forming a "flying wedge" and attacking a group of nonunion drivers and independent distributors. Management claimed that there were eyewitnesses and/ or videotapes that supported its allegations.

Theodore Kheel labeled these actions "a grandstand effort to get publicity" and a libelous attempt to portray the unions as violent conspirators. Kheel supported his reaction with a statement John Sloan had issued earlier in the day that noted that the *News* was rebuilding its circulation day by day without Kheel and his "violent thugs" who continue threats against news dealers.

James Hoge had a second opportunity to present his conspiracy allegations at a New York state legislative hearing concerning the possible outlawing of strike replacements. Making his first public appearance since the first day of the strike at the November 26 hearing, Hoge testified that the strike's first four weeks experienced some 700 incidents of assaults, harassment, and damage to property and persons. Further, centralized planning and execution were involved because the events were both sudden and sustained. Hoge documented his allegations by noting that arrested union members were able to put up "instant cash bail," were using union lawyers, and had "computerized lists" of distribution points.

Hoge's charges were refuted by Police Chief Robert Johnston, Jr. who said that as of the hearing date he knew of only 229 serious incidents, including 107 arrests, 75 of whom were strikers. Chief of Detectives Joseph Borrelli further regarded each arrest as an isolated incident with absolutely no basis for a conspiracy.

Frank J. Barbaro, cochairperson of the committee and an assembly member from Brooklyn, expressed anger at Hoge for not considering several offers made by Mayor Dinkins, Governor Cuomo, and John J. Cardinal O'Connor to mediate the dispute. Barbaro also bristled when Hoge suggested that he should look at arrest sheets to obtain correct insights into the issue. Barbaro loudly informed Hoge that his comments were "self-serving" and "totally inappropriate."

George McDonald, who also testified at the hearing, indicated that this occasion was the first time that he or any of the union leaders had been in the same room with Hoge in two years. McDonald had also informed Hoge the day of the hearing that labor–management negotiations were "more likely to be more productive if you are in charge."

After the hearing, Hoge might not have heard two reporters taunting him. Juan Gonzales shouted, "Jim, you set a record for lies," while Mark Kriegel indicated Hoge was "nothing but a mistress for the *Chicago Tribune.*" Several other union placards around the city read, "Get rid of the Hog(e)!" Hoge said that blaming management for the violence "was the wrong message to send to the city." His remarks were seconded by an editorial in *Editor and Publisher* that defined "conspiracy" as "agreement between two or more persons to do an evil act in concert," and cited related events such as 12 men attacking a *News* delivery truck with baseball bats and bombs and 15 men invading a store to stop *News* sales. The editorial concluded:

The unions and their members seem determined: If they cannot have their own way about the operation of the *News,* then nobody else has the right to work there, nobody has the right to print the paper, and nobody has the right to read it. So much for the rights of everyone else.[39]

Three days after the hearing, management again displayed its conspiracy hypothesis in a lawsuit filed in the United States District Court in Manhattan. The 109-page complaint charged the striking drivers' union, 23 of its members, and the Allied Printing Trades Council (APTC) with violating federal racketeering laws (RICO) with conspiring to coerce *News* management either to accept a labor agreement featuring featherbedding or to sell the newspaper to the striking unions. The suit sought treble damages in excess of $150 million and

- described Theodore Kheel's offer to purchase the *News* and related violence that was conducted to further that purchase to his personal benefit;
- contended that Michael Alvino, president of the drivers' union, and George McDonald, president of the APTC, "ratified, condoned, and incited" the unlawful actions of drivers' union members; and
- described the "notorious history" of the leadership of the drivers' union, including convictions or guilty pleas for crimes of "extortion, income tax evasion, operating a union as a racketeering enterprise, kickbacks, payoffs and bribery."

Alvino was not specifically mentioned in the suit but attempted to put this peripheral bargaining tactic into a traditional bargaining perspective:

I haven't seen [the suit], I haven't talked to the lawyers. . . . I'm not involved in any organized type of thing outside of legal boycotts. We're asking people not to buy the paper in a legal manner. . . . I've negotiated in good faith. . . . I've offered them relief. . . . I've given my best to try to avoid this strike.[40]

Unions' Responses

A spokeseperson for the APTC called management's charges in its RICO suit "false and malicious." She also noted that Kheel and the unions would file a $100 million civil libel action against the newspaper, Hoge, and the Tribune Company, along with its chief operating officer, Charles T. Brumback. Kheel indicated that the statements made by police officials at the state legislative hearing, November 26, blew management's conspiracy charge out of the water forever, although the large number of subsequent/related lawsuits would create a lawyer's paradise.

The striking unions had also responded to allegations of violence before management filed the RICO lawsuit. Union officials had reiterated that management's strike preparations had provoked the strike with its emphasis on "mental violence" and the "napalming of the human spirit." They also noted throughout November various incidents/ arrests caused by management security guards, "goon squads" supplied by such firms as the Special Response Corporation of Towson, Maryland. In one incident, for example, they charged that a woman organizer from Local 1199 had been bruised when a security guard hit her with a walkie-talkie as she and others were destroying *News* copies they claimed they had bought from a street vendor.

George McDonald formally notified Mayor Dinkins and Police Commissioner Brown of management violence in a telegram on November 11 that read, in part:

The *Daily News* has unleashed a private army of terrorists onto the streets of New York City. . . .

This army of combat-ready troops comprised of men in ski masks, combat boots, and black body suits are unleashing a reign of terror on the people of the city of New York. Published police reports state that Special Response Corporation troops are using martial arts sticks and other illegal and life-threatening weapons on not only striking union members, but on the general public as well.

These mercenary terrorists must be stopped before they take an innocent life. I await your immediate response.[41]

Shortly after this telegram, union leaders urged the New York State Attorney General, Robert Abrams, to investigate whether management violated the state laws governing use and licensing of out-of-state security guards. The General Business Law, for example, prohibits a company involved in a labor dispute from furnishing any of its out-of-state hired employees with weapons.

Management responded that none of these individuals were armed, although some of these employees had told others they had been licensed to carry firearms. Spokespersons further maintained that any investigation of strike-related violence would "undoubtedly lead to the union strikers" and that the unions could better spend their time eliminating "the marauding of their own members."

Yet these remarks were not strengthened the next day when Jim McCully indicated to a *New York Times* reporter that he responded to an advertisement placed by Securex, Inc. of London, Kentucky. His subsequent assignment in Fairfield,

New Jersey, was to pay him a $150 advance, approximately $700 for an 84-hour week, working 12 hours on, 12 off, as well as a $1,500 bonus if he completed the full tour estimated at 120 days.

McCully indicated that he only received a $50 advance, and that he had to pay for food even though the company paid for the motel rooms that did not have telephones, "when they get you there, they pretty much know you are broke [and treat you] like hostages." He further described his job assignment:

They had us equipped with camcorders and 35-millimeter cameras. . . . They had a chase car that was supposed to follow the trucks. In the chase cars, too, were camcorders and 35-millimeter cameras. The bottom line was they were going to get some documentation on film of union members beating up on the heads of these guys so they could take them to court and freeze their assets. We were put there as bait.[42]

James Hoge informed Max Frankel, executive editor of the *New York Times,* that his newspaper's "bait" article was "distorted," "unfair," and based on "skimpy, unsubstantiated talk," since one of the two sources quoted in the article had never worked for the security firm while the other had only worked one day. Hoge further stressed that the *Daily News* was prudent, not conspiratorial, in cautioning all its employees "to be nonviolent and to restrict their activities to documenting the violence perpetrated *against them* by striking workers."[43]

Union leaders also questioned the role of the New York City police in strike-related violence. There were some specific allegations of police brutality. One reporter, for example, claimed he was arrested, punched in the stomach, and denied a telephone call for several hours after asking for the badge numbers of police at a rally. This incident prompted Norman Siegel, the head of the New York Civil Liberties Union, to label the police as the *News*'s "private security force," since they expressed a "complete nonrecognition of the strikers' First Amendment rights."

Unions also criticized the police for providing too much protection for delivery operations at taxpayers' expense. The bill for police overtime from the date the strike began until November 18 was $3.2 million, an average of $145,000 a day, although police had also stopped the practice of escorting delivery trucks during this time period. George McDonald and Theodore Kheel met with Police Commissioner Brown on November 19 to discuss alleged police hostilities against strikers and their more general, expensive role in the strike. Hoge suggested the union leaders were seeking less police protection because it would expose *News* operations and distribution to "even *more* shocking levels of arson and assault."

McDonald said that he was "very satisfied" with the meeting. Commissioner Brown said after the discussion that the police's dual roles of neutrality and maintaining the peace would not change. One strike observer revealed two common denominators between union and management charges and countercharges regarding violence. "Both sides have denounced violence, but neither has said their people will be punished if they are found to have participated in any attacks."[44]

NOTES

1. Edwin Diamond, "The Incredible Shrinking Newspaper," *New York*, December 3, 1990, 41–42, 43. See also, "Labor Lawyer Makes Offer to Buy New York Daily News," Bureau of National Affairs, Inc., *Daily Labor Report* 213 (November 2, 1990): A-16, A-17.

2. David E. Pitt, "Daily News Unions Said to Be Ready to Take Cuts," *New York Times*, November 9, 1990, A-18.

3. David E. Pitt, "Emotions High During Seminar on Daily News," *New York Times*, November 17, 1990, 26.

4. Hoge had indicated that as of November 3d he had personally briefed Governor Cuomo and Cardinal O'Connor and had met twice with Dinkins—in addition to frequent telephone conversations.

5. Martin Gottlieb, "The Newsroom: Doubts and 14-Hour Workdays," *New York Times*, November 3, 1990, 2.

6. Pete Bowles, "Braving the Line," *Newsday*, October 30, 1990. Dialog File 638, item 05809154.

7. Alessandra Stanley, "A Union: The Staunch, the Desperate, the Undecided," *New York Times*, November 2, 1990, B-3.

8. David E. Pitt, "News Sues 11 in Strike, Citing Acts of Violence," *New York Times*, November 21, 1990, B-2.

9. David E. Pitt, "News Hopes to Lure Minority Journalists," *New York Times*, November 6, 1990, B-4. The AAJA had 1,000 members, the NAHA had 900 members, and the NABJ had some 2,000 members.

10. David E. Pitt, "Black Journalists Won't Assist News," *New York Times*, November 7, 1990, B-2.

11. Sheryl McCarthy, "Striking Lesson in Loyalty," *Newsday*, November 12, 1990. Dialog File 638, item 05822129.

12. George Garneau, "Daily News Shifts Strategy," *Editor and Publisher*, November 10, 1990, 15.

13. Elaine Rivera, "Reporter's Notebook: Breaking News on The Picket Line," *Newsday*, November 4, 1990. Dialog File 638, item 05814228. McAlary returned to the *News* some two-and-a-half years later. For related details see Chapter 8, Note 35.

14. "It's Organized Terror: Hoge," *New York Daily News*, November 3, 1990 (Located in News Bank), Media and Communications, 52: A-4.

15. Garneau, "Daily News Shifts Strategy."

16. Kenneth C. Crowe and Paul Moses, "News' Hawkers Pit MTA, Unions," *Newsday*, December 1, 1990. Dialog File 638, item 05842077.

17. David E. Pitt, "News Upheld on Hawking in Stations," *New York Times*, December 1, 1990, 27.

18. Katherine Foran and Curtis Rist, "RR Unions: Hawkers Would Bring Anarchy," *Newsday*, December 2, 1990. Dialog File 638, item 05843169.

19. Scott Ladd, "Jackson Has News for Hoge," *Newsday*, November 3, 1990. Dialog File 638, item 05813102.

20. Andrew L. Yarrow, "Alexander's Joins Large Retailers That Won't Advertise in the News," *New York Times*, November 27, 1990, B-5.

21. Thomas B. Rosentiel, "Woes of N.Y. Daily News Go Way Beyond Current Strike," *Los Angeles Times*, November 14, 1990, D-1 and D-5.

22. Edwin Diamond, "The Incredible Shrinking Newspaper," *New York,* December 3, 1990, 41–42, 43.

23. At a November 26 state legislative hearing on a proposal to ban replacement employees (discussed later in this chapter), James Hoge said the *News* would lose about $85 million in 1990, pushing 11-year losses to $200 million. The yearly loss exceeded analysts' predictions and included between $15 million and $30 million in strike preparation and operation costs.

24. Hoge said daily circulation was 500,000 copies in November's last week. Also, 4,000 sales outlets and 1,000 hawkers were selling the *News* at this time.

25. Dennis Duggan, "New York Diary: Army of News Hawkers Paper's Key to Survival," *Newsday,* November 20, 1990. Dialog File 638, item 05830218.

26. James Warren, *"Odd Couple:* The News Strike Is Not Without Its Domicile for Post Editor Nachman," *Chicago Tribune,* December 16, 1990, sec. 5, p. 2.

27. Duggan, "New York Diary."

28. "McDonald Blasts Hoge for Exploitation of Homeless," PR Newswire, November 10, 1990. Dialog File 613, item 0320581–NYSA002. For a rather detailed account of the hawkers' experiences and attitudes similar to McDonald, see Keith M. Brown, "New York Forum About Labor. I Sold My Body to the News," *Newsday,* December 11, 1990. Dialog File 638, item 05852061.

29. Kieran Crowley and Michael Shain, "New York's Homeless Paper," *New York Post,* November 9, 1990 (Located in News Bank), Media and Communications 52: A-8.

30. James Taranto, "The Homeless Are Ill-Served by Advocates," *Wall Street Journal,* November 14, 1990, A-16.

31. "Visited by Enforcers," *New York Daily News,* November 3, 1990 (Located in News Bank), Media and Communications, 52: A-13.

32. David E. Pitt, "Daily News and Police Vary on Degree of Violence," *New York Times,* November 8, 1990, B-18.

33. Edwin Diamond, "The Incredible Shrinking Newspaper," *New York,* December 3, 1990, 42.

34. John Kifner, "Daily News Strike Becomes A Battle for Advertisers," *New York Times,* November 4, 1990, 1, 38.

35. "Duel of Bludgeons and the Voice" (editorial), *Chicago Tribune,* November 25, 1990, sec. 4, p. 2.

36. David E. Pitt, "Circulation Hurt, News Gives Away Many of Its Copies," *New York Times,* November 3, 1990, 1.

37. Mitch Gelman, "Strike Costs City $465,000 in Police OT," *Newsday,* October 30, 1990. Dialog File 638, item 05809154.

38. Michael Shain, "Daily News Boss Rips Hometown," *New York Post,* December 6, 1990 (Located in News Bank), Media and Communications 56: F-4. Hoge's newspaper had noted about a month earlier that the *New York Times* had become the first competitor of the *News* to renounce violence. The editorial indicated that union leaders had made "barely dutiful statements until they reject violence sternly and unequivocally, and work to restrain their members, they're more likely to repel the public than attract its support." "Assails Union 'Crime,' " *New York Daily News,* November 3, 1990 (Located in News Bank), Media and Communications 52: A-14. Hoge was also no doubt aware that articles and editorials in other nonlocal publications condemned violence during this time period. For example, an article in *MacLean's* (November 12, 1990, 72) was titled, "A Violent Standoff: Strikers Attack New York's Daily News," whereas an editorial in the *Christian*

Science Monitor ("Save the Daily News," November 9, 1990, 20) noted that some union workers had resorted to "inexcusable goon tactics." An editorial in the *Wall Street Journal* ("City to News: Drop Dead," November 30, 1990, A-14) reported in the last week in November that one of the few remaining midtown news dealers selling the *News* was shot at after a visit from more than a dozen union members.

39. "Acting in Concert-Conspiracy," *Editor and Publisher,* December 8, 1990, 6.

40. Scott Ladd and Paul Moses, "News Hits Union with $150M Suit," *Newsday,* November 30, 1990. Dialog File 638, item 05840102.

41. "Text of McDonald Telegram to Mayor Dinkins and Police Commissioner," PR Newswire, November 11, 1990. Dialog File 649, item 09589611–1112NYSU002.

42. John Kifner, "Guards Say They Were Hired by Daily News as 'Bait' in Strike," *New York Times,* November 15, 1990, B-10.

43. "New York Daily News at Odds with the New York Times," *Editor and Publisher,* November 24, 1990, 38–39.

44. Rose Marie Arce, "Both Sides Wage War of Tabloid Words," *Newsday,* November 12, 1990. Dialog File 638, item 05822104.

5

Seventy More Days of Peripheral Bargaining

Violence and the involvement of governmental officials and agencies continued in the labor dispute through December 1990 and January 1991. Management and union negotiators also focused on various concerns within their respective organizations. Management became preoccupied with advertising and circulation losses while unions, particularly the Newspaper Guild, were concerned with building a membership consensus. The external developments, coupled with the self-absorption of the union and management organizations, ensured that peripheral bargaining (nonexistent bargaining table activities and results) also continued through this time period.

CONTINUING EXTERNAL DEVELOPMENTS

Intensification of Violence

On December 5, management added three civil suits to the four filed in November. These suits sought actual and punitive damages in excess of $100,000 from eight individuals for alleged unlawful interference with distribution of the *News* through assault, battery, theft, and vandalism. The first suit alleged that a *New York Times* truck driver slammed his vehicle into the back of a *Daily News* truck, then assaulted the *News* driver who had to be treated at a hospital for severe injuries.

A second suit named four individuals who were charged with attacking *News* hawkers with baseball bats and crowbars, while the third charged a single defendant with illegally harassing, threatening, and/or assaulting two independent contractors who delivered the *News*. The fourth suit charged two individuals with attacking and injuring two *News* employees. James Hoge indicated why these suits were filed:

We are not going to let people use violence and intimidation to prevent the newspaper from getting into the hands of our readers. . . . If they try, they will be brought to justice and forced to pay for any damage they cause.[1]

The next day at 4:45 A.M. a *Daily News* driver, Carlos Chacon, and his helper were attacked by 12 to 15 men who beat them with baseball bats and bottles. Chacon was also stabbed with a knife three times (twice in the abdomen and once in the buttocks). According to the victims, one assailant said, "These people that work for the *Daily News* are taking my job. I'm going to kill you."[2] Chacon was left bleeding on the street while the truck was stolen and subsequently abandoned by the assailants.

Hoge responded to this most serious, violent incident since the strike began by offering a $100,000 reward for information leading to the arrest and conviction of those involved in the stabbing. He also called for a task force of federal, state, and local law enforcement agencies to probe what he said was a "criminal conspiracy of violence." Hoge urged the police to face up to the situation that "gangsters are running free" in New York City. Barry Lipton responded angrily to Hoge's comments: "Jim Hoge repeating something over and over like a parrot doesn't make a conspiracy. . . . This is meaningless babble from a desperate man."[3]

The day after the Chacon stabbing, police reported six strike-related incidents that resulted in ten arrests, some damage, and minor injuries. These incidents included protesting over the selling of the *News,* fighting directed at delivery truck replacement drivers and helpers, breaking delivery truck windows with baseball bats and pipes, scattering newspaper bundles, and hurling a fire bomb onto the roof of a delivery truck.

Two days after these arrests, fourteen tractor-trailer cabs were set afire, and five others were vandalized at a company that provided paper to the *Daily News.* Damage was estimated in the hundreds of thousands of dollars. An editorial in *Editor and Publisher* indicated that these events represented an extension of intimidation of *News* vendors to *News* suppliers.

A press release issued by management on December 12 furnished an update on violent incidents since the strike began on October 25 and also reflected growth in its financial reward policy:

Serious incidents: 888

Number of arrests: 144

Injuries: 66

Persons hospitalized: 11

Trucks and busses destroyed or damaged: 147

The reward for information leading to an arrest has been doubled from $500 to $1000; and the reward for information leading to a conviction has been doubled from $5,000 to $10,000. Rewards are offered for information on strike-related violence, threats, theft, or vandalism toward the *Daily News* or any persons representing or selling the paper. A 24-hour reward line (212-949-2308) is available for those who wish to report acts of strike-related violence.[4]

News management continued to file civil suits against unions and individuals charged with strike-related violence. On December 17, the *News* sought damages in excess of $50 million against nine striking unions and the Allied Printing Trades Council (APTC). The suit (not to be confused with the RICO suit filed on November 30) charged the defendants with violating federal labor law when they took action against neutral third parties, newsstand dealers, and advertisers who were uninvolved in the labor dispute.

Three days later, *News* management also filed four more civil suits (for a total of eleven since the strike began) against eight individuals. These suits charged violence similar to that in preceding cases, although new weapons such as a flare gun and flare loads, a flammable liquid, and a bayonet could have been used in these activities. (Another three suits were filed against six strikers on January 10, 1991.)

Violence and related arrests intensified just before New Year's Day. Two striking *Daily News* employees were arrested for the Chacon stabbing at about the same time that a security guard scared off a person who had placed a bomb underneath the gas tank of a bus used to transport nonunion employees to their temporary hotel lodging. Another arrest occurred when three persons opened the rear of a *News* truck in the Bronx and threw a firebomb that failed to ignite. This same day, police sought another striking driver who had been identified by a newsstand dealer in Suffolk County as having consistently stolen copies of the *Daily News* since the strike began.

In December, a Congressional hearing was held to examine the impact of using permanent replacement employees in the *Daily News* strike. George McDonald, one of the union officials who testified at this hearing, concluded that the *Daily News's* eventual use of permanent replacements was consistent with its stance as an "antiunion employer," one that

looks at collective bargaining negotiations as an opportunity to destroy the rights of his employees rather than an opportunity to arrive at a mutually acceptable contract. This is contrary to the national labor policy, to sound social policy, and to the most basic notions of decency.[5]

James Hoge, who had earlier pressed for a federal, state, and local task force to look into strike-related violence, indicated that he was unable to attend this hearing and chose not to send a representative from the *News* and/or Tribune Company. However, his prepared statement submitted at the hearing urged the committee to condemn violence, "hooliganism," and the "breakdown of law and order" in New York City's streets, instead of questioning the employer's right to hire strike replacements, which Hoge did not regard as a "solution to this problem." He further chided the subcommittee for sending "the wrong message" — considering a bill that would reward the criminals and punish the victim, the *Daily News*'s organization, and its employees. He reasoned that far more employees were lost to companies going out of business because of inefficient, costly work rules than those replaced when they were out on strike.

Hoge had another chance to demonstrate his contentions about union violence in an almost automatic fashion on February 7, when four striking pressmen were arrested and charged with criminal mischief and possession of a firearm. The pressmen allegedly used a sling shot and steel balls to break a window of a Hillside Bedding store in Queens, an organization that advertised in the *News*. The president of Hillside Bedding, aware that two of his other stores were vandalized the same night and that more than 20 acts of violence had occurred at his stores, supported Hoge's assessment of coordinated union violence.

Involvement of Public Officials

James Hoge sent an advance copy of his prepared remarks before the Congressional hearing on strike replacements. His cover letter, released at a news conference, admonished New York's Cardinal John J. O'Connor for suggesting that hiring permanent replacements was "immoral":

In continuing to conduct its business, the *Daily News* has followed strictly the laws of New York State and of the United States. We also have continued collective bargaining with striking unions, indeed urging that the pace and frequency of negotiations be stepped up. Therefore, I have been troubled by press reports of your questioning and morality of the *Daily News* exercising its lawful right to employ replacement workers. We would not have done so unless the very survival of the business was not threatened after a strike began. I am also troubled that the illegal, massive, and continuing violence against *Daily News* employees and thousands of small businesspersons has not been seen as the moral outrage which it is against the entire civilized community and against the rule of law.[6]

O'Connor stated and restated management's "immoral" strike replacement tactics at the hearing, and at a rally held the night before the Congressional hearing and the quarterly board meeting of the Tribune Company. The Reverend Jesse Jackson also attended this rally of some 6,500 union supporters in front of the News Building at E. 42d Street, and he indicated that the strike was "immoral," "illegal," and "wrong," since it used the homeless to make other people homeless. Richard Trumka, AFL-CIO vice president, told the crowd that strike replacements will "burn in hell" for crossing the picket lines. He likened the *Daily News* organization to other companies that support apartheid in South Africa because it spent $24 million to break a union, "but not one penny" to put clothes on the backs of union members and their families. (Another rally drawing some 2,000 individuals was held at about this time at the *Daily News* Garden City facility.)

New York Mayor David Dinkins, who did not appear at the 42d Street rally, was loudly booed when his name was mentioned in a speech. Hoge might have also joined the chorus of boos if he had been in the audience since he wanted the Mayor to condemn specific conspiratorial acts of urban violence more forcefully and specifically instead of issuing a general declaration of all violence at any time. Dinkins had repeatedly offered to mediate the strike but had not taken a public stand on the issues. He did speak briefly at a benefit for the Newspaper Guild four nights after the rally that also featured Jessica Hahn, Lou Reed, Pete Seeger, and the Roches. Dinkins stopped short of endorsing the strike but reiterated his strong union ties, expressed his concern for how the strikers had "suffered," and opined, "It's pretty clear that the *Daily News* should get back to the bargaining table."[7]

Dinkins also held a January 17 breakfast meeting with union and management negotiators at Gracie Mansion. The session represented the first time that Hoge and union leaders had been in the same room since the November 16 legislative hearing. Mayor Dinkins thought that some progress was made because each side understood the other and indicated a desire to focus on future relationships instead of debate where they had been.

Governor Mario Cuomo's speech at the rally symbolized his most overt support of the unions since the strike had begun. Cuomo compared the *News* strike to the equally publicized, if not more acrimonious, and disastrous labor dispute at Eastern Airlines, and indicated that the *News* situation must have a successful ending. He also urged the strikers to "stay strong," since they were fighting for the necessary balance between the people who work and the people who invest and manage, and asked rhetorically, "Where would this country be without a strong union movement?"[8] Cuomo's speech was frequently interrupted by crowd chants of "Mario, Mario." Barry Lipton said that the unions were "extraordinarily pleased that the Governor came and indicated his support."

Yet Cuomo also received criticism for his rally appearance. James Hoge's near automatic reaction to any strike assessment made by an elected official (Dinkins or Cuomo, for example) was disappointment that New York public officials excused away many violent acts. Hoge's remarks were echoed in editorials from the *Daily News* ("Cuomo threw himself, body and soul, on the side of the men of terror")[9] and the *Wall Street Journal* ("Last Hurrah"), which chided Cuomo and other speakers at the rally for failing to realize the obvious; namely, that it was impossible to distribute the newspaper in an atmosphere of threats and violence. Cuomo responded that he was glad *Daily News* reporters were less "distortive and hysterical" than their management counterparts. Barry Lipton echoed Cuomo's assessment, as he regarded Hoge as "cowardly" for making accusations without further explaining them in televised debates with the president of the Newspaper Guild.

A more significant and persistent challenge to Governor Cuomo's rally remarks came from officials of New York State's public employee unions. Four such organizations, representing more than 200,000 members, formally accused Governor Cuomo with failure to negotiate in good faith over proposed state employees' layoffs. The president of the Public Employees Federation thought Cuomo's statements represented the "height of hypocrisy" since "every time the Governor shows his disdain for labor, he goes out and tries to get press coverage for how he's labor's best friend."[10] Cuomo countered that union leaders supporting these statements were leading their members "off the side of a cliff."

SELF-ABSORPTION OF UNION AND MANAGEMENT ORGANIZATIONS

Worsening Revenues and Corrective Alternatives

Management experienced continued advertising/circulation losses during this time period, which they hoped to correct through new and evolving distribution approaches. These factors prompted management to consider and resolve a stay-or-sell decision, which was announced January 16.

Advertisements in the *News* declined rather sharply after the strike began largely because of the sharp dip in circulation figures. Around December 1, 1990, management broke with its tradition of not giving daily circulation figures, and furnished a "stone-cold number" at 525,000 copies sold. Union officials scoffed at this report and estimated a more realistic figure between 200,000 and 300,000 newspapers. But this circulation decline gave no assurance that other New York City newspapers would realize circulation gains and/or increased advertisements as other media options such as television or radio were available.

At least one rival newspaper executive, Jerry Nachman of the *New York Post,* thought that hundreds of thousands of readers lost to the *Daily News* strike would never return to any newspaper. Nachman's fears went unrealized. The *New York Post* had picked up nearly 250,000 additional readers since the *News* strike began with its circulation reaching 750,000. Many advertisers, seeking to attract the blue-collar, former audience at the *News,* joined the *Post* and paid as much as 20 percent more than old advertising rates for this switch. The *Post's* advertising volume (71,374 column inches) in the first three weeks of November 1990 had already surpassed the volume (57,980 column inches) for the entire month of November 1989. This increase was even more impressive considering that the 1989 figures included a Sunday edition of the *Post* that did not exist in 1990. By December 7, the newspaper was at its maximum press capacity of 128 pages; about 90 of them were devoted to pre-Christmas advertisements.

New York Newsday also experienced a large (56 percent) increase in daily circulation since the *News* strike, from 225,000 to 350,000 copies,[11] and the newspaper had added some 60 advertisers as a result of this circulation increase. Publisher Robert Johnson suggested that the *News* had to have suffered a severe blow when its advertisers left, although John Sloan regarded this defection as temporary.

Conversations between executives at the *News* and *Newsday* became more directly focused in early January when the *Daily News* filed a $1 million suit against the owners of *New York Newsday* and two independent home-delivery companies. The suit charged that *Newsday* "willfully induced" the distributors to begin delivering *New York Newsday* to *News* subscribers. A different strike-related dimension of the *News-Newsday* feud was added a couple weeks later when *News* security guards detained a *Newsday* driver for allegedly gluing the locks of a store that sold the *News*. Johnson contended that the store owner could not identify the vandal and that the driver was not on duty, therefore not present or guilty, when the locks were glued, but *News* guards still held him at gunpoint until police eventually arrested him.

Management attempted to improve its circulation-advertisinig problems through continued and innovative efforts. The temporary restraining order issued by Judge Miriam Cedarbaum in late November enabled the *News* to employ hawkers to sell the newspaper in the New York subway system through the following month. Her order was not well received by transit and rail officials of some 22 unions representing MTA employees, and they held a December 10 meeting in the office of Sonny Hall (author of the "their ass belongs to us" quote) to discuss the situation. The participants were eager for action, anything that would get the hawkers out of the subways. Then George McDonald spoke and indicated that a shutdown of service would be the worst idea since it would be illegal and could likely turn millions of riders against the *News* strikers. Hall eventually agreed with McDonald even though someone asked, "What about Mike Quill?" who had held Hall's presidency of the Transport Workers Union (TWU) years before. Quill was a legendary militant who once commented about a judge who enjoined his organization from striking, "May he drop dead in his black robes." Hall responded, "Mike Quill was the greatest . . . but that was in his day."[12] (Before the Taylor Law, which made strikes by public employees in New York illegal, management extorted particularly hard-line bargaining stances). The meeting terminated with a joint resolution to "monitor" this situation.

A few days later, about 80 TWU volunteers handed out, for one day only, thousands of free copies of the *Post, New York Times,* and *Newsday* at a number of major subway locations. The newspapers cost the TWU $3,500; however, a spokesperson for the union contended the action symbolically countered MTA management's support of the strike when they allowed hawkers to sell the *News* in the subway, yet urged the public to continue their support of the strike.

The New York Civil Liberties Union (NYCLU), however, regarded Cedarbaum's decision consistent with the *Daily News* rights under the Constitution and past practice in the subway system.

The MTA already permits leafletters, political orators, religious, and charitable solicitations as well as street musicians within its facilities. The sale and distribution of newspapers by individual vendors is entirely compatible with the activity already taking place on MTA property.[13]

On December 18, Judge Cedarbaum granted the *Daily News* a preliminary injunction that allowed the organization to continue selling its newspaper in the subways. She concluded that management could establish that the MTA revoked the permits because it feared illegal conduct by strikers and the transit unions, and that it would be unreasonable for the government to tolerate such interference with freedom of speech and of the press.

Many hawkers selling the *News* outside of the subways had a "shadow"—a union member standing nearby, who urged potential customers not to purchase the strike-affected newspaper. One customer might have provided a typical response to this situation when he indicated that he did not know whether the hawker or union member was right, "But I'm not about to get caught anywhere between those two."[14]

On December 4, the *News* released 30,000 copies of an afternoon newspaper nicknamed "Big Blue," the first afternoon daily in New York City since the *Post* had ended this type of publication in 1987. James Hoge noted that this rather limited publication (particularly when compared to a reported printing of 740,000 edition of the A.M. *News*) represented, a "go home" paper available from 3:00 P.M. to 6:30 P.M. that would have morning news, particularly from overseas, and updated local and sports stories. Hoge also indicated that the goal of this paper, given free to a force of more than 1,000 hawkers, was to improve circulation, not advertising, and that advertisers had not been approached for this edition.

Some wondered why the *News* undertook this effort since the company had previously encountered a poor experience with its last afternoon edition in 1981 when $20 million was spent to attract some 70,000 readers—far fewer than the hoped-for 200,000. Striking reporter Tom Robbins speculated that this new (and unneeded) publication effort represented Jim Hoge's "vanity press edition."

Hoge indicated in early December that publishing would continue for the foreseeable future regardless of the collective bargaining progress or settlement. He did note, however, that given the cost of funding at this time (12 to 13 percent), the *News* would have to turn a profit of 10 percent after another year of operation if very large investments in the newspaper were expected to be made in a short time span. This figure might not be easily attained since the newspaper had only been profitable once in the past 25 years (5.5 percent return in 1979). Hoge also angrily refuted the unions' charge that he was merely the conduit for strike strategy since he took orders from Tribune Company executives in Chicago: "I've never received an order like that in my life, that you do this or that. It is simply not true."[15] Newspaper Guild president Barry Lipton noted that Hoge's remarks regarding profits and investment represented the "first specific thing he has said," and he hoped that Hoge would bring this information to the bargaining table and open related financial books so that a settlement could be reached.

Lipton and other union leaders likely discounted Hoge's remarks, however. They sent letters to 200 managers at institutional organizations that owned 35 percent of the Chicago Tribune Company stock. The letters explained that many of the strikers held Tribune Company stock, and shared with other stockholders an interest in the newspaper's survival and profitability. They reiterated the union's offer to bargain, noted that the strike was costing between $12 and $15 million a month in lost revenue, and maintained that closing the newspaper would not serve the interest of strikers and/or stockholders. The managers were further encouraged to urge the Tribune Company's 14-member board of directors at a December 11 quarterly meeting to direct *Daily News* management to reach an amicable collective bargaining settlement. Yet several management executives suggested that Charles Brumback had a long-range view of collective bargaining and that any decision to sell or close operations would not be made until mid-1991.

One financial analyst observed that Tribune Company stock had been on the rise since the strike had begun and maintained that the board would decide the *News*'s fate just before the company's annual meeting in April 1991. This decision would then depend on the price of Tribune Company stock at that time and on the extent to which Hoge had achieved a break-even point by regaining advertisers and a daily circulation around 575,000 copies. The analysts predicted that the Tribune Company would easily accept a $100 million loss since 1990's fourth quarter was already written off as a loss, and that it was best to take an eventual hit entering a recessionary time period. A Tribune executive, aware of the positive performance of Tribune Company stock since the strike, agreed with the analyst's opinion, and maintained that investors did not want the Tribune Company to shed the *News* from its organization.

The Tribune's board did express "continued strong support" of *News* management. Hoge reflected that people involved with this financial decision realized that significant progress was being made and that there was a 100 percent certainty that the newspaper would be alive in December 1991. Tribune Company stock closed at $37.75 a share the day of the board's announcement. This figure was up from $33.75 when the strike began.

The Tribune Company's support for the *News* was symbolically reemphasized at a Paine Webber Media Outlook Conference three days later. Charles Brumback and James Hoge sat side by side and posed for photographers. Then, Brumback introduced Hoge with an effusion that was regarded quite unusual for this forum, calling him his "friend," who "had his highest regard."

Yet management did not present a consistently optimistic picture at this forum. Scott Smith, chief financial officer of the Tribune Company, noted at a meeting shortly after the board's endorsement of the *News* that strike losses would significantly affect the Company's profits. Analysts pegged the *News*'s operating loss for 1990 at $85 million; however, Tribune executives said the company would publicize the exact losses at the *Daily News* at its February 1991 meeting when fourth-quarter earnings were reported.

Hoge also indicated at this meeting that advertising revenues would return because of increased circulation and the possibility that the *News* would file lawsuits against the striking unions for "intimidating" advertisers. Hoge's statement was not as well received by leaders of the unions' boycott, who maintained that *News* management's strategy was to force them to spend time and money on "nonsensical legal suits."

About a week after the board's statement of support, John Sloan indicated that the *News's* total daily circulation was 600,000 copies: 125,000 at newsstands; 200,000 through hawkers; 200,000 through home delivery; and 75,000 through suburban distribution. These figures were further being subjected to the Audit Bureau of Circulation, which monitors circulation sales, and, unlike self-serving underestimates made by unions and competitors of the *News,* should be regarded as "hard data."

Circulation figures notwithstanding, Hoge announced on January 16 — the 83d day of the strike — that investment banker Lazard Freres had been retained to put the newspaper up for sale because the newspaper's losses of more than $200 million over the past decade, coupled with continued workplace inefficiencies and the strike's violence against vendors and operators, made long-term operations responsible. He noted further, "In the little time left, we will make every effort to reach cost-efficient contract settlements and to achieve the other business conditions necessary for the *Daily News* to continue to serve New York."[16]

A second alternative was closing the operation if a potential purchaser could not be found. Hoge indicated that current employees and strikers at the *News* would be informed that the paper might close down in 60 days as required under the federal Worker Adjustment and Retraining Notification Act (WARN). Theodore Kheel said the provisions of this act, including a 14-day extension of the statutory 60-day WARN period, suggested April 3, 1991, as the likely "D-Day" by which the newspaper must sell or close.

Investors responded positively to Hoge's announcement. Tribune Company shares on the New York Stock Exchange rose $2.625 to close at $37.25 the day the statement was made. One newspaper analyst maintained that this sharp gain resulted because any resolution of the situation (sell, shut down, or a negotiated labor agreement) was better than continued reported financial losses.

Hoge was hopeful that the January 16 close-or-sell announcement would prompt a collective bargaining settlement, but he also indicated that there was no basis for his optimism other than that the *News* closure "is in nobody's interest." Hoge further noted that the *Daily News* was "prepared to negotiate around the clock" although he indicated that there was little immediate possibility of a settlement.

Many union leaders were surprised, dismayed, and suspicious when informed of this latest development. George McDonald responded "I'm not optimistic" because "the company is still not looking to reach a settlement. They summoned Hoge to Chicago and laid down the law that that's the end of the line."[17] Barry Lipton of the Newspaper Guild further suggested that the announcement represented a "squeeze-play designed to create a pressure cooker situation" in labor–management negotiations.

Union leaders, despite their apprehensions about management's bargaining sincerity, had to realize that a potential purchase for the *News* would be difficult to find in a time marked by economic recession and the uncertainties of the Persian Gulf War. This dire situation was reinforced by public, if not private, responses of potential *News* purchasers. For example, Robert Johnson, of *Newsday* and *New York Newsday,* indicated that the purchase of the *News* was "an option we discarded a long, long time ago" while an executive of the Gannett Company, when asked if they had any purchasing contact/interest in the *News,* responded, "No, no, and no." A senior vice president for communications and planning for Knight-Ridder suggested when asked about purchasing the *News:*

Nobody in their right mind would touch it. . . . That thing is dead as a doornail. It's a totally untenable situation. Anyone who would be interested in buying the *Daily News* would lose lots and lots and lots and lots of money.[18]

There was some resumption of bargaining table issues and behaviors during January. These considerations and efforts were at a minimum suggested and shaped by the *News*'s announcement to sell the newspaper.

Developments Within the Unions

George McDonald indicated the nine striking unions were "100 percent united together" as the strike approached three months. This assessment was no doubt bolstered by various actions involving judges, the AFL-CIO, and other unions in December, January, and February. For example, a federal judge in Manhattan ruled that the striking unions could have up to 51 days to file and argue motions in the *News* RICO suit filed in late November. The judge also denied management's request to begin interviewing witnesses and gathering evidence, activities that would have cost the unions "many hundreds of thousands of dollars" in legal expenses. Theodore Kheel maintained that this decision in effect placed the suits on the "back burner."

The AFL-CIO was concerned about the strike for symbolic as well as legislative reasons. Thomas Donahue, secretary-treasurer of the organization, observed that the *News* was one of the world's most visible newspapers, thereby making management's use of strike replacements also visible. He further hoped that this situation would press Congress to pass legislation prohibiting the use of strike replacements in 1991. The AFL-CIO's special assistance to the striking unions included the full-time support of three staff members, outside legal and public relations help, and $300,000 to underwrite strike activities. The organization even paid strike benefits to drivers, whose union was not an AFL-CIO member, which enabled all *News* strikers to receive some form of benefits.

Several unions not directly involved in the strike also furnished support during this time. A national corporate campaign was launched by these organizations to "put as much pressure on the Tribune Company board as possible, in as many different ways as possible," according to union spokesperson Deborah Friedman.[19] One phase of this campaign concerned bringing the strikers' story into areas where Tribune Company subsidiaries were located.

Trade union leaders from across the country, including Jack Sheinkman, the international president of the Amalgamated Clothing and Textile Workers Union, gathered in front of the Tribune Company's *Fort Lauderdale Sun-Sentinel* office in Fort Lauderdale and formed an informational picket line. The major message according to a union press release was that readers' payments for the *Sun-Sentinel* were "helping to bust unions in New York," thereby hurting thousands of men, women, and children. The AFL-CIO conducted a press conference and subsequent rally on February 8 in Chicago to announce an expanded offensive against Tribune Company properties outside New York in the union's corporate campaign.

Some strikers also became directly involved in this campaign. In late January, the *Chicago Tribune* reported that the Tribune Tower in Chicago and the North Side home of Charles Brumback were "picketed peacefully" by a small group of strikers. John Madigan, publisher of the *Chicago Tribune* and a director of the Tribune Company, was also confronted on his doorstep by a group of strikers. When informed that it was his fiduciary responsibility to end the strike, he responded that Brumback and Hoge, not he, represented the proper channels for related discussions.

Nevertheless, the accord between and within unions was not complete during this period. Management told the printers' unions that if the paper folded or incurred a "permanent suspension," it would not be responsible for the lifetime job guarantees. This announcement no doubt caused tensions between the printers and the other unions as George McDonald pledged that if the *News* closed, the unions would press their boycott campaign against the Tribune Company and its holdings "forever."

Tensions between the drivers' union and the other striking unions no doubt occurred in early December when there was speculation that this union would be holding its first back-to-back collective bargaining sessions with management since February 1990. Theodore Kheel strongly believed that management was trying to reach a deal with Michael Alvino, the president of the drivers' union, and Alvino was pressed into assuring the heads of other unions that he would not enter into any agreement with management unless the other unions concurred.

The drivers' union also had to be distracted by a $30 million class action suit filed against them in December by two newsstand dealers who claimed that "violence, intimidation, vandalism, and theft" by union members had deprived them of "the ability to make a fair living." A lawyer for the Newsstand Operators Association, which represented the city's 300 freestanding newsstands, suggested, however, that this suit did not represent all of the city's vendors because these alleged actions had not been experienced by every member.

The Newspaper Guild was affected by internal and external diversions during this time. In early January, ten striking *Daily News* reporters and artists barricaded themselves inside an empty news bureau office in Brooklyn. After entering the office, they began calling the Tribune Company board members, informed them of the takeover, and urged them to encourage the newspaper's management to negotiate "in good faith." Eighty police officers in some 30 vehicles approached the building, snarling traffic in the process.

Juan Gonzalez, a striking reporter who was the leader of this incident, admitted that he had only been to one Guild union meeting when the strike was initially called. But he became a quick convert to the union cause, a regarded, unofficial strike leader according to some Newspaper Guild members, and a sometime critic of Barry Lipton's direction of the Newspaper Guild for not calling more membership meetings before the strike occurred. In public, Gonzalez and Lipton had furnished joint praise for each other's strike roles. Gonzalez suggested that Lipton's performance had not been "uniformly excellent," although he felt Lipton tried to do a good job in leading the union in difficult times. Lipton expressed his gratitude that the Guild had received "some vital new activists."

The sit-in lasted for four hours; then the ten strikers were arrested and charged with criminal trespass, a misdemeanor. Gonzalez maintained that the sit-in represented a symbolic gesture, intended to rejuvenate public interest in the strike and force a conclusion of the dispute. He wanted to make sure that *News* strikers did not end up like their counterparts at Eastern Airlines, whom the public eventually forgot. A judge subsequently dismissed the trespassing charges against the ten *Daily News* strikers, on the condition that they stay out of trouble for the next six months.

One article in the *Chicago Tribune* indicated that this situation melded labor relations with "journalistic guerrilla theater," while *News* executive John Sloan dismissed this episode as "just another publicity stunt" indicative of a flailing union that had seen 53 percent of its members cross the picket line. Barry Lipton reported that Sloan's crossover percentage of Guild members was "grossly exaggerated and inaccurate," but he declined to cite specific numbers.

Lipton was not indifferent to members who had crossed the picket line, however. At this time, the Newspaper Guild announced that it had filed charges of illegal strikebreaking against 98 of its own members. Lipton contended that all of these individuals had crossed picket lines to return to their jobs but had never resigned from the union. About 170 other members had crossed picket lines but had resigned either before or during the strike. The 98 members, if convicted at the internal trial proceeding, could face fines and expulsion from the union, although the convictions and related penalties could also be appealed.

The Newspaper Guild also experienced a membership difficulty in a broader sense. The Guild's international constitution provides that if its strike defense fund falls below $4.5 million, dues of Guild locals will automatically increase by 50 percent until the fund rises above $6 million. Moreover, the International's executive board voted not to transfer any money from the general fund into the defense fund.

Some leaders of Guild locals did not at least publicly blame Lipton's organization for the drained funds and looming hike in their members' dues. They were concerned, however, that some of their members working under labor agreements by which union membership was not a condition of employment would leave the Guild if a forced and significantly higher dues increase occurred. According to one leader of the Los Angeles Guild local:

When newspapers across the country are making cutbacks and some of our members are losing their jobs, it's unrealistic for the Guild International office to expect to fully fund itself by using money that would otherwise be transferred to the defense fund.[20]

Some leaders urged the International headquarters to "bite the bullet" by using alternatives to a dues hike, such as cutting back in international operations and obtaining loans from either locals with large defense funds or from the AFL-CIO.

Management claimed that the Newspaper Guild was also subjected to an external diversion when it filed an unfair labor practice charging that the organization failed to identify and provide the *Daily News* with copies of all past agreements and memoranda that it sought to include in a successor contract. The Guild agreed to furnish the information in accordance with the National Labor Relations Board's remedy. This settlement likely represented the quickest, cheapest, and perhaps only legal/quasi-legal dimension of this dispute resolved to date. Yet the implications of this settlement did not prompt significant bargaining table behaviors or results in December, January, or early February.

PERIPHERAL BARGAINING EFFORTS

Involvement of Federal Mediators

There had been some 200 bargaining sessions that occurred from January 1990 to December 1990, but only a dozen since the strike began on October 25. On December 3, the Newspaper and Mail Deliverers' union participated in their second negotiation since the strike began. Management's attitude regarding its 200-word management rights provision (cited in Chapter 2) appeared to be a major stumbling block for all unions in seeking a negotiated settlement. Wayne Mitchell of the mailers' union indicated that management appeared unwilling to take the prerequisite action of putting its machismo aside.

Michael Alvino, the drivers' union president, indicated that whenever he asked Robert Ballow what management specifically wanted in negotiations, Ballow would always respond, "Give us management rights and we'll tell you." As previously noted, the drivers' union did have bargaining sessions with management on December 3 and 4 at the offices of a federal mediator in lower Manhattan. James Hoge declined comment on these talks on the grounds that it would be improper "to conduct collective bargaining in public." Hoge did say, however, that there was no immediate deadline for a bargaining settlement even though the *News* had experienced a precipitous circulation and advertising decline by this time:

The company is quite comfortable that we're on the right road and that we're making steady progress. . . . The unions want everybody to think that, "My God, if The *News* doesn't get everything straightened out by this week or next week, they're through." Fair enough. Only problem is, it ain't true.[21]

On December 7, Bernard E. DeLury, director of the Federal Mediation and Conciliation Service (FMCS), issued an invitation to the Allied Printing Trades Unions and the *New York Daily News* management to meet under the auspices of the FMCS in Washington, D.C. Both union and management representatives accepted DeLury's offer a day later, and indicated that each side would meet separately with him. They also stressed the positive and urgent dimensions of this development. John Sloan indicated that management agreed to "fully cooperate" in this development because it represented "a step forward in the negotiations process." Theodore Kheel called DeLury's invitation "the last clear chance for a settlement." Kheel and the union officials were concerned that differences were emerging between Chicago and New York executives of the *News,* with the former group poised to close the newspaper at the December 11 meeting of the Tribune's board of directors. Continuing this line of reasoning, Hoge accepted the mediation offer to show Tribune Company management that a settlement was possible, even imminent. John Sloan did not dispute this scenario but did exhibit optimism that the *News* would continue to receive the Tribune Company's support after the board reviewed the newspaper's financial performance and labor situation.

The Tribune Company board did not seek closure of the *News* in spite of, or because of, the renewed mediation efforts. DeLury reported on the meeting held a day after the board meeting[22] (the first time since the strike began that management officials and the leaders of all nine unions had negotiated under the same roof) that the negotiators were "quite far from reaching an agreement." McDonald indicated that he was "very embarrassed" that the unions went to Washington and participated in a "charade" on the part of management who clearly did not wish to reach an agreement, since it rejected all of the unions' three proposals made at the meeting.

The first proposal asked management to drop or at least postpone a series of damage suits seeking more than $150 million from the unions,[23] then all strikers would be allowed to return to work. Kheel indicated that the second proposal received "absolute unanimity" from the Allied Printing Trades Council's members unions, that no one would return to work "without all of the strikers."

A third union proposal requested that management conduct future collective bargaining discussions with all the unions instead of separate meetings with each union. John Sloan indicated this proposal reflected the unions' "ever-changing position with regard to the ground rules"; moreover, negotiating on a union-by-union basis was necessary since the bargaining issues with each union varied. This position was not surprising since management had previously filed an unfair labor practice charge with the National Labor Relations Board, charging that the unions were bargaining in bad faith by insisting on coordinated bargaining.

Sloan further urged the unions to realize the potential benefits of federal mediation. Both sides indicated that they would attend another meeting, possibly in New York City, if DeLury requested one. About a week later, Hoge publicly called for the appointment of a federal mediator to compel the parties to reach a settlement: "What we are in favor of is a very high-powered, supermediator . . . to come in and knock everybody's heads together." Newspaper Guild president Barry Lipton responded, "We're willing to consider anything that will bring about a fair and equitable settlement."[24] Lipton's noncommittal response appeared justified for at least two reasons. He might have thought that Hoge was trying to convince Chicago Tribune management that a settlement was near. A day after Hoge's mediation request, *News* management might have reflected its true bargaining intentions when it filed its second major lawsuit against the unions alleging their varied and serious illegal activities.

Additional union skepticism over mediation's potential to resolve the dispute was likely caused by a negotiations meeting with the paperhandlers' union held soon after Hoge's desire for an appointed mediator. According to union participants at the session, Bud Johannsen, management's negotiator, walked into the session, threw a contract on the table, and informed the union the strike would be settled if they signed it.

Few, if any, negotiation sessions were conducted for the remainder of December. Indeed, the three previously discussed sessions between the mailers' union and the drivers' union were the only publicized collective bargaining efforts during this month.

Bargaining Efforts in January

Management urged the Newspaper Guild's members to return to the bargaining table on January 3; however, its related press release had to send mixed, if not opposite, messages to the Guild's members and leaders.[25] The union was also urged to examine the names and numbers of those who returned to work, thereby verifying John Sloan's previous statement that 53 percent of the Guild membership had crossed the picket lines. This announcement also contended that Barry Lipton's "credibility has become a wasting asset even with his own membership." Further:

To the Guild, we say come back to the table. Our readers are back. Our advertisers are starting to come back. Now you come back. But negotiations must take place at the bargaining table — not in the streets, not through illegal actions, not through the intimidation of innocent people.[26]

The next day, Lipton, along with a large union negotiation committee and nearly 100 rank-and-file members-observers, arrived at the Roosevelt Hotel. Management refused to negotiate with this large contingent, and the two parties adjourned to separate rooms. The union negotiators then submitted written questions to management officials concerning strike replacements, and management responded with a list of its own handwritten questions that it wanted answered first. Lipton refused this request, contending that he could not respond to management's question in a "vacuum" that existed without the union's questions. A mediator announced the meeting's nonexistent results when the union further refused management's proposal that both sides exchange written answers simultaneously.

A subsequent, alleged bargaining development involving the drivers' union in mid-January, demonstrated that the media's coverage of related interpersonal and sometimes private activities can be fragile and possibly incorrect. A *New York Times* reporter, who had frequently covered the *News* strike, wrote:

A Tribune Company official, speaking on the condition of anonymity, asserted last night that The *News* and the drivers had been on the brink of an important agreement on staffing levels in a 14-hour bargaining session on Monday night. But the official said that the Tribune Company board of directors shot it down in a special meeting on Tuesday. "Mr. Hoge, who appeared at the meeting in Chicago, had thought he had a deal," the official said, "but Tribune said they couldn't do a contract with specific numbers in it" because that would suggest to the other unions that management was willing to compromise on management rights. "That is something Chicago simply will not do," the official said.[27]

James Hoge quickly responded that he was "absolutely mystified and flabbergasted" about the reported development and called the account a "total fabrication." Hoge acknowledged that he had felt hopeful in recent weeks that a settlement with the drivers was near, and Michael Alvino of the drivers' union had indicated that bargaining progress had been made after a January 12 meeting and a nearly 14-hour negotiation session on January 14. But, as Hoge indicated, "The idea that we had an agreement with the drivers – or even a significant part of an agreement – is just wrong";[28] moreover, the subject had not been discussed in any "special" board meeting involving Tribune Company officials.

About a week after this story broke, the *New York Times* indicated that the report of the board meeting had come from an anonymous caller who had often represented himself as a Tribune official, eager to assist the reporter, who, in turn, never learned the identity of his telephone source, but still quoted the individual. The newspaper further noted that the reporter's actions in this situation "violated the *Times* standards of check and corroboration."

The reporter was "severely reprimanded" in writing by *Times* editor Max Frankel, who apologized to Hoge for the coverage. Though failure to check the accuracy of sources is an offense that can lead to dismissal, the reporter was reassigned to the page makeup desk because of his "12-year record of meritorious service as desk editor." Tom Robbins, striking reporter for the *News,* commended the reassigned reporter for his previous aggressive, fair, and accurate coverage of the strike, and further speculated that the disputed story was correct:

The tragedy of this situation is (that) his source's version of what happened, most people believe, is accurate. . . . There's no doubt in my mind [the reassigned reporter] had a real live fish on the line. The problem was the fish wasn't telling him his name.[29]

Robbins's assessment was at least partially supported by a member of the drivers' 30-member negotiating committee, who acknowledged management's past practices of spreading rumors about a settlement to divide the unions; however, the union member thought that management wanted to make enough serious concessions due to the possibility of war in the Persian Gulf: "I think they're finally realizing that they are losing the strike, and that unless they settle soon, they're going to lose out on the jump in circulation that occurs in time of war."[30]

The mid-January negotiations with the drivers might have also been prompted by Alvino's split with the other union leaders, who wanted the strike replacement issue resolved for each union before negotiations could occur on other issues. The two negotiations with the drivers were predicated on Alvino's preference to discuss and resolve other bargaining issues (staffing, for example) before settlement was reached on the issue of replacements for striking workers.

For the eight other unions in the Allied Printing Trades Council, Theodore Kheel proposed a new bargaining position and strategy that would be compatible with the perspective of the drivers' union. Kheel suggested that union negotiators would not demand the dismissal of the permanent replacement workers as a condition of any settlement. They would instead leave the fate of those employees up to management. However, the union officials would continue to insist that all 2,300 strikers be reinstated simultaneously as a condition of any final settlement. Thus, the drivers and the eight other unions would be on the same footing since they all could feel free to negotiate other issues ahead of the replacement employee situation. Kheel's revised strike replacement position might have been made to avoid discrimination suits and negative public opinion since many of these individuals were women and minorities who replaced mainly white, male union members.

Management's tentative decision on January 16 to close or sell the newspaper unless its long-term profitability could be assured did prompt Hoge to schedule collective bargaining sessions with each of the unions "as soon as possible." Hoge also indicated that he could not comply with the unions' request for an umbrella or coordinated bargaining meeting.

The mailers' union subsequently met with Bob Ballow on January 28 to exchange bargaining proposals. Ballow presented to the union a 36-page contract proposal that included the 200-word management rights clause and a 3 percent raise when circulation reached the level it had been a year before the strike began.

George McDonald, who headed the mailers' union in addition to the Allied Printing Trades Council, countered with a four-point plan that included a wage freeze and a 25 percent cut in the mailroom staff (estimated to be 100 employees before the strike). McDonald indicated that management refused his proposal and that the negotiation session was "a complete failure."

James Hoge's rather nebulous position regarding strike replacements seemed to represent the only basis for bargaining settlement optimism as January ended. Hoge had been deliberately ambiguous about any commitments made to the 800 strike replacements hired since the start of the strike. Replacements were required to sign a release giving management the right to dismiss them at will. Hoge indicated that the replacements' employment status was currently secure but required by law to be open subject to collective bargaining negotiations.

Kheel's second attempt to purchase the *News* on January 29 symbolized the avoidance of bargaining issues to date. Under this purchase plan, approved in principle by the unions, employees would own about 20 percent of the company, a situation similar to that reached with the *New York Post* in the summer of 1990. Kheel indicated that he had met with two potential purchasers, Robert Maxwell and Peter Kalikow of the *New York Post,* several times to discuss the matter.

The purchase effort would parallel continued efforts by the unions to settle bargaining issues when the strike began and two subsequent issues: the strikers' return to work, and management lawsuits against the union. Discussions over shutdown issues such as severance pay and pensions could also be conducted, depending upon the extent that management expressed good faith cooperation with any purchase attempts.

Kheel indicated that he would continue to be unpaid for his efforts in the purchase venture as "[my] sole objective is to try to save the *News* and the jobs of the employees."[31] Hoge responded that Kheel would be treated "like any other potential buyer" and given information any such individual needs to put a deal together.

Entering the Second Year of Negotiations

Few, if any, tangible bargaining results had occurred when management and union officials entered the second year of negotiations in February 1991. Hoge's initial attention at this time appeared focused on the reluctance of his newspaper's major competitors to support his positions on the adverse collective bargaining climate.

The *News* had pressed its crime wave/conspiracy views with big headlines such as "Bodega Bombed in News War"; "It's Organized Terror: Hoge"; and "They Live in Fear of Violence." Hoge was dismayed that other local newspapers had not recognized and promulgated these messages:

I can't conceive of this amount of sustained criminal activity against a prominent business and *Newsday* and the *Post* having nothing to say about it. . . . We've seen no expression from the mayor, the governor or any other public official that this kind of criminal campaign against a business is unacceptable.[32]

One reporter from the *Washington Post* partially agreed with Hoge that only the *Times* had editorialized against strike-related violence; however, James Troedtman, managing editor of *New York Newsday,* said that his newspaper's inactions did not represent a media conspiracy against the *News.* He instead contended that dozens of bombs exploded in New York City every day, and that his newspaper would never report each event. Jerry Nachman of the *New York Post* retorted that Hoge's accusations of a media conspiracy represented "tragic" grandstanding since he blamed the competing press along with the unions, the governor, the mayor, the police department, and the Cardinal.

Hoge's concerns notwithstanding, February's collective bargaining efforts were introduced by a *Miami Herald* editorial that was consistent with most, if not all, of the other nonlocal, print editorials on the subject. It ignored/absolved management's role in the bargaining impasse, patronized/blamed unions for not acknowledging bargaining realities, and, in part, read:

The need for labor unions has not disappeared. But today's bankruptcy rates are as much a risk to job security as abusive management practices were 50 years ago. In some cases, organized labor must come to recognize when its demands jeopardize an indispensable employer, and must find an honorable ground for principled retreat.

At the *Daily News* — what's left of it — that time has come. For the labor movement's own sake, it's time to settle.[33]

The dire economic conditions at the *News* suggested by the above remarks were further illustrated by the Tribune Company's rather unusual issuance of preliminary operating results that isolated one property's financial performance. Overall results for the Tribune Company showed a 99 percent decline in fourth-quarter 1990 operating profits ($1.2 million) when compared to performance for fourth-quarter 1989 ($118.8 million), and a 45 percent decline for the full-year 1990 operating profits ($237 million) when compared to 1989 figures ($433.1 million). The report also indicated that the *Daily News* operations played a large part in this financial reversal since it posted operating losses of $69.3 million in fourth-quarter 1990 and $114.5 million for all of 1990.

The Tribune Company's fourth-quarter net loss, or a specific charge against profits that would result if the *News* closed, was not released. But at least one analyst downplayed the role of the *News* in the Tribune Company's stock value, maintaining that a worst-case, closing scenario of $150 million would cost the company no more than 15 cents a share and not affect 1991 earnings. The analyst's assessment must have been shared on Wall Street as Tribune Company stock posted a $2.37 per share gain, to $44 the day of the report's release.

Thus, Tribune Company management, while desiring to either sell the *News* or to minimize a special charge if the newspaper closed, had no strong financial incentive to bargain with the unions, particularly if it attached great financial and/or symbolic cost to not receiving its 200-word management rights clause. Theodore Kheel did issue a rare public compliment to *Daily News* owners, maintaining that they appeared to be "sincerely interested" in reaching an agreement to sell the newspaper. Yet Kheel quickly amended the compliment by indicating that the cooperative attitude and actions in seeking a potential purchaser "bore no resemblance" to the negotiating stance it had taken in bargaining with the unions.

Kheel believed that management was uninterested in reaching a bargaining settlement since it had failed for one year to resolve basic issues that had been routinely settled in American industry.

Kheel's assessment of management's bargaining intransigence was punctuated by an unfair labor practice complaint filed by an administrative law judge of the National Labor Relations Board (NLRB) on February 6. The complaint pertained to the "Battle of Wounded Knee" incident, and management's subsequent permanent replacement of some 60 employees represented by the drivers' union. It determined that management's actions were "inherently destructive" of this protected and concerted employee activity under section 7 of the National Labor Relations Act since management used a "lockout" as a pretext to permanently replace bargaining unit employees.

The impact of this tentative finding was more symbolic than substantive. A hearing before an NLRB administrative law judge was scheduled for June 3, a date far after management's intended sell-or-close decision; at the hearing, the initial complaint would be reviewed and likely subjected to the full NLRB and subsequent judges in court appeals that could linger over several years. A *News* spokesperson suggested this scenario when she refused to comment on the initial complaint but indicated that management favored an impartial third party giving a full and fair review of the situation.

Union leaders were aware of the potential awards of back pay to be made to the drivers and employees represented by other unions if subsequent and prolonged legal appeal procedures determined that the October 25 incident represented an unfair labor practice strike. Irwin Bluestein, an attorney for the Newspaper Guild, maintained that strikers in an unfair-labor-practice dispute would be reinstated with back pay, thereby nullifying the strike replacement issue. Along with other union officials such as Michael Alvino, Bluestein realized that the NLRB's initial decision gave unions an immediate public relations advantage since it labeled management as the strike's provocateur, thereby refuting management's claim that the unions caused the bargaining impasse and continued it through violence and intimidation.

Kheel was somewhat smug in his reaction to the NLRB's actions, noting that those familiar with the situation knew that management's "patently outrageous" conduct would result in a complaint being issued. He further concluded that the complaint also sent a message to management hard-liners that "anyone hiring Robert Ballow should anticipate extensive litigation."

NOTES

1. "Daily News Brings Further Suits," PR Newswire, December 5, 1990. Dialog File 649, item 09657287–1205NY073.

2. Guy Sterling, "Two Daily News Workers Injured in Mob Attack on Irvington Street," *Newark (New Jersey) Star-Ledger,* December 7, 1990 (Located in News Bank), Media and Communications 56: F-6.

3. Ibid.

4. "Daily News Issues Summary of News Releases, Commentary and Advisories," PR Newswire, December 12, 1990. Dialog File 649, item 09677201/9–121NY023. *News* management updated its strike violence statistics in another press release on January 11, which tallied serious incidents – 1,331; arrests – 180; personal injuries – 80; people hospitalized – 11; and vehicles damaged or destroyed – 200.

5. U.S. Congress, Senate, Committee on Labor and Human Resources, *New York Daily News Strike and Permanent Replacements:* Hearing Before the Subcommittee on Labor, One Hundred and First Congress, December 11, 1990, p. 21.

6. "Daily News Publisher Sends Letter to Cardinal O'Connor," PR Newswire, December 10, 1990. Dialog File 649, item 09670313–1210NY082A.

7. Kenneth C. Crowe and Rose Marie Arce, "Stars Meet Press at News-Aid," *Newsday,* December 15, 1990. Dialog File 638, item 05856138.

8. Alison Carper, "Thousands Rally for News Strikers," *Newsday,* December 11, 1990. Dialog File 638, item 05852035.

9. Rose Marie Arce, "News Ad Criticizes Governor; Strikers, Management Air Complaints in Public," *Newsday,* December 17, 1990. Dialog File 638, item 05858103.

10. Elizabeth Kolbert, "State Employee Unions Say Cuomo Exploits Strike at News," *New York Times,* December 12, 1990, B-8.

11. On Sunday, when the *Post* does not publish, *New York Newsday*'s circulation increased from 225,000 to 375,000. The *New York Times* indicated that it had increased daily sales by 50,000 with little increase in advertising. By January 17, 1991, the combined circulation of *New York Newsday* and *Newsday* had risen about 25 percent, to 872,000 copies, and its Sunday circulation by 43 percent, to more than $1 million since the *News* strike began October 25.

12. Ellis Henican, "In the Subways in New Era, It's Not Easy to Kick Scabs," *Newsday,* December 11, 1990. Dialog File 638, item 05852037.

13. "Summary of New York Daily News Releases, Commentary and Advisories," PR Newswire, December 10, 1990. Dialog File 649, item 09670291–1210NY046.

14. Ellis Henican, "In the Subways, Hoge Letter May Heat up Subway War," *Newsday,* December 9, 1990.

15. Scott Ladd, "News Must Earn 10%, Says Publisher Hoge," *Newsday,* December 4, 1990. Dialog File 638, item 05845030.

16. "Daily News Announces Tentative Decision to Close or Sell; Prospect For Material Charged Against Earnings," PR Newswire, January 16, 1991. Dialog File 613, item 0336130–NY006B.

17. Howard Kurtz and Robert J. McCartney, "New York Daily News Warns of Possible Shutdown Soon," *Washington Post,* January 17, 1991, E-1 and E-5.

18. Ira Teinowitz, "Buy or 'bye' for Daily News," *Advertising Age,* January 21, 1991, 3 and 56.

19. "Unions Express Some Hope for New Talks After Meeting with Daily News Publisher," Bureau of National Affairs, Inc., *Daily Labor Report* 13 (January 18, 1991): A-9, A-11.

20. "Trouble in the Ranks?" *Editor and Publisher,* December 29, 1990, 15 and 28.

21. David E. Pitt, "Daily News Adds Edition for Commuters," *New York Times,* December 5, 1990, B-1 and B-5.

22. The *News* was represented by its two principal negotiators, Ed Gold and Robert Ballow. The nineteen union participants included two officials from each striking union and Theodore Kheel.

23. There did seem to be at least some recognition by the unions that various civil suits filed by management against employees for strike-related violence would continue if a settlement were reached.

24. "New York Daily News Asks for Mediator," *Chicago Tribune,* December 17, 1990, sec. 1, p. 8.

25. The press release gave the following employment statistics for Newspaper Guild members:

	Currently at Work	Before 10/25/90	Percentage at Work
Advertising	116	166	70
Administration	1	1	100
Promotion	10	17	59
Marketing	5	5	100
Human Resources	1	4	25
Production	7	23	30
Circulation	84	115	73
Finance	50	103	49
Editorial	152	365	42
TOTAL	426	799	53

26. "The Daily News Schedules Negotiation Session with Newspaper Guild," PR Newswire, January 3, 1991. Dialog File 613, item 0333202–NY071.

27. David E. Pitt, "The News Says It May Close Or Seek A Buyer," *New York Times,* January 17, 1991, B-1 and B-3.

28. David E. Pitt, "Tribune Didn't Scuttle Talks with Union, Publisher Says," *New York Times,* January 18, 1991, B-1 and B-3.

29. George Garneau, "Anonymous Source Leads to Reporter's Reassignment," *Editor and Publisher,* February 2, 1991, 11.

30. David E. Pitt, "News Strikers Ease Stance on Critical Issue," *New York Times,* January 15, 1991, C-5. There was one report by a union official, however, that the drivers had made concessions worth as much as $15 million in annual savings but were met by management intransigence on staffing level issues.

31. "Employee Stake in Daily News Proposed as No Progress Is Reported in Contract Talks," Bureau of National Affairs, Inc., *Daily Labor Report* 20 (January 30, 1991): A-10. Members of Kheels' purchasing team included Patrick A. Flanagan, managing director of Fidelis Group Inc. of Quincy, Mass.; Eugene Keilin and Ron A. Bloom, investment bankers specializing in employee stock ownership; Robert M. Siper, principal of KPMG Peat Marwick; Harry F. Weyher, partner in the law firm Olwine, Connelly, Chase, O'Donnell & Weyher; and Kermit J. Berylson, vice president of Hickok Associates, a management consulting team associated with KPMG Peat Marwick.

32. Howard Kurtz, "N.Y. News Publisher Faults Rivals in Strike," *Washington Post,* February 3, 1991, A-1 and A-9.

33. "Labor's Lost Loves" (editorial), *Miami Herald,* February 4, 1991, 14-A.

6

Bargaining Table
Behavior and Results

As suggested in the previous chapter, union and management officials did not immediately enter the second year of negotiations with apparent objectives or efforts to reach a settlement at the bargaining table. Some peripheral bargaining dimensions remained in early February, but these were eclipsed by potentially serious mediation initiatives as mid-February approached. These efforts encouraged Robert Maxwell to purchase the *News* in March although the newspaper's sale would be conditioned upon completed labor agreements with the nine striking unions. In this chapter will be discussed related activities, as well as significant labor–management considerations, including contract ratification, after the tentative bargaining settlements had been reached.

TRANSITION FROM PERIPHERAL BARGAINING
IN FEBRUARY 1991

Vestiges of Peripheral Bargaining in Early February

Peripheral bargaining continued into February 1991 with one rather novel example pertaining to the strikers' return of hundreds of copies of the *Daily News* to the newspaper's headquarters on East 42d Street. This effort symbolized the presumed attitude of many newsstand dealers, who refused to sell the *News,* and authorized the strikers to return the unsold bundles to management. Some 599 newsstand dealers signed letters that informed management that they were receiving poor service from replacement workers and did not want to be included in "fabricated circulation figures" released to the media, advertisers, and the general public. Another group of local merchants, florists, also agreed not to advertise in the *News* in the days just before Valentine's Day, traditionally their biggest week of the year.

Violence had not been eliminated by February, although an analysis of related incidents (2,072 tallied by the *News* security staff, or 586 strike-related incidents confirmed by police and 153 arrests of strikers through February 21) reflected the following trends:

- a sharp decrease in the number and seriousness of the incidents after the first six weeks of the strike;
- an overall less violent strike situation at the *News* when compared to two recent publicized labor–management confrontations at Pittston Coal Group (more than 3,000 incidents in Virginia alone) and Greyhound Bus Lines, where there had been 52 sniper attacks on busses carrying passengers; and
- the shift in the nature of the violence from ambushes and assaults on trucks and drivers (only four after January 1) to vandalism against vendors and advertisers, particularly Hillside Bedding and Save-Mart Electronics.

Union leaders continued to discount their roles in violent incidents. For example, Michael J. Alvino of the drivers' union indicated:

I didn't order it, I don't condone it. . . . I wish I had the power to turn everything off like a faucet, but I don't have that power. Nobody calls me up on the phone and tells me Hey, we're going to do this. If they did, they'd be out of the union.[1]

Mediation Initiatives Approaching Mid-February

Juxtaposed against these peripheral bargaining activities were mediation efforts conducted by William J. Usery, former Secretary of Labor and an exceptionally experienced mediator, who had met secretly with four of the largest striking unions on February 4, and with publisher James Hoge two days later in his Washington, D.C. offices. A mediator has no binding authority to resolve a labor–management dispute. Instead, he or she is an invited guest at the bargaining table who can be ejected by one or both of the union–management negotiation teams. Therefore, a mediator cannot take credit for a collective bargaining settlement, since related endeavors focus on labor and management negotiators reaching a collective bargaining agreement that they can live with. Usery's mediation capability, while statistically meaningless in a settlement or no settlement sense, was verified by Richard Trumka, president of the United Mine Workers, who experienced Usery's "outstanding" mediation skills in a widely publicized ten-month labor dispute involving Pittston Company and exuded, "If a settlement is possible, [Usery] can do it."

Both union and management negotiators agreed on February 11 to have Usery mediate the *News* dispute although no related ground rules for this effort had been set. Hoge accepted Usery's involvement because of his reputation, belief in the collective bargaining process, and success in difficult circumstances. Theodore Kheel, union advisor, agreed that Usery was a skilled mediator but did not think that his efforts would prompt a negotiated labor agreement. Usery, chairman of Bill Usery and Associates, a Washington labor–management relations firm, did not indicate who initiated his involvement in the dispute but did say that he was initially acting in a private-sector, yet unpaid capacity, although he hoped "to be successful enough for them to want to pay me."

Four days later, top union and management officials (McDonald, head of the Allied Printing Trade; Brumback, CEO Chicago Tribune Company; Kheel; two representatives from each striking union; Hoge; Ballow, management's hired negotiator; and Edward Gold, the company's director of labor relations) had separate (union/management) closed-door meetings with Usery for about 90 minutes, the first time the union and management had met (if not bargained) face-to-face since the strike began October 25. After a midafternoon break for lunch, Usery went back into separate sessions with each side. The emphasis was on resolving procedural issues for future negotiations, not on actual bargaining. One such resolved issue was the union coalition's selection of the 400-member pressmen's union to negotiate first and one-on-one with management. The Newspaper Guild had also volunteered to serve in this capacity, but the other eight unions felt the bargaining objectives had more in common with the majority of union members involved. Usery also thought if management could reach agreement with the pressmen, it should be relatively easy to obtain settlements with the other unions.

Usery requested that negotiators for management and the pressmen only discuss minor issues (no management rights provision, for example) at their first two-hour session. Afterward, he noted that there was a potential for a negotiated settlement since management and union negotiators who could settle the dispute were present and expressed a commitment to work with each other. However, he further added a sense of urgency to the procedure saying that a settlement had to be reached in days, not weeks. Usery also indicated that he might lock the doors, a tactic used in past marathon labor negotiations to prevent people from leaving. Hoge thought that management both listened to and was heard well by Usery, and he also echoed Usery's requirement for urgent negotiations. McDonald commented after the meetings that the negotiators should "forget about the past" and noted cryptically that it was unfortunate that the meetings had not started one day earlier, on Valentine's Day. One report indicated that management was seeking an estimated $70 million reduction in labor costs while the unions were willing to concede as much as 25 percent, or $32 million in payroll costs.

Negotiations involving Usery were held with the pressmen's union the next day, and a day-long bargaining session was held the following day, Sunday, February 18. (Much of this time consisted of four hours of closed-door discussions with Usery, Hoge, and Ballow.) Management indicated at the end of this latter session that the union would receive a proposal by early afternoon February 18, and additional bargaining could occur that evening. Hoge hoped management's proposal would cover "all the important issues," a sentiment shared by Usery, so that serious thrashing out of differences could occur in this very critical session. John Kennedy, head of the pressmen's union, also indicated his awaiting of management's offer but further noted that the mediator had spent most of the day with management officials, who, in turn, did not characterize the proposed new offer as a final proposal.

Management's three-year labor agreement proposal was presented on February 18 and represented a significant reversal of its previous, long-standing bargaining position that staffing levels should be determined solely by management. Hoge noted that management had dropped its earlier position that it reserved the right to determine the staffing at any point in time. Management officials instead proposed bargaining over staffing issues and suggested a reduction of more than 50 percent in the number of employees on each press. More specifically, this offer sought reduced staffing levels at the paper's 23 presses, from a prestrike average of eight to thirteen operators to no more than five, with no provision for more operators when additional units were operating. According to John Kennedy, some of the staff reductions (about 150 "apprentices" having 14 years or less seniority and about 83 of the 250 journeymen) would be terminated or offered an undisclosed amount as a buy-out. Kennedy also indicated that this proposal represented the first time that management had discussed staffing levels with his unions. The proposal also included a rather large wage concession. More specifically, the prestrike hourly rate of $22.50 would be paid to 40 percent of the remaining journeymen with the other 60 percent of their employees having this figure reduced to $12 an hour. Management also continued to seek a management rights clause covering anything not specifically addressed in its proposed labor agreement.

Union officials were not enthusiastic about management's proposal despite the elimination of management's previous insistence that it unilaterally determine staffing levels. Some called it a "suicide" proposal while Barry Lipton said the proposal "was made to be rejected."

The pressmen rejected management's proposal the next night (February 19) and offered a counterproposal, a six-year labor agreement with a gradual 25 percent reduction in either or both staffing levels and wages. Hoge felt the pressmen's proposal was "too vague," and management rejected the union's proposal; the marathon bargaining session was ended by Usery at 2:10 A.M. with further talks being recessed for two days.

Kennedy, however, indicated that while he was "always hopeful" he did not envision the pressmen modifying their February 19 proposal and that the two sides were far apart. Hoge agreed with Kennedy that the parties were far apart, and the Tribune Company board of directors meeting in Chicago on February 19 indicated that they received a bargaining update from Hoge over the telephone. A Tribune Company spokesperson issued a formal statement that said no final decision was made on whether to sell or shut the *News* with its losses estimated at $750,000 to $1 million a day but also cautioned, "Time is very short." Usery attempted to put an optimistic spin on the lack of bargaining results, contending that the sessions involved "some fruitful and in-depth discussions"; moreover, "it would be almost like having a miracle to expect something to happen this quickly, what with all the rancor and deep divisions of the last four to ten months."[2]

Management thought that Kheel's presence at the resumed negotiation talks on February 22 represented a "conflict of interest" since Kheel was actively seeking a purchaser for the newspaper. Kheel did name two of these interested purchasers — Mortimer B. Zuckerman, owner of *U.S. News and World Report,* and Robert Maxwell, the British communications mogul. One of Maxwell's spokespersons agreed that his level of interest in the *News* was high.

Negotiations continued through February 24 with neither optimism nor substantive accounts of these sessions being publicized. Alan Finder, who reported on the labor negotiations at the *News,* observed these activities reflected journalistic "KP duty," since many negotiators, unlike politicians, or even generals in the Gulf war, give very little information to the media:

That kind of elusiveness has left reporters frantic for information. They dissect each small remark and passing comment. They sit for hours in hotel hallways, watching Mr. Usery and his two aides shuttle from one closed meeting with management to another closed session with the unions.

They analyze his body language and facial expressions. Some desperate reporters, including this one, began noting the exact time of Mr. Usery's arrivals and departures, as if that would somehow provide clues about the fate of the 72-year-old newspaper. (It has not.)[3]

Theodore Kheel thought both union and management negotiators wanted to terminate the sessions but they also sought to avoid being held publicly responsible for refusing to continue bargaining. Barry Lipton regarded the scheduled resumption of negotiations on February 27 as a "turning point" from which bargaining progress had to be made if a settlement were to be reached with *News* management and unions.

Lipton never experienced this session since Usery postponed the meeting until the next day. James Hoge did make an announcement on February 27 that the decision on whether to close the newspaper would be made Monday, March 4 if striking unions failed to grant concessions by then. If Hoge decided to close the newspaper, he would set a specific date for a shutdown, and the Chicago Tribune Company would make the final decision. Then, on February 28, Hoge and Kennedy announced that they had reached a bargaining impasse.

Usery adjourned the sessions after this meeting because he thought the parties were too far apart to resolve their differences. He also indicated that management had held firm to its proposal made to the pressmen on February 18 and further noted that mediation in this situation had come too late because management's positions were already established and buttressed by lawsuits that "inhibited us from getting to the merits of the case in some instances." Usery felt that this peripheral collective bargaining element generated bitterness between the parties and that "both sides begin to protect their lawsuits instead of openly talking about settling."

New York Governor Mario Cuomo indicated that he had never had any confidence that management would seek or reach a bargaining agreement with the unions. He further contended that management's unlikely, continued bargaining efforts would occur for the wrong reasons—to protect themselves against union unfair labor practices or "set themselves up to be able to sell the paper to another operator." Hoge maintained Cuomo's bargaining assessment was "unfortunate, uninformed speculation."

MARCH AND THE MAXWELL FACTOR

Initial *News* Sale Considerations

Usery also pulled out of the bargaining sessions on February 28 to give the unions and management some time to reach an agreement with a potential purchaser. While Mort Zuckerman was reported not to be interested in purchasing the *News,* James Hoge met with some of Robert Maxwell's representatives to discuss purchase possibilities on the evening of February 28 with another meeting scheduled the next day. Maxwell had repeatedly asked Hoge over the years if the *News* were for sale, and each time Hoge had replied in the negative. Now, Maxwell again declared interest in purchasing the *News,* but only if no other competition/potential investors were involved in these actions. Hoge noted that if progress resulted in these talks, the unions would be negotiating with Maxwell's representatives.

Hoge's previously promised statement regarding the *News's* sale or closure deadline was made, as scheduled, on March 4:

The New York Daily News will cease publication on March 15, 1991, unless a binding agreement to sell the newspaper is reached by that date. . . . Barring a sale, I regret that a shutdown of the business will be necessary. . . . The problems facing the Daily News remain unsolved—challenging economic and competitive conditions in the New York area, the failure to achieve new labor agreements with the unions, and a violent strike that has significantly damaged the circulation and advertising revenues of the newspaper. With operating losses still mounting at the rate of $700,000 a day, it is simply not possible to continue publication. . . . In the time left . . . the company will continue to explore intensively a possible sale of the newspaper.[4]

This potential sale announcement shortened by five days the earlier March 20 closing deadline made in January that included the 60-day notification mandated by federal law. Thus, the newspaper was obligated to pay its employees for five days if it shut down March 15. This potential expenditure could be justified to put additional pressure on Maxwell and the unions to reach agreement in the following 11 days.

Unions were unsure about management's real intentions at this time. As Deborah Friedman, a spokesperson for the Allied Printed Trades Council, stressed:

The *News* has to want to sell the paper. . . . If they really want to sell it, they'll sell it to Maxwell. . . . If this paper closes, it's because the *News* wants it to close.[5]

Maxwell, in turn, wanted a firm newspaper purchase agreement before bargaining with affected unions. He also stressed his active participation in these efforts because of a lesson learned from a previous purchase and $50 million failure with an afternoon tabloid: "Never again would I launch a paper and leave it in the hands of the professionals." There was a good chance that Maxwell or any purchaser would not have to put any up-front money for the newspaper. Purchase negotiations would likely consider which liabilities the purchaser would assume and which the Tribune Company would honor.

Under the original sale offering, the purchaser would assume the largest potential obligation, an estimated $100 million in lifetime employment guarantees made to *News* printers although some thought this liability could be as low as $20 to $30 million if many of the printers who were in their fifties would accept early retirement buy-outs at $100,000 each. Lazard Freres and Company, the investment bank handling the potential sale, estimated that an additional $50 million would have to be spent by someone to restore the newspaper's advertising and circulation to prestrike levels.

The Tribune Company would accept liability for five years of underfinanced pension funds (estimated at $25 million) and the cost of severance pay if the newspaper were shut down (another $25 million). It might also be liable for legal suits and remedies involving the dismissal of strike replacements if the new purchaser and the labor unions reached an agreement to terminate these individuals as a condition of reaching satisfactory collective bargaining agreements. Finally, the Tribune Company might be obligated for most of the purchaser's liabilities if the new owner failed to meet them.

New York News Inc., a subsidiary of the Tribune Company, announced on March 5 that it entered into a letter of intent to sell the *Daily News* to Mirror Group Newspapers Inc. and its chairman, Robert Maxwell. The sale was subject to a number of conditions including satisfactory collective bargaining agreements with the unions by March 15. Terms were not initially made public although one person participating in the negotiations said that Maxwell would receive about $60 million from the seller in exchange for assuming responsibility for about $25 million in potential severance costs and for the printers' lifetime employment guarantees.

Union officials now directed their attention toward Robert Maxwell's management approach in general and his collective bargaining style in particular. Maxwell had exhibited neither a prounion nor a participative, cooperative approach in his previous management experiences. He provided an insight into his managerial philosophy: "When I pass a belt . . . I cannot resist hitting below it."

A reporter informed Maxwell of another caveat regarding his managerial dealings with others: "You can charm the birds out of the trees and then you shoot them." Maxwell did not deny this characterization.

Well, if I have to shoot the birds, I shoot them. But I get no fun out of it. If the implication is that I charm you into making concessions and then shoot you just for the fun of it, that's not true.[6]

In England, union employees cursed Maxwell as "Captain Bob," for his autocratic approach toward labor relations and the hypocrisy they perceived when the billionaire called himself a socialist. One observer claimed Maxwell also cultivated and pampered union leaders with various perks such as rides in his helicopter, and persuaded them to serve as a police force to keep their restive members in line. This same observer further contended that Maxwell had plundered the *Scottish Daily News* and *London Daily News* under his ownership and concluded:

In the past [Maxwell] he has dealt with the unions, picked up businesses cheap and been hailed as a savior. The euphoria has never lasted very long, and the betting among London journalists is that the *Daily News* in New York will not last long.[7]

Another account of Maxwell's earlier experiences with 11 unions in England established his ability if not desire to negotiate in a concessionary bargaining atmosphere. Maxwell expressed his attitude concerning this situation: "We have too many employees and we pay them too much."[8]

Union leaders were aware of Maxwell's past bargaining behaviors and predilections, but subsumed them. Jack Kennedy, of the pressmen's union, knew that the survival of the *News*, not negotiators' personalities, had to be addressed at this time, while Barry Lipton thought Maxwell would deal in good faith with the unions.

George McDonald acknowledged previous accounts of Maxwell's hard-nosed, antiunion reputation and the need to reduce Maxwell's negotiation statements to writing. However, he also thought Maxwell could not be worse than *News* negotiators and indicated that he would reserve any judgment until he met Maxwell. McDonald also indicated that he had had a six-minute telephone conversation with Maxwell, who was not forceful but instead asked McDonald, "Do you think it's worth my time to come?" McDonald indicated that the unions would give concessions. McDonald also felt that he had achieved more with Maxwell in this conversation than he had in two years of bargaining with Tribune Company management. He further sensed that Maxwell wanted to be owner of the *News* at all costs because "owning the *Daily News* is like a visiting card for sheiks, kings and queens. It opens the door for people and I guess he wanted it that bad."[9] Maxwell indicated that he wanted negotiations to begin March 6 and be concluded no later than March 11.

The Unions' First Bargaining Meeting with Maxwell

Unions awaited the March 7 meeting with Maxwell prepared to make large concessions so long as the framework of the old labor agreement (the absence of the 200-word management rights clause, for example) remained in place. According to Tom Bower, a biographer of Maxwell, union leaders ought to be prepared as well for several marathon bargaining sessions, where Maxwell would personally try to wear them down to win large concessions:

[Maxwell] has extraordinary energy and will go from now to Monday without sleep. . . .
He will put unions in different rooms and go from one to another, bombarding them with
threats, cajolery, and promises.[10]

Some who had bargained with Maxwell found the experience both unique and
unforgettable since his normal work week of seven 18-hour days became accel-
erated when crucial negotiations were involved. One union officer in England,
who had dealt with Maxwell, described his habit of conducting three or four
meetings at one time, one in person and the others by telephone. Moreover, his
conversations could also switch from English to French to German since he was
fluent in six languages. The union leader noted that the results of these lengthy,
disconcerted sessions, coupled with Maxwell's brinkmanship skills, were aimed
at keeping union officials off guard to extract concessions:

You walk into a building to negotiate with Maxwell and you never know when you'll get
out. . . . With Maxwell, you think you've got a deal and you haven't. . . . It's just bi-
zarre.[11]

Yet this same union official offered optimism to her American union counterparts bargaining for the *News*'s survival when she indicated that Maxwell wanted
to become a household name in America, a feat that would be accomplished by
operating the *News*. One of Maxwell's top executives for the years 1986 to 1989
noted that Maxwell was deeply offended that he was seen as merely a *printer* of
his previous U.S. purchases of Macmillan and the Official Airline Guides. Maxwell's purchase of the *News* would "demonstrate to the world that he was a publisher as well."

The March 7 meeting involved Maxwell and the ten union leaders (of the nine
striking unions and the typographical union) in a small auditorium in the Macmillan building at Third Avenue and 53d Street where Maxwell described his
social and political beliefs and his business experiences/strategies. He acknowledged that unions had a legitimate role to play and that a harmonious relationship with union leaders was necessary to save the *News* through successfully
obtained labor agreements.[12] He also quickly obtained the union leaders' favorable attention by promising that replacement employees and legal suits filed
against the unions would be eliminated if a settlement were reached.

Both Maxwell and McDonald remarked that the first-day sessions conducted
with the unions in separate rooms had been very successful. Maxwell noted that
his imposed March 11 deadline was "very tight indeed," and that the parties
would "sit all night and work all over the weekend." A subsequent session between Maxwell and the union leaders was conducted in the Macmillan building's
board room at 9:30 P.M., March 8. Maxwell started out the session by saying "no
lawyers." Lawyers for Maxwell and the unions then left the room. Theodore
Kheel, however, remained, presumably because his role was unpaid advisor, not
legal counsel.

Maxwell moreover suggested to the press that the controversial management rights clause that had held up negotiations at the *News* would not be an issue in these negotiations. George McDonald agreed with Maxwell and further contended that the management rights issue was "not going to be the problem that the Tribune Company and the *News* made it out to be. Management has the right to manage. That's what Mr. Maxwell wants and that's what he's going to get."[13] McDonald further explained that Maxwell reflected some bargaining weakness with his revised management rights' stance,

When the cameras had gone he told me, "I want that paper," so I knew that we had a deal if I got all nine unions into line and gave a few concessions and redundancies which the Tribune was paying for.[14]

McDonald also said that an amnesty was being discussed for union members involved in alleged physical altercations on the picket lines and elsewhere. Each alleged striker misconduct action would be assessed, and those who had been convicted of a strike-related issue would not be reemployed. In return, Maxwell wanted the elimination of some 800 to 900 of the newspaper's 2,300 union jobs, a figure that was lower than the 1,000 jobs the *News* previously wanted eliminated. (The particular job elimination breakdown by union was not made public at this time.) Kheel indicated that union leaders found these negotiations "refreshing," particularly when they were compared to frustrations in dealing with Ballow and to the lack of access to Hoge and other *News* executives.

Additional Bargaining Considerations

On the second day of negotiations, Maxwell did confirm the Tribune Company's offer to pay him $60 million for purchasing the newspaper and, for the first time, placed a dollar value on union concessions. He contended that the *News*'s operating costs had to be cut by $1.4 million to $1.6 million a week ($72.8 million to $83.6 million a year), which was higher than McDonald's originally anticipated $50 million in necessary union concessions, and likely more than that requested by *News* management, who had indicated in an April 1990 news release that "solid financial performance" could only be achieved if $50 to $70 million in annual operating costs were eliminated. Maxwell described the collective bargaining situation at this point as being into very serious "meat-and-potatoes" items.

McDonald did not apparently regard Maxwell's bargaining concessions/objectives as unsurmountable, and his attitude might have been due to previous negotiations with *News* management who did not establish a specific dollar figure for union bargaining concessions but sought instead vague and snarled labor agreement language concerning management's rights. According to one report, some of the other union leaders appeared "almost elated" at the prospect of working for Maxwell, who, despite his announced proposal calling for union concessions, would be an owner who did not question the place of union leaders at the *News* and who wanted the newspaper to continue its operations. Wayne Mitchell of the mailers' union said, "He wants the paper, and if he wants the paper, we want him."[15]

Some of this sentiment was likely also due to the fact that Maxwell provided a most comfortable bargaining environment, including secretarial help, according to a spokesperson for the Allied Printing Trades Council. He also paid for all negotiation costs, from takeout food to carfare, and provided food prepared by his corporate chefs to the union officials.

Union and management negotiators had far less optimism after the third day of extensive negotiations. Maxwell wanted to close one of the *News* printing plants, but also said he would hire back affected union employees as circulation increased.

Perhaps more serious was the management rights contract language that Maxwell proposed and that the union leaders found virtually identical to that of the controversial *News* proposal. George McDonald estimated Maxwell's management rights proposal to be "60 percent Ballow, 20 percent the old contracts, and 20 percent new." Theodore Kheel noted that Saturday's labor agreement language "didn't reflect what Mr. Maxwell had agreed to" on Friday.

Charles Wilson, Maxwell's chief negotiator, who had told his wife on Friday that the odds of a negotiated settlement were 50 to 1, was even more skeptical when union leaders expressed their displeasure over the management rights language on Saturday, March 9, which, Wilson said, completely destroyed the atmosphere bringing the parties back to "ground zero." Wilson acknowledged that his role as chief negotiator was not to study former, even proposed, *News* labor agreements. Instead, he had to quickly

talk face-to-face with people and get them to trust me. I had to show them that I knew newspapers, even if I really didn't know anything about their contracts.[16]

Maxwell left the discussions late Saturday (March 9) to celebrate his wife's birthday and their 46th wedding anniversary. He informed reporters that he intended to return to bargaining sessions scheduled for the next day at 6:00 P.M. But Kheel said Maxwell gave a different message to the unions, one that indicated that he was uncertain both about the reasons for the unions' unrest as well as his specific return plans. This negotiation setback was eliminated the next day, however, through a Sunday morning explanatory, possibly apologetic, letter delivered by Charles Wilson. The letter basically reflected concern that the spirit of cooperation and optimism about the saving of the *Daily News* had been damaged by Saturday proposals; moreover, time constraints prompted Maxwell to rely on the only material available. The letter also expressed a hope that both sides could "recreate the spirit of Friday evening." At 3:00 P.M. Sunday, George McDonald telephoned Maxwell, who was still in London. Kheel gave the following account of this conversation:

Maxwell asked George how it was going, and George said he thought the letter from Wilson was very good and that the tone was better. . . . George said, "Are you coming back?" . . . And Maxwell said, "I will come back if you ask me." And George said, "I'm asking you."[17]

The messages were apparently well received by union negotiators. McDonald said Maxwell's Saturday proposal was made in haste, and Maxwell's management "rewrote what we didn't like." Kheel also opined that Maxwell was not trying to pull a "fast one" on the unions with the Saturday proposal; instead, Maxwell had relied on some *News* representatives who had "slipped in a couple of Mickey Finns." These assessments were supported by James Hoge, who maintained that he and the unions realized that Maxwell would not walk away because he would "do anything to get the newspaper."

Sunday's letter also proposed a three-year labor agreement with common expiration dates (March 31, 1994), which had been previously offered by the Tribune Company. Wages would not be reduced the first year; however, "upward readjustments" would be negotiated by the parties on common 1992 and 1993 contract anniversary dates. If a settlement was not reached on this issue after 60 days, then the matter would be resolved by binding arbitration. This proposal retained several previous benefits that were often points of contention with *News* negotiators: paid holidays and vacation, compassionate leave, jury service, optional leave, publisher-paid group life insurance, contributions to jointly trusteed health and welfare and pension funds, employer-financed sick leave, a 401(k) plan, and a Newspaper Guild scholarship fund. Other issues such as recognition for the union's jurisdiction and security, automatic dues collection, and the right of supervisory personnel to join the unions (major stumbling blocks in previous negotiations at the *News*) were also included in the proposal.

Bargaining did occur on Sunday as scheduled between management and union representatives and continued well into the night and into Monday morning (Maxwell arrived in New York at 2:30 A.M. Monday). Don Singleton, a reporter and member of the Guild's negotiating team, described this and other sessions that followed as "free-floating and chaotic—no structure at all." Singleton further said that the only commonality during this process was Maxwell who was "popping up and saying 'oh Hallo,' and bestowing handshakes."

The lawyers had returned along with Charles Wilson, and these individuals were successful in settling disputes in the few remaining hours before Maxwell's deadline. But George McDonald played a major role in making sure that Maxwell saw the individual union leaders when bargaining points remained unresolved. Stanley Aslanian, president of the photoengraver's union, noted management's successful bargaining approach when union leaders had to cool their heels waiting to see Maxwell.

Obviously, there were a lot of waits because they did not have nine top men. . . . If you wanted to see Charlie [Wilson] or wait for Maxwell, there was a lot of dead time. They were smart enough to fill it by bringing in sandwiches and pizzas.[18]

Kheel confirmed Ashanian's assessment, indicating the sessions represented the "best-fed negotiation I have ever attended."

Maxwell had wanted about 85 percent of the employee reductions to come from three unions: the pressmen (from 400 current employees/members to 200), the drivers (from 700 to 400), and the Newspaper Guild (from 700 to 580). At least one union leader, Michael Alvino of the drivers, suggested Maxwell's proposed reductions would not come easily, "I'm willing to give, but I'm not willing to let him have the whole farm. . . . I'm trying to keep the back quarter acre for the people."[19]

George McDonald said that several unions appeared to be close to a settlement by 10:00 P.M. on Sunday but did indicate that some confusion was caused by language. For example, "vacations" in America are called "holidays" in England, and these heretofore unrecognized differences occupied two days worth of bargaining. McDonald also indicated that Maxwell's proposed $40,000 buy-out for each employee who agreed to retire as part of a plan to cut labor costs would be higher by the time the unions agreed to a settlement. McDonald also said that the stereotypers, engravers, and typographers were seeking higher buy-outs, up to $100,000, in exchange for lifetime job and benefit guarantees. McDonald further raised the possibility that Maxwell could seek an additional $3 million from the Tribune Company to cover the steeper-than-proposed buy-outs.

Despite these obstacles, Maxwell found enough optimism to extend the "absolute" Monday, March 11, 10:00 A.M. deadline for 14 hours, to 12:00 A.M. The possibility of a negotiated settlement had to be regarded differently by strike replacements who were working at the *News* and knew they would be terminated after labor agreements with the unions were reached. At least one Guild replacement employee offered a rather calm reaction to the bargaining progress at this time: "We knew what we were getting into" she said, despite receiving a telephone message on March 11 from an anonymous caller who said, "Start clearing out the desk that wasn't yours."

A Settlement Between Maxwell and Nine Unions of the APTC

Maxwell's optimistic extension of the labor negotiations was no doubt influenced by the tentative settlements reached with four unions after an earlier deadline had been extended. The mailers' union was the first to reach a tentative agreement, which included a reduction of its members from 107 to 72 with related buy-outs of $40,000 per employee. Maxwell acknowledged that job losses were neither right nor pleasant aspects of these negotiations. Other accords were reached with the paperhandlers, machinists, and electricians, and negotiations with the other five unions resumed at 1:30 A.M. on March 12.

Maxwell acknowledged this development meant that the second "deadline" was no longer applicable: "We will work all night again." He also stressed that major changes/concessions were needed from some if not all of the remaining unions since, he said, "I don't belong to the Salvation Army." Maxwell indicated, for example, that no employee buy-out would exceed $50,000. The drivers and press workers reportedly differed from Maxwell on staffing levels, and some members of the Newspaper Guild said Maxwell did not clearly guarantee dismissal of all permanent replacements hired during the dispute. The typographical union was also bargaining, but at a location different from the other nine unions who were housed at the Maxwell-owned Macmillan building.

At 2:00 P.M. on March 12, Maxwell set a final deadline of one hour later, and indicated that he would leave the country if deals with all unions were not reached. The drivers' union was the last to reach a tentative bargaining settlement about an hour after that deadline, around 4:00 P.M. on March 12.

The three-year labor agreements mirrored the previously discussed management proposal made on Sunday, and resulted in some $70 million in concessions and the elimination of some 800 jobs, or about one third of the prestrike unionized work force at the *News.* Replacement employees would be terminated and rehired only when all union members were employed; however, *crossovers,* union members who had crossed picket lines to return to work during the strike, would continue to be employed and would retain all their seniority except that obtained during the strike. The settlement also indicated that unions would drop all charges filed against management with the National Labor Relations Board and give up five days of vacation or personal leave. Maxwell also obtained another union concession which had been sought unsuccessfully by the Tribune Company—that is, a longer work week (37½ hours, versus the previous 34½ hours). Employees would receive three more hours of straight-time pay per week; however, the paper would likely reap a large net gain through fewer overtime expenses.

A major bargaining settlement issue, the number of employees by job/union classification who would be severed from the *News,* is outlined in Exhibit 6.1. These reductions would be accomplished by a combination of buy-outs and layoffs. Buy-outs would be offered in the order of seniority, with those having the most seniority offered the buy-outs first—if attrition for each group of unionized employees was insufficient, then layoffs would be made in the reverse order of seniority.

Employees for most of the unions could receive severance pay of two weeks of pay per year of service or a $40,000 buy-out, whichever was greater. Members of the printers, stereotypers, and photoengravers' unions would be eligible for a $50,000 buy-out alternative plus medical benefits through age 65 because of lifetime guarantees in previous labor agreements. These buy-outs were considerably less than those given by other New York newspapers including the *Daily News* in the 1980s; however, union leaders had compared this amount to that received by *New York Post* employees (8 weeks severance pay), which was 25 percent of the amount that *News* employees without lifetime guarantees would receive.

Barry Lipton of the Newspaper Guild had not attained agreement with Maxwell on the precise effects of seniority on buy-out payments and layoffs one half hour before the bargaining deadline (3:00 P.M. on Sunday, March 12). Indeed, Maxwell expressed a desire to completely remove seniority from these considerations. Maxwell met with Lipton between 2:30 P.M. and 3:00 P.M. on March 12, and these somewhat complex issues were resolved. Lipton's reflection of this situation appeared similar to the experiences of many of the other union leaders during the final stages of negotiations, as he suggested that even complicated issues could be resolved in 20 to 25 minutes if the meeting included a management representative who has the authority to make decisions.

Maxwell reflected that bringing an end to a "long, terrible dispute" was similar to "a miracle on 42d Street," through which he and the unions were giving the newspaper back to New York's readers and advertisers. He further indicated that he would serve as the *News*'s publisher for 6 to 12 months and promised a profit, barring any unforeseen circumstances in the first year of circulation, an indication of the "realism of this bargaining." Related promises/expectations included spending $10 million in the first six to eight weeks to rebuild the newspaper's circulation and advertising, and using color presses within the next two to three years.

Maxwell also suggested that this settlement would benefit his recognition in yet another part of the world—New York. He had been surprised, even shaken, over his reception in New York and the United States, where his appearances in the streets and restaurants of New York City were acknowledged by applause, and where he also lunched with President George Bush and sat in the reviewing stand with General Norman Schwarzkopf when Desert Storm troops received a ticker tape parade on Broadway. Maxwell basked in this situation: "In my whole

Exhibit 6.1
Summary of Approximate Number of Jobs Lost After Tentative Settlement Was Reached with Robert Maxwell on March 12, 1992

Union	Prestrike work force	New total	Jobs Lost Number	Percent
Newspaper Guild (Editorial, clerical, and some advertising and circulation workers)	759	521	238	31
Drivers	702	450	252	36
Pressmen	410	**	**	**
Printers	199	100	99	50 L
Mailers	107	72	35	34
Paperhandlers	79	40	39	50
Machinists	49	**	**	**
Stereotypers and photoengravers	55	35	20	36 L
Electricians	37	21	16	43

Source: New York Times March 14, 1991, B-2.

L—Lifetime job guarantees: All printers and some photoengravers have guarantees. *News* workers with guarantees are to be offered inducements of $50,000 each to leave the paper or retire early. Payments offered to others will be $40,000.

**—Figures for pressmen and machinists are not shown because the unions refused to confirm any information before final written contracts were available.

life in London, no one's ever acted like this. I'm here a month and look what's happening."[20]

Maxwell also publicly indicated his thanks for the constructive and cooperative efforts of James Hoge and the leaders of the ten unions whose leaders were

Runyonesque—straight out of *West Side Story*. . . . They have a great sense of humor—I had not realized how the Irish dominate the crafts here. I hold them in high regard. They have good spirits and are as tough as boots.[21]

James Hoge publicly labeled Maxwell's contribution "extraordinary" and "central to the results announced" and looked forward to successfully completing the sale on the schedule specified in the letter of intent. Union leaders also acknowledged Maxwell's collective bargaining role in favorable terms. Lane Kirkland, president of the AFL-CIO, indicated that his organization was "delighted" at the settlement, which he contended was made possible when the strike replacement issue was removed from the table. George McDonald also appreciated Maxwell's willingness to indicate what he needed, a tactic he said was not found with *News* negotiators.

The unions' advisor, Theodore Kheel, praised Maxwell's collective bargaining involvement:

It was a performance to end all performances. . . . He was in everything. He dominated. He cajoled. He met with the full committees and he met with the small committees. He got involved in the minutiae.[22]

Kheel also took a last shot at Robert Ballow, the *News* negotiator, who, unlike Maxwell, was "the world's greatest dealbreaker," and who had established himself as "the Saddam Hussein of collective bargaining."

SIGNIFICANT CONSIDERATIONS INCLUDING RATIFICATION

After the Tentative Bargaining Settlements

News hawkers during the strike, many of whom were homeless, had no role in achieving a collective bargaining settlement and knew that their employment at the *News* would be ended when negotiations were successfully concluded. One hawker, a welfare mother, said that she made $25 a day selling the *News*, a sum that enabled her to buy her baby a rather full set of winter clothing. Another hawker did not want his job to end because he liked giving people something (a copy of the *News*) in exchange for his monetary requests. Mary Brosnahan, director of the Coalition for the Homeless, reiterated her position that *News* management exploited these individuals during the strike, regarding them as disposable after they had served their purpose.

March 21 was the estimated date for the strikers to return to the *News* if the labor agreements were ratified by the unions' members. At least some replacement reporters, if not all replacement employees, were told that March 20 should be their last day and that they would be paid through March 28.

Many striking employees were relieved that a quick settlement ended previously lengthy, brutal, and futile collective bargaining activities involving *News* management. As one striking reporter, Tom Robbins, indicated:

People are either on the verge of tears or laughter. . . . We are all still in a kind of giddy free fall. We feel like giants, but that's a momentary feeling. After being told for so long by so many smarter and more powerful people that we were on a quixotic mission that would never succeed, to have won is amazing.[23]

Robbins also wondered why previous management officials did not prevent this event from happening since the Tribune Company could have received $150 million in union concessions a year before this figure was included in the settlement reached with Maxwell.

This cautiously optimistic reaction could bode problems when the tentative labor agreement settlements were subjected to the membership for their approval. George McDonald indicated that no striking members would return to work until all unions ratified the tentative collective bargaining settlements. Lipton indicated that only Newspaper Guild members at the *News* would vote on its union's tentative labor agreement, but some other unions, including the pressmen and drivers, would have all their members (including those working at the *New York Post* and *New York Times*) voting on the proposed labor agreements. Some thought that this voting procedure would doom contract ratifications since negative votes would likely be registered by unions at other New York newspapers because they would not want the *News* concessionary settlement to serve as a depressionary precedent on their subsequent collective bargaining negotiations, particularly those at the *New York Times,* which expire in 1993. Yet, at least some union leaders and members reasoned that the *News* labor–management settlements, while concessionary, nonetheless reflected a long and effective shutdown of the *News* with competitors gaining at the struck newspaper's expense. This reasoning further contended that the *New York Times* management would not risk this situation, including removal of its newspaper from the newsstands for a similar settlement. Therefore, union members at the *Post* and *Times* could ratify the *News* labor agreements without incurring adverse effects to their future bargaining positions.

Nevertheless, contract acceptance by all unions was not automatically assumed by union leaders. John Kennedy, leader of the pressmen, conceded that labor agreement ratification would be a "hard sell." George McDonald thought all unions would ratify the settlements but only after a lot of "hollering" occurred. Alvino of the drivers union at least recognized potential membership dissension but said that these opponents, not voting for the agreement, would "be committing suicide for the union."

Pressmen were no doubt concerned that reduced staffing levels per press could reduce overtime guarantees specified in the previous labor agreement. All *News* unionized employees did not know how much time they had to accept or reject proposed buy-outs/severance payments. Their decisions would be complicated by eligibility requirements. Union members who accepted other employment during the strike could claim buy-out pay only if they had not resigned and received severance pay. Buy-outs were likely a more generous option for members of craft unions, while many longtime Newspaper Guild members would benefit more from the severance pay option. Many union members would not accept either bargained option, however, because of existing financial commitments such as college-tuition payments for their children.

If those accepting buy-outs or severance pay per union fell below related figures reached with Maxwell, then layoffs could occur with additional complications that would have to be clarified and explained before the labor agreements could be ratified. Some unions enabled laid-off members to use their seniority to obtain employment at other newspapers, creating a complicated situation because many of the craft members at the *News* had also worked on a part-time basis at other newspapers. It was not clear whether these individuals could bump craft employees having less seniority at other newspapers.

At least some union members eligible to return to the *News* might vote no on the contract ratification vote because they would have to work with colleagues who were perceived to be less talented than those who were laid off. Even more no votes might be recorded if union members did not want to work with those who had crossed the picket lines. This situation was intensified by individuals who had made eloquent strike speeches only to cross the picket line a few days later. Even worse, under terms of the tentative settlements, returning strikers would have to work with some employees who had crossed the picket lines, and after some time had passed, waved their paychecks in picketers' faces. Don Singleton, a reporter for 26 years, predicted that volcanic tempers could erupt, possibly resulting in "blood on the newsroom floor the first day."

While union leaders discussed the terms of tentative settlements and the timing and prospects of the ratifications, James Hoge met with Robert Maxwell on Maxwell's yacht, *Lady Ghislaine,* on March 13 to discuss the details of the proposed sale of the *News.* The March 15 closure deadline for the newspaper remained if a sales agreement could not be reached.

Charles Brumback announced the next day that a definitive sales agreement of the *News* had been reached between the Tribune Company and Robert Maxwell, one in which Maxwell would receive $60 million to assume Tribune Company operations and long-term liabilities, including severance pay if there was a subsequent shutdown, and lifetime job guarantees to the members of the printers' union. This agreement's settlement was scheduled for March 20, subject to the prior ratification of the ten collective bargaining agreements. The Tribune Company would continue to operate the *News* through March 20, and Maxwell would assume control of the *News* March 21. Brumback's press announcement congratulated Maxwell for his accomplishments; however, no mention was made of the union's role in precursory bargaining efforts. When asked if his organization might have facilitated the *News* strike and sale, Brumback responded that his company would be looking forward, not backward in the days ahead.

Robert Maxwell also spoke at the news conference and indicated that 16 of the newspaper's top 20 prestrike advertisers had pledged to return. This announcement was significant because of the large, possibly irreversible, inroads that the *News's* competitors, the *New York Post* and *New York Newsday,* had made on circulation and advertising revenues. *Post* editor Jerry Nachman reflected, "I get letters that say: 'We were forced to read you; now we're addicted.' " *New York Newsday* editor Donald Forst retorted that Nachman's only strike gains were his body weight, and some circulation outside of the city, which was not sought by *Newsday.*

When asked why the Tribune Company could not achieve these collective bargaining results Maxwell replied, "The mistrust went so far and deep." Maxwell acknowledged that union leaders had had to give up a lot in bargaining sessions with him because they realized there would be no jobs and *News* otherwise. He further stressed that ratifying the labor agreements was urgent and necessary, and that union members should put bitter strike experiences behind them so that current bargaining table efforts were not lost and the *Daily News* could resume publication. Maxwell's comments were seconded by James Hoge, who sent a message to union members which, in part, read, "Tribune Company has done its best to contribute to the survival of the paper. . . . I've done my best."[24] The sales agreement concerning the *News* would lapse if the labor agreements were not ratified by March 20.

On March 16, the day after the tentative sale announcement, union officials from at least five unions (mailers, machinists, paperhandlers, electricians, and the Newspaper Guild) met with Maxwell's lawyers to work out differences in contract language and interpretation. Some union leaders maintained that there were differences between what they had agreed to in principle and the labor agreement language prepared by Maxwell's lawyers. Many reporters further felt that the March 20 ratification deadline did not give them enough time to decide whether to take the $40,000 buy-out. They were also concerned that they had to make this decision without first knowing what their new assignments would be in the reconfigured newsroom if they returned. Barry Lipton of the Newspaper Guild did not think that these differences were insurmountable, however.

Leaders of the Newspaper Guild were also considering the possibility of instituting internal proceedings against members who had crossed the picket line during the strike. Some felt that what should be imposed was a fine of a day's pay for each day's work during the strike, which would be dropped if the crossovers leaving the *News* would generate enough vacancies so that all striking members could return to the *News.* Another concern was for minority members who represented about 20 percent of the *Daily News's* employees and typically had little seniority and would be disproportionately affected if a layoff occurred.

Layoffs could also affect the drivers' union, which had signed a consent decree more than ten years ago concerning racial discrimination. The decree meant in part that the union would hire a minority driver for every white driver hired. At contract settlement time, 35 percent of the union members were minorities; however, this proportion would be greatly reduced since many of them would be laid off because of their relatively low seniority.

The photoengravers union was the first to ratify the labor agreement on March 15. Then the pressmen's union ratified the labor agreement (409 to 39) after a three-hour meeting two days later. John Kennedy indicated about half the pressmen's jobs would be eliminated, which would result in some nine employees on each press instead of the 12 to 13 prestrike total and the five-employees-per-press figure once proposed by the Tribune Company. Under the new agreement, union supervisors would determine the number of pressmen required for each day's operation, and the positions would be filled on a seniority basis. This agreed-upon staffing level appeared higher than that enjoyed by many publishers for years. For example, the *Chicago Tribune* and the *Sun Times* have employed no more than seven press operators per press.

The typographers union also ratified its labor agreement with an estimated 10 to 20 members accepting buy-outs. Of course, no member of this union was obligated to leave because of lifetime employment guarantees, which were further assured when this union did not go out on strike. James Grottola, president of the typographers union, indicated, "We learned from the Chicago experience," where 213 of the 235 printers, who also had lifetime guarantees, struck the *Tribune* in 1985 and were permanently replaced, at least until related unfair labor practice charges were resolved.

The Newspaper Guild postponed its initial ratification meeting, scheduled for March 17 to March 19. Barry Lipton indicated that he had convinced Maxwell to save an additional 38 jobs for its members (membership reduction would be 200 instead of 238). This adjustment was in effect giving the Guild credit for retirements and voluntary separations that had occurred during the strike. Lipton termed "impossible," however, Maxwell's mandate that eligible members, strikers and nonstrikers with ten years of service, would have to make their buy-out decisions by the night of March 20.

The drivers' union also had last-minute concerns before its contract ratification vote. Union officials in collective bargaining sessions strongly urged Maxwell not to retain at least 40 nonunion foreman who had been hired during the past year. Officials also gave Maxwell names of ten supervisors who might spark violence. Maxwell promised orally that most of them would be gone in a year but did not give a flat guarantee according to a union official who met with Maxwell on March 16 and reflected, "He understands what we're saying about those guys, but he may not really believe how much we hate them."

Collective bargaining resumed in effect after the tentative labor agreements were reached when Maxwell held a last-minute meeting with members of six unions on March 19, a day before the sell-or-close deadline. The paperhandlers, stereotypers, electricians, and mailers ratified their labor agreements on March

19, but Maxwell adjusted the mailers' labor agreement by adding 3.5 hours to the members' work week and restoring nine of the 35 jobs that were to be cut from a total of 107.

The drivers' union voted unanimously to accept their labor agreement, which replicated the reduction from 702 to 450 members specified in the tentative settlement. The last-minute discussion between drivers' union officials and Maxwell did produce assurances that no driver would be forced to accept a buy-out but instead could elect to be placed on the "One List" where they would be first called to fill temporary and/or permanent vacancies as they arose at the *News, New York Times,* and *New York Post.* One driver indicated that the settlement reflected "a lousy contract, but it's something we can live with." Michael Alvino of the drivers' union noted the ratified labor agreement would enable 500 families to eat again.

Less than one hour later, the Newspaper Guild's members ratified their agreement. Barry Lipton did arrange a compromise with Maxwell whereby Guild members would have until March 27 to determine who would take the buy-outs. Guild members would not return to work until this date but would be paid for this time. Their jobs would continue to be performed by management employees and union members who had crossed the picket line to return to work during this time period.

On Wednesday, March 20, the machinists completed the ratification process when they voted 36 to 3 to accept their labor agreement. A rally was held in front of the *News* building to celebrate this event, which concluded the 147-day strike. Union leaders congratulated Maxwell on his willingness to purchase the *News* and to bargain with the unions. AFL-CIO Secretary-Treasurer Tom Donahue termed the situation a "victory" of 2,300 people, who effectively used solidarity to fight the "union-busters to a standstill."

John Kennedy indicated at the rally that the *News* strike contrasted with the Professional Air Traffic Controller's Organization (PATCO) strike in 1981 where the strikers were successfully replaced, "This is the end of the PATCO era. . . . It's over." Barry Lipton gave some credit for this agreement to New Yorkers, who had "refused to buy a paper put out by greedy bums and scabs." George McDonald regarded the union's victory as more of an "educational lesson":

Now the Tribune Company can leave New York and go back to Chicago. . . . This agreement shows that if the labor movement stays together, it can overcome these obstacles. . . . If management really wants to use collective bargaining and really wants to talk, then the process will work.[25]

Maxwell appeared last at the ceremony and declared, "In a free society, if collective bargaining is destroyed, you destroy democracy and, in due course, prosperity." Charles Brumback of the Tribune Company sent his congratulations to Maxwell before the rally and his best wishes to Maxwell and *News* employees for "long-term success in publishing New York's hometown paper." Brumback also commented on another occasion, "We were looking at a fifty-year investment," while also realizing that Maxwell was sixty-seven and wanted to enjoy a piece of "his lifetime's ambition." Brumback's comments no doubt reflected relief that the labor relations and financial problems of the *News* were behind him, and likely placed in the hands of Maxwell, who some thought made a vanity purchase.

Yet some financial analysts noted that $160 million in strike-related costs represented about half the amount it would have taken to purchase new color presses and make the newspaper more competitive. One reporter for *Newsday* indicated these figures were understated by over $100 million. He figured that direct strike-related costs were $75 million a year for two years and that indirect costs (hiring and training replacement workers, resolving various unfair labor practices, and so forth) of $50 million should be added to the $60 million paid to Maxwell to take the newspaper off its hands. He further maintained that the Tribune Company's decision to throw this money "down a sewer . . . in a fit of pique" was not business. "That's just nuts."[26]

The Tribune Company's official financial figures for the fourth quarter and for 1990 totals included the nonrecurring charge relating to the sale of the *New York Daily News*. The organization had a fourth-quarter 1990 net loss of $191.4 million compared to $67.6 million in fourth-quarter 1989. For year 1990, the reported net loss was $63.5 million, versus a net income of $242.4 million for 1989. The news release also indicated:

The nonrecurring charge totaled $295 million on a pretax basis [$185 million on an after-tax basis] including: $60 million paid to Maxwell Newspapers, Inc., the purchaser of the *Daily News,* to fund employee buy-out costs and other transition expenses; $86 million of accrued employee compensation costs and other expenses resulting from the sale; $57 million of 1991 *Daily News* operating losses through the date of sale; and a $92 million noncash charge for the write-down of *Daily News* assets to net realizable value.

In addition to this nonrecurring charge, the *Daily News* incurred pretax operating losses of $69.3 million for the fourth quarter and $114.5 million for the full year.[27]

The rally also featured chants of "Hoge must go," a response to an earlier published interview with Maxwell, who had said that he would become actively involved in the newspaper's affairs and then gradually began to turn the paper over to James Hoge. Maxwell, when asked about his decision to retain Hoge, commented "I didn't ask them. It's none of their business." George McDonald did volunteer before the rally that Hoge's retention represented "a colossal mistake. . . . like George Bush making Saddam Hussein Secretary of State." McDonald also noted, however, that Maxwell's decision could be lived with. Edward Gold, the newspaper's director of labor relations during the strike, was also retained by Maxwell.

Maxwell and the union leaders entered the *News* building after the rally ended, presumably to symbolize the new publishing arrangement. However, a miscommunication had the strike replacements working the night of March 20 while union leaders had also informed their members to report to work for this shift as well. This potentially explosive situation was diffused when the returning employees were sent home after being told they would be paid for this shift they did not actually work.

Far less scheduling doubt occurred over replacement reporters and copy editors, who had their last work days on March 20. They did receive a tote bag and a coffee mug as a going-away present, but some contended they had been offered three weeks severance pay if they signed releases pledging not to sue the paper over their dismissals.

NOTES

1. David Gonzalez, "Violence and the News Strike: Anger, Blame and Distrust," *New York Times,* March 2, 1991, 1 and 26.

2. "Daily News Negotiators Report No Progress After Three Days of Mediated Bargaining," Bureau of National Affairs, Inc., *Daily Labor Report* 34 (February 20, 1991): A-7 and A-8.

3. Alan Finder, "Quietly, He Keeps Foes Talking," *New York Times,* February 25, 1991, B-5.

4. "Tribune Company Announces Daily News to Cease Publication on March 15," PR Newswire, March 4, 1991. Dialog File 613, item 034922–NY077.

5. "Daily News Sets March 15 Closing Date Unless It's Able to Sell Newspaper," Bureau of National Affairs, Inc., *Daily Labor Report* 43 (March 5, 1991): A-13.

6. "Playboy Interview: Robert Maxwell," *Playboy,* October 1991, 70.

7. Timothy Gopsill, "After the Cheering Ends at the News," *New York Times,* April 14, 1991, A-11.

8. James M. Perry, "Would-Be Press Mogul Maxwell Grapples with the British Unions," *Wall Street Journal,* December 6, 1985, 34.

9. Tom Bower, *Maxwell: The Outsider* (New York: Viking, 1992), 452. McDonald at this time also announced that his last meeting held with *News* management negotiators was March 5, 1991. He said the meeting amounted to no more than discussing "cleaning out our lockers" in the event of a shutdown.

10. Alex S. Jones, "Warily, Labor at Daily News Awaits Talks," *New York Times,* March 7, 1991, B-1 and B-2.

11. Steve Lohr, "British Tycoon Tries Proven Tactics to Negotiate A Daily News Takeover," *New York Times,* March 11, 1991, B-2.

12. Maxwell indicated that this labor relations philosophy was suggested by an article written by Jack Sheinkman, president of the Amalgamated Clothing and Textile Workers Union, who had participated in the earlier leafleting of the Tribune Company's *Fort Lauderdale Sun-Sentinel* office, and wrote a piece for the March 7, 1991 *Wall Street Journal,* A-15, entitled, "Daily News Scoop: Busting Labor Is Bad Economics."

13. "British Publisher Opens Talks with Unions in Bid to Purchase New York Daily News," Bureau of National Affairs, Inc., *Daily Labor Report* 46 (March 8, 1991): A-13, A-14.

14. Bower, *Maxwell,* 433.

15. "$70 Million Annual Savings Is Goal for Purchase of News," *New York Times,* March 9, 1991, 27.

16. James Warren, "Paper's Unions Cheered by British Publisher's Apology," *Chicago Tribune,* March 11, 1991, sec. 1, p. 9.

17. Alan Finder, "Rescuing the Daily News: Struggle Down to the Wire," *New York Times,* March 14, 1991, A-1 and B-2.

18. Ibid.

19. "Robert Maxwell, N.Y. Daily News Unions Extend Bargaining Deadline by 14 Hours," United Press International, March 11, 1991. Dialog File 649, item 10442332/ 9–0311U1337.

20. Edward Klein, "The Sinking of Captain Bob," *Vanity Fair,* March, 1992, 186.

21. Alessandra Stanley, "Rushing from Yacht to Jet, Maxwell Relishes New Role," *New York Times,* March 13, 1991, 1 and C-19.

22. Alan Finder, "Unions in Accord Allowing A Sale of New York News," *New York Times,* March 13, 1991, 1 and C-9.

23. James Barron, "At The News, Anxiety, Elation and Darting Eyes," *New York Times,* March 15, 1991, B-2.

24. James Warren, "Accord Completed on Daily News Sale," *Chicago Tribune,* March 15, 1991, sec. 1, pp. 1 and 8.

25. James B. Parks, "Unions, Maxwell Agree to Save Daily News," *AFL-CIO News,* March 18, 1991, 1 and 2.

26. Alan Sloan, "Tribune's Expensive Fit of Pique," *Newsday,* March 17, 1991. Dialog File 638, item 06079344.

27. "Tribune Company Reports 1990 Fourth-Quarter, Full-Year Loss Due to Daily News Losses," PR Newswire, March 27, 1991. Dialog File 613, item 0355635–NY008. Wall Street did not respond positively to this financial announcement as it had to others in the past. Tribune shares lost $5/8$ to $41 3/4$. These statistics were lower than those (gain of $2 3/8$ to $45 1/4$) previously recorded when the Tribune Company announced its intent to sell the *News.*

7

Developments After the Sale of the *Daily News* to Maxwell

Maxwell's flamboyant approach to labor relations and publishing continued after his March 1991 "purchase" of the *Daily News* for about eight months, until his mysterious death off the Canary Islands. These influences and the appointment of Maxwell's son Kevin to operate the *News* will be discussed in this chapter, along with the eventual dissolution of Maxwell's empire and its impact on the *Daily News*. This time period of some nine months witnessed discussion between union and management representatives over the financial and organizational future of the *News*. The survival of the newspaper, particularly after labor agreements had been previously reached, should have provided a superordinate goal for both union and management officials, along with reinforcement of a more traditional labor–management relationship. Few, if any, tangible outputs resulted from these discussions, however.

LABOR RELATIONS AND MANAGEMENT CONSIDERATIONS AFTER MAXWELL'S TAKEOVER

Initial Aspects of the Labor–Management Relationship

Maxwell indicated his intention to retire soon as chairman of Maxwell Communications Corporation Public Limited Company (PLC) to devote more time toward operating the *News*. His involvement came early; both Maxwell and the returning strikers were jointly responsible for the March 22, 1991 edition of the *News* although this inaugural event was marred by vandalism that had apparently occurred on the strike replacements' last shift on March 20. The damage caused the *News* to generate only 600,000 to 700,000 copies of Maxwell's first edition, far below his estimated 1.2 million circulation target. Another dubious event occurred on the first day of Maxwell's operation of the *News* when a *Daily News* editor who had served as a reporter during the strike was roughed up by angry, returning union pressmen. Tensions and bitterness also occurred between returning employees (many of whom wore T-shirts with the phrase "The Daily News Strikers") and those who had previously crossed the picket lines. One returning reporter noted that he had some tense moments with a couple of "scabs," who had better not "expect to be my friend," while another indicated that it would be enjoyable "bumping into a scab someday knowing you fought for dignity and integrity and you won, and they fought for money and they lost."[1]

This situation did not disappear during the weeks following the strike, as many strikers continued to be silent toward their nonstriking coworkers. Juan Gonzalez, a striking reporter, said these actions were necessary to let crossovers and replacements "know that's not something you get away with." Tensions between strikers and nonstrikers were also likely generated by (1) the anticipated move of the nonstriking International Typographical Union from the *News* headquarters on 42d Street to the Brooklyn printer's plant that housed striking pressmen, drivers, and mailers and (2) the Newspaper Guild's continued practice of fining members.

The Guild initiated proceedings in June 1991 to extract damages from more than 140 members who had crossed picket lines during the strike. Union procedures require the accused employee to appear before a five-member trial board with no member of the board being a *News* employee. Charges are then read aloud by a team of "prosecutors," five *News* employees/Guild members. Then the employees can present a defense, with or without a lawyer. Guild members' attitudes toward this exercise probably were often attributed to whether they remained on strike or crossed the picket line. Reporter Jerry Capeci had been an active striker and supported the fines, because, he felt, crossovers

made what should have been a four-to-six week strike into a five-month strike. . . . They gave the Tribune Company false hope the rest of us were going to come back to work. . . . That made them tough it out much longer.[2]

At least one member, who was a target of Guild charges, disagreed with Capeci, contending that his action prolonged the hostility; moreover, he maintained that the strike had been caused by "poor" Guild leadership before the strike, who "set up," "lied to," and "deceived" the members. Six members were found guilty during the first round of convictions and were fined from $850 to $6,500, which represented 30 percent of the income they had earned during the strike. If members refused to pay the fines, a court order would likely be needed to enforce them.

During Maxwell's first operating week, *News* production of an estimated 800,000 daily copies continued to fall behind the goal of 1.2 million copies. Maxwell labeled this situation as "teething problem," but did wonder publicly if production delay was caused by some union members who were dragging their feet to create overtime situations. John Kennedy of the pressmen's union said that the early editions were being printed and delivered to the suburbs, which required the most delivery time. But the prohibition on overtime had often meant that the presses were shut down before they could print enough copies of the late edition, which is distributed in New York City.

Another incident involving Maxwell and Kennedy occurred after Maxwell had assumed ownership, related in a conversation from Maxwell's end of the telephone and recorded in an October 1991 *Playboy* interview, gives some insights into Maxwell's bargaining approach. Kennedy had telephoned Maxwell to indicate that his members could not cross a picket line established by the Teamsters, who claimed they were entitled to some cleaning jobs at the *News*. Maxwell informed Kennedy that the Teamsters' representative had never given him any previous indication of this possibility and that the pressmen's union should cross this picket line or the newspaper would "disappear." When Kennedy put the Teamsters' official on the line, Maxwell replied:

Hello. It's not so nice talking to you unless you withdraw the picket line. Absolutely. If you don't threaten me, you'll find me as a friend. Threaten me and the paper shuts and it never reopens. Good. Well, if you're off the (picket) line, you come and talk to me. Call me and we'll be happy to make an appointment. But not until you're off the line. You agree to that? That's very nice of you. I won't set an appointment until there is no line. Call me any time tomorrow and we'll fix up a mutually agreeable appointment. Jack has all my numbers. God bless. (He hangs up.)[3]

Kennedy also indicated that Maxwell's labor–management approach featured aloofness on an international scale:

You think you'll have him chased down in London, a secretary says he'll get back to you, and he doesn't. . . . If a major crisis came along, I don't know what we'd do.[4]

Maxwell faced another initial production/revenue problem, namely, allegations that some *News* employees were stealing newspapers and selling them to dealers at a discount. Two such forms of theft include (1) "tapping," where two or three newspapers are removed from a bundle and assembled into a new bundle, which is, in turn, sold to dealers at a discount and (2) falsification of newspaper returns, through which thefts are covered up in inflated, nonsalable returns by legitimate dealers. Maxwell, unlike the *News* executives before him, did not openly accuse employees of theft; however, he hoped to install computerized counts instead of relying on newspaper production numbers supplied by union employees.

Theft allegations surfaced publicly some ten months later (January 1991) when *Newsday* reported a two-year investigation during which state and local police had raided the *New York Post, New York Daily News,* independent distributors, drivers' union offices, and some homes of members of the drivers union. Part of this investigation concerned alleged thefts at the *Daily News* of possibly 80,000 newspapers and $50,000 in lost revenue a day. Two days after the raids, the number of "unaccountable" newspapers in a day dropped from 17,000 to 5,000.

The investigation pertained to the broader issue of mob infiltration into the drivers' union. According to a *Daily News* account, wiretaps and videos of the Gambino and Colombo crime family social clubs recorded union officials meeting and talking to top mobsters. Douglas LaChance, president of the drivers' union before Michael Alvino, who spent five years in prison for taking kickbacks from distributors and subsequently wrested control of the union's presidency from Alvino, said that he would be "the most surprised guy in America" if any union officials were implicated. A member of the drivers' union, who was also a strike leader, also reacted to the investigation:

Ninety-five percent of the members of this union are hardworking men and women. But if it takes this kind of (probe) to clear us for the future then that is what is needed.[5]

Management Changes and Circulation Problems

Although an absentee owner, Maxwell was concerned with supervision and circulation during the *News*'s first month of poststrike operations. An estimated 260 of 550 nonunion employees were informed that their services would not be needed on the first day of *News* operations under Maxwell. Replacement employees in the newsroom were given until April 1 to determine whether they wanted one-week severance or four weeks (the latter option available if employees would sign a written pledge not to sue the Tribune Company for breach of promise). This situation's magnitude and swiftness stunned many in the organization, while also pleasing at least some returning strikers. Two *News* spokespersons who had raised the unions' ire during the strike, Lisa Robinson and John Sloan, were immediately discharged and given 90 days' notice respectively.

Near the end of March, some 35 to 40 management supervisors of mailers, paperhandlers, and pressmen were laid off, according to George McDonald, who regarded the action as a "very constructive move" since the managers had been holding back production after Maxwell's takeover because they did not understand *Daily News* operations. These layoffs came a day after Maxwell named K. Tomasieski vice president for production and delivery. Tomasieski had been vice president of production for three years under the paper's previous owner and left under what was publicized as a "mutual separation."

Another management change was made about this time in the circulation department. Donald A. Nizen, a former circulation executive at the *New York Times* and the *New York Post*, was apparently hired to "work with our unions to make sure all our readers have the paper on time." Maxwell's refusal to pay overtime still created problems similar to those that occurred during the first days of the strike. Drivers were still not making all their scheduled deliveries due to Maxwell's overtime restrictions, and Nizen's responsibilities included redrawing drivers' routes and considering the reopening of its Garden City, Long Island printing plant for logistical/delivery purposes. Problems notwithstanding, the return of the *News* hurt the circulation of its rivals. The *New York Post,* which was selling slightly over 1,000,000 daily copies when the Persian Gulf War began (and the *News* was struck), experienced a daily circulation of 500,000 to 600,000 at the end of April while *New York Newsday's* Long Island daily circulation was about 25,000 copies fewer than the 535,000 figure attained during the strike.[6]

The *News* could not automatically capitalize on its competitors' circulation losses even though Nizen became familiar with drivers' routes and some overtime was restarted for longer routes. Nizen realized that routes between Brooklyn and Montauk could not be scheduled on straight time although all overtime work still had to be approved by Maxwell. *News* management estimated daily and Sunday sales of 754,000 and 887,800 copies respectively for the period April 1 through June 30, 1991. These figures were well below its 1.2 million daily and 1.5 million Sunday prestrike circulation, a less-than-enthusiastic readership reception when the *News* shed its pre-Maxwell "scab" status.

News advertisers' and related rates associated with poststrike circulation were also qualified. Nineteen of the top 20 advertisers in the prestrike *News* returned to Maxwell's operation; however, there was an overall downturn in newspaper advertising during this time period. One financial analyst also indicated that Maxwell was unrealistic to expect the *News* to prosper in the severe economic recession found in New York City. Charles Brumback expressed this situation for the Tribune Company *after* it sold the *News:* He regarded the 1990s as being off to a "very slow start," and predicted 1991 would be a very difficult year.

Brumback repeated his assessment when 1991 financial figures were released for the Tribune Company. When the nonrecurring charges related to the sale of the *New York Daily News* and its operating losses were excluded from the Tribune Company's 1990 results, there was a 26 percent decline in net income when 1991 was compared to 1990. Brumback attributed a large part of this situation to a "steep decline in advertising revenues."

Advertiser loyalty to the *News* was shored up through a variety of introductory rates that were minimal, according to newspaper executives, and tied to circulation figures. Maxwell offered rebates to advertisers if daily and Sunday circulation figures were below 800,000 and 1 million copies respectively for the six months ending September 30, 1991. These figures would be obtained from an independent organization, the Audit Bureau of Circulation (ABC).

James Hoge's public voice was stilled during the *News* distribution, circulation, and possible advertising problems following Maxwell's takeover. Many union members and leaders wanted Hoge removed since he had served as a lightning rod for his ultimate employer, the Tribune Company, which had been perceived as being focused on breaking the *News's* unions. Despite these protests, Hoge continued to be employed after the sale of the *News* and was given the new title of chief operating officer. Hoge's long-range future at the *News* was doubtful, however, despite the new title and Maxwell's previously noted comments that Hoge had a prominent future in the organization. Hoge had taken a six-week vacation during the Maxwell purchase negotiations and aftermath and resigned from the *News* on July 12. His next assignment was "consultant" to "assist the further development of the Maxwell group's media position in the Western Hemisphere." However, Maxwell's public response to this situation — "We wish him well for the future" — when seen with Maxwell's assumption of the position of publisher of the *News,* and Hoge's acceptance of an appointment to Harvard's John F. Kennedy School of Government for the fall 1991 semester, suggested that Hoge's days at the *News* were numbered.

Hoge's separation arrangement of some $2 million was publicly revealed ten months later when copies of his W-2 form were tacked to *News* bulletin boards in March 1992. Some of his settlement might have been at least partially paid from Maxwell's purchase agreement, which required the Tribune Company to pay severance allowances, from two weeks' pay up to a maximum of one year's salary, for a maximum of 60 *News* executives who were dismissed by Maxwell within 90 days of the *News* sale. At least some *News* executives could also receive this financial arrangement if they left voluntarily, ten days after the 90-day period. At least one union official thought Hoge's previous antiunion stance and related inability to work harmoniously with unions during this transition period caused his "unavoidable departure."

Maxwell exuded confidence in the *News's* future as the audit date approached. He indicated that the survival of the *News* was "the surest thing on this earth" and that the newspaper would be profitable and sell 1 million daily copies by early 1992. Moreover Maxwell wanted to be judged by his predictions. The ABC audit for the six months ending September 30, 1991 revealed daily and Sunday circulation figures of 762,078 and 911,684 newspapers. Both figures were below Maxwell's earlier predictions, however, thereby prompting likely rebates to advertisers.

THE FINANCIAL DISSOLUTION OF MAXWELL'S EMPIRE

Maxwell's Death and Related Organizational Considerations

The rather lackluster circulation figures reflected a larger financial problem at the *News,* which, according to analysts, was continuing to lose money some three months after the strike. Labor costs remained higher for the *News* (40% to 50% of revenues) than for other newspapers (25% of revenue). The *New York Post* had less circulation and far fewer advertisers than the *News* but was profitable because it had only one-third of the *News* work force. *Post* editor Jerry Nachman said the *News* had to slash its payroll to make money. A *New York Times* editorial contended that future purchasers would learn from Robert Maxwell that *News* production and distribution costs were far higher than necessary and demanded further labor concessions.

Maxwell Communication Corporation PLC (MCC) had incurred financial problems from its other operations subsequent to Maxwell's purchase of the *News.* Some analysts contend that Maxwell's purchase of communication properties represented an overpriced and confused agglomeration with little, if any, long-term strategy and integrated resources, including management direction:

Analysts find it increasingly difficult to follow Mr. Maxwell's empire because he has sold off and acquired so many businesses, swapping others around among various of his corporate entities. They worry that if one subsidiary collapsed, hidden financial ties to some other Maxwell enterprise might pull that down, too.[7]

Maxwell frequently shuffled assets between publicly held companies organized under MCC and Mirror Group Newspapers, privately owned companies under Robert Maxwell Group Ltd., which included the *Daily News,* and the family-owned Maxwell Foundation, which was rumored to contain a horde of gold in its tax haven base, Liechtenstein.

This financial situation assumed greater publicity on November 5, 1991 when Maxwell's dead body was retrieved from waters off Grand Canary Island. Employees last saw Maxwell on board his $26.2 million floating office, the *Lady Ghislaine,* pacing the decks alone around 4:45 A.M. The yacht's captain attempted to find Maxwell six hours later. After three unsuccessful searches of the yacht, the captain then called Spanish shore crews, who located Maxwell's body at 6:00 P.M. Mystery surrounded Maxwell's death. The Spanish autopsy did not indicate a likely cause of death, only that drowning could not have occurred because there was not enough water in Maxwell's lungs; moreover, death certainly took place before his fall in the water.

Insurers were concerned because they would have to pay up to $35 million if Maxwell did not die of natural causes. In February 1992, Lloyd's of London maintained that the inconclusive results of a second medical report on Maxwell's death did not exclude a possibility of suicide, which the organization found "more compelling than any other cause." Lloyd's suicide theory was based on Maxwell's locking of his stateroom door, his uncharacteristically genial manner toward his employees, and indecisiveness. This transformation of his personality was regarded as remarkable and as an indication that he was already contemplating suicide because his empire's collapse was inevitable and would lead to the end of his flamboyant life-style. The insurance company basically challenged Maxwell's family to change its suicide conclusion and related refusal to pay Maxwell's accident policy.

Maxwell received somewhat better eulogies from the *Daily News* and union members who negotiated with him. The *Daily News* devoted its entire front page to a photo of Maxwell with the words, "Farewell, Robert Maxwell, 1923–1991." As *News* editor James Willse noted:

Whatever else [Maxwell] may have been, he was a masterful negotiator. . . . We'll never know what would have happened if he had not arrived. All we know is he did, and pulled the paper out of the big hole.[8]

Barry Lipton noted that Maxwell would be a missed "character," while Juan Gonzalez wrote, "We whose jobs he saved never got to see his dark side. We're thank-
ful enough we got a chance to see the good."[9]

George McDonald professed optimism for the *Daily News*'s survival on the day
of Maxwell's death. He thought that the *News* was "back in good shape," and that
Maxwell's sons, Kevin and Ian, who became acting chairpersons of MCC and
Mirror Group Newspapers respectively, could sell the newspaper if they did not
wish to retain it. Kevin Maxwell also assumed the leadership (publisher) of the
Daily News the day of Robert Maxwell's death.

Both Maxwell sons enjoyed favorable reputations in the publishing industry for
their management experience, capabilities, and demeanors. Yet one media observer noted that their abilities were almost hidden when their father was around;
they behaved as if they were in a "Stepin Fetchit routine." He remembered one
meeting with Maxwell and analysts in which the two sons were reduced to "passing around the nuts in trays." One of Maxwell's executives claimed that Maxwell
would publicly berate Kevin with foul language. Another observed that Maxwell's sons were in "mortal fear of their father," while a third suggested that

no one can understand the enormous pressure he put his sons under. . . . He bullied them.
He castigated them. He told them they were no good, to fuck off. When he said 'Sign,' they
signed.[10]

Kevin and Ian Maxwell knew severe financial difficulties surrounded their in-
herited positions. At the time of Maxwell's death, revenues from MCC, Mirror
Group Newspapers and Robert Maxwell Group Limited totaled $2.58 billion,
while debts were estimated at $3.13 billion to $4.38 billion.[11] Moreover, Maxwell Communications had to come up with a $750 million payment to creditors
by October 1992 plus a $1.25 billion installment two years later. (One estimate
placed Maxwell's total bank debt from $1.5 billion to $2.53 billion.)

In effect, no Maxwell property was secure at the time of his death because he
had put up four-fifths of his family's MCC stock holdings (68 percent of total
shares outstanding) and the Mirror Group as collateral for much of the $1.3 bil-
lion in loans made to his private companies. Thus, MCC's earnings and share
prices were necessary to establish credit worthiness of other properties; however,
this conglomeration could not even pay its own interest, tax, and other dividends.

It was unlikely that Robert Maxwell would have used one option in this dire
financial situation, namely, reducing MCC's stock dividends. His family controlled 68 percent of MCC's shares, and he needed to receive these dividends to
pay interest on his private debt. Moreover, Maxwell needed to maintain an "un-
usually generous dividend to prop up the price of MCC shares" so that the banks
would not demand even more collateral, which would generate additional pressures on his empire.

This situation (and related Maxwell properties to be discussed later) came to
light at the time of his death:

Banks, alarmed by sliding prices of the Maxwell Communication and Mirror Group Newspaper stock he had pledged as collateral for their loans, were asking for more collateral — and some answers. Maxwell apparently had neither.[12]

Kevin Maxwell also had to be aware of positive and negative economic indicators at the *Daily News,* which had circulation gains and weekly advertising revenues of $3 million and had broken even in three recent weeks before Maxwell's death. These figures supported McDonald's optimism cited earlier; however, some analysts indicated that the newspaper could still lose $1 million a week and/ or $40 million in 1991. One analyst doubted that Kevin Maxwell would continue his father's interest in the *News,* which was based more on personal, ego trip considerations instead of financial investment realities.

Yet on the day his father died, Kevin Maxwell expressed his determination to continue *News* operations:

My father was tremendously excited by the *News* and its prospects. . . . We are completely committed to continuing the marvelous comeback of the newspaper by providing the support it needs to prosper in the years ahead.[13]

He also expressed his family's "total commitment" in these endeavors to readers and advertisers in a statement in the *News* made the day after Maxwell's death, and met two days later with union leaders in New York City to make this pledge operational. Union leaders said they were assured by their 30-minute meeting with Kevin Maxwell. Barry Lipton was impressed that Kevin Maxwell "met with us even before the funeral took place" and further indicated that he did not share his father's March 1992 deadline for the newspaper's survival.

Organizational Changes in December 1991

Despite Kevin Maxwell's publicized commitment to the *News,* he and his brother abruptly resigned their positions as chairmen of Maxwell Communication Corporation and Mirror Group Newspapers PLC on December 3, 1991. Kevin's resignation occurred over a disclosure made by Britain's Serious Fraud Office that some $930 million to more than $1.09 billion in the Mirror Group pension fund had been transferred or loaned "apparently without due authohrity" to counter the higher-than-previously-estimated debts of privately held Robert Maxwell Group Limited. Kevin Maxwell said the *News* had spent more than the $60 million that his father received from the Tribune Company for taking over the newspaper and added another $20 to $25 million to *News* operations from Europe. Yet he expressed surprise that these and other monies came from stolen pension funds. When asked if his father had hidden this information from the sons, he replied that his father informed him on a "need-to-know" basis instead of "sharing information all the time." James Hoge also expressed ignorance over this situation—while he did not regard Maxwell as "milk and cookies," he did not think he was a "crook."

Kevin Maxwell indicated that he resigned to avoid potential conflicts of interest in handling the Maxwell family's public and private holdings. Some 30 British banks had lent his family's business millions of dollars and would decide the eventual Maxwell properties to be sold. Maxwell did think that the *News* would be profitable in 1992 but thought that the sale of the *News* would be unlikely since the newspaper leased its building and some equipment and had little to sell except its name and some outdated presses.

James Kennedy of the pressman's union indicated that the *New's* $77 million in pension funds were intact, safeguarded by independent management at the Bank of New York. Also, the Tribune Company was responsible for any pension-fund shortfall for five years after its sale to Robert Maxwell.

Two announcements having a potentially significant impact on the *News* were made on December 5. The first concerned a British court appointment of four administrators from Arthur Andersen and Company to oversee the Maxwell family's private holdings that included the *News*. Kevin and Ian Maxwell announced this arrangement after being unable to reach agreement with British bankers to restructure the debt-laden family businesses. Under British law, court-appointed administration is a step short of receivership and may help a company avoid bankruptcy. An editorial in the *New York Times* blamed both Robert Maxwell and British Bankers (but not fellow newspaper owner, the Chicago Tribune Company) for this situation:

Mr. Maxwell deserves the blame for his financial shenanigans. But lax British regulation contributed; it's unlikely that he would have succeeded in a country with tough financial disclosure laws, like the U.S. And he almost certainly would not have succeeded without the complicity or inattentiveness of others, including the lenders who happily ignored his reputation as a financial rogue. All of them loved the color of Mr. Maxwell's money as long as he seemed to have plenty of it, and any fair and final reckoning will hold them to task as well.[14]

The administrators indicated that the two public companies partially owned by Maxwell, MCC, and Mirror Group Newspapers would continue to function and not be under their direct control. They did, however, intend to sell the Maxwell family shares in both companies. Estimated returns for the sale of Maxwell's shares in the Mirror Group Newspapers ranged from $360 million to $1.4 billion. But some thought nothing could be obtained from selling shares in MCC and that this company would likely have to file for bankruptcy protection. These administrators could also move swiftly to petition the federal bankruptcy court in the United States to close or sell the *Daily News* operations if they concluded that the *News* was not a viable business.

This situation prompted the second major announcement on December 5—management at the *Daily News* indicated that it had filed for Chapter 11 bankruptcy protection. Under this arrangement, the *News* would continue its operations while a creditor's committee was formed to develop a reorganization plan. The announcement indicated that the *News* was ahead of its 1991 business goals, but nonetheless required a continuing short-term investment of funds to maintain operations and achieve consistent profitability.

Bankruptcy proceedings are often lengthy and expensive. One financial analyst estimated that these efforts could take up to two years, while others pegged the costs for this experience between five to ten million dollars in professional fees. A bankruptcy attorney indicated that the estimate's top figure would represent over 30 percent of the *News*'s assets and therefore prompt resolution of this financial dilemma by January 1993. Bankruptcy Judge Tina Brozman urged the *News* and its creditors to keep expenses down by sharing accounting and financial information from the same advisors. This situation did occur in the early months of these proceedings. Moreover, there was much more emphasis on resolving the problem personally in order to keep expenses down and save the newspaper rather than through court appearances and contested legal motions.

Management further noted that the newspaper had assets of $37 million and liabilities of $53 million. The liabilities basically reflected trade debts to ink and paper suppliers and lawyers who negotiated Robert Maxwell's takeover of the *News*. There were some 2,000 creditors, who were owed $5.3 million during this time period. The biggest individual creditors were James Willse, John Campi, and James Hoge, who were owed $72,964, $54,796, and $44,283 respectively for salaries/bonuses. Also owed were the Waldorf-Astoria and Helmsley Palace, which claimed Maxwell ran up a combined tab of $142,000 for the period September 1 to December 4, 1991. Little, if any, long-term bank debt was reported. However, $4.3 million in advertising rebates was added to debts at the *Daily News* shortly after its bankruptcy protection petition. Don Nizen, vice president for circulation, said that Robert Maxwell had informed him "to be creative" with readership figures when Maxwell heard that his guarantees of 800,000 and 1 million daily and Sunday circulation fell to 720,000 and 860,000 respectively.

Kevin Maxwell responded to a question from ABC-TV's Sam Donaldson, who asked if this and other Robert Maxwell activities suggested that his father "was a crook":

The straight answer to that is that that kind of quote is fair comment under the circumstances. But . . . I think after all the inquiries, after the due process and all the rest of that, you know, we'll be able to take a balanced view about him. But for the time being, that's fair comment.[15]

Donaldson's "tough" questions came too late, as most of the press in the United States pandered to Maxwell and ignored warning signs of his dubious financial holdings and intentions. Scott Ladd, a reporter for *New York Newsday,* explained this situation:

We looked at it mostly from the point of what is it going to mean for the *Daily News*. . . .
When Maxwell bought the *Daily News*, the Tribune Company gave him $60 million to
take it. He wasn't paying for anything.[16]

Some of the press's docility was also due to Maxwell's legal counterbarrages
whenever a critical investigation of his financial arrangements was attempted.
Maxwell had initiated this strategy to mute the press thirty years before when he
filed five libel actions against the *Sunday Times* of London, which had conducted
the first expose of Maxwell's operations.

James Willse, editor of the *News,* said the bankruptcy filing was taken to insu-
late the newspaper from the legal and financial collapse of Maxwell's empire in
Britain, and the possibility of the Maxwell family's bankers urging the sale or
closure of the newspaper. As previously noted, British-appointed administrators
could still seek closure or sale of the *News;* however, this situation was more
complicated and thus unlikely with the bankruptcy petition under judicial scrutiny and protocol in the United States. This action might have also enabled Kevin
Maxwell (not the British bankers and other creditors) to use American law to
hold onto the *News* and effect his previously stated commitment.

Employees at Maxwell's Mirror Group Newspapers quickly reviled the publisher after the December announcements. At one bar near Robert Maxwell's
London headquarters, known to patrons as "The Stab in the Back," employees
were conducting contests for best headline. The winner—"Mirror Mirror On the
Wall, Who Is the Biggest Crook of All?" Some sang a song about Maxwell's
posthumous nickname, "Captain Bob Bob Bob Bob," while another Maxwell employee commented that Maxwell was similar to Julius Caesar because "No one
can wait to stick the knife in." In the United States, union reactions to the December announcements focused on what, if anything, could be done to solidify the
preexisting, albeit financially shaky, relationship with Kevin Maxwell.

A day after the December 5 announcement, Kevin Maxwell informed union
officials that sufficient funds were available to meet any obligation in the foreseeable future and told them that "the paper is not for sale." Maxwell further indicated that all financial information would be given to unions, and two individuals
selected by the unions would join other advisors in preparing a reorganization
plan. Also, two union representatives would be placed on the board if the newspaper emerged from bankruptcy.

George McDonald did not rule out Maxwell's plan. He said that Theodore
Kheel would be one of the union representatives on the reorganization advisory
board and "planning committee." (The unions also appointed Eugene Keilin, an
investment banker at Keilin and Bloom, to serve as their second representative on
the board shortly after the Kheel appointment.) McDonald was still concerned
that a subsequent purchaser of the *News* would use any concessions given to
Maxwell as a "floor" for additional concessionary bargaining.

Subsequent meetings between Kevin Maxwell and union leaders at the *News*
were doubtful, however, since a British judge imposed a freeze on Maxwell's

assets estimated at $815 million (he was subsequently declared bankrupt by a British Court on September 3, 1992). The court order prohibited Kevin and Ian Maxwell from leaving Britain until they gave the provisional liquidator affidavits that detailed their personal assets as well as additional information that could help secure these assets. An exception was made for Kevin Maxwell to meet with the unions in New York City to help fashion a reorganization plan for the *Daily News*. However, the judge also indicated that Maxwell had to return before the evening of Friday, December 13th and surrender his passport.

The *News* announced on December 10 that the newspaper had received a $7 million cash infusion from the Maxwell family since March 1991, and a full investigation would be made of any other cash transaction possibilities from this source. This information would be given to the planning committee, which would include a member of the "creditors' committee" (representatives of those owed money by the *News*) that was scheduled to be formed a week later.

Union leaders on this day also announced they would become buyer of last resort should this action be needed to keep the newspaper alive. They knew that their ability to cover the purchase of the *News* financially was limited, if not impossible; however, their willing consideration of further concessions for equity could entice a potential purchaser. After reviewing financial figures supplied by the *News,* Theodore Kheel maintained that the newspaper must cut approximately $400,000 from its weekly operating costs of $6 to $7 million in order to survive. Union leaders sought to counter this situation in a December 10 meeting with New York Mayor David Dinkins to seek possible financial breaks that the city could give the *News*. Dinkins pledged his support but also noted that he could not come up with immediate, related, and specific assistance.

George McDonald indicated that a union takeover of the *News*, while possible, was unlikely at this time since the newspaper was not officially for sale. Kevin Maxwell continued to represent the top management official in day-to-day union–management contract adminsitration—possibly negotiation—activities at the *News*. He also came under increasing investigation for his father's financial debacle and indicated that he would step down as publisher and chairman of the *News* when he was told by colleagues that he was a liability to the *Daily News*. At least one union leader, who spoke on the condition of anonymity, thought Maxwell's offer to remove himself was most appropriate given his financial uncertainty.

Management and union representatives on the *News's* planning committee met for two hours on December 11 to consider related alternatives. No cost-cutting concessions were sought from the unions, and Kheel thought there was enough cash on hand or receivables to give labor and management enough time to solve the *News's* financial and operational problems. Kheel's assessment was likely predicated on an estimated shortfall at the *News* that would not exceed $400,000 a week.

Union involvement in the *News's* future was formalized in another forum about a week later when representatives of the drivers, pressmen, mailers, and Newspaper Guild were named to 4 of the 13 positions as the creditors' committee established in the bankruptcy proceedings. They wanted to strongly influence the creditors' committee to keep the *News* operating despite its financial obstacles. Yet there was no evidence that any of the newspaper's creditors had sought liquidation, because they knew the *News* would have little if any value at this point.

Union leaders also effectively asked two *News* representatives on the creditors' committee, James R. Willse (editor) and Larry Bloom (chief operating officer), to replace Kevin Maxwell as the intended chairperson. Leaders were concerned that Maxwell could not devote sufficient attention to a reorganization of the *News,* even if he was not charged with a crime relating to the dissolution of Robert Maxwell's empire. Stanley Jablonski, an executive of Kruger Inc., a newsprint company, was elected chairperson of the creditors' committee, while George McDonald was elected vice chairperson.

The planning committee conducted its second meeting shortly after the creditors' committee had been appointed. Kevin Maxwell emerged from this meeting and indicated that the financial "scandal" in Britain had not directly harmed the *News* since the newspaper had just recorded the best week of advertising revenues in the previous three years. Maxwell indicated that his potential resignation was not discussed at this meeting but repeated that he would step down if he perceived himself to be a liability to the paper.

Maxwell did resign his positions of chairman, publisher, and board member of the *News* four days later. He gave no reason for his decision, effective January 1, 1992, but indicated that he was "proud" to have been involved with the *News* and that the newspaper's future was "well assured." Barry Lipton likely reflected general union sentiment when he contended that Maxwell's resignation was inevitable, given his legal difficulties. Kevin and Ian Maxwell were arrested some six months later in London with Kevin charged with stealing pension fund money, and both charged with conspiring to defraud banks.

James Willse succeeded Maxwell as chairman and publisher, while also continuing as editor. His appointment was likely subject to three factions of *News* employees. One faction thought he was a fine No. 2 executive but was in over his head as editor-publisher. A reporter indicated another somewhat-shared employee sentiment that the new owner should get rid of the personnel brought in by the Tribune Company, including Willse. Another group of veteran employees, experienced in the Tribune Company and Robert Maxwell campaigns, likely reflected the response of one *News* union official, who thought Willse was the best available person. Willse indicated that the *News* hoped to replace the board vacancies of Kevin and his brother Ian, who also resigned from the five-member board effective January 1, with individuals who had previous management experience under adverse financial conditions. The two other remaining board members were Larry Bloom, chief operating officer, and Jay Swardenski, general counsel and vice president for labor relations. Willse assessed the outlook for the *News* as good but not immediate, since all employees were "working for the good of a paper," but, he added, "We're a long way from having a real reorganization plan."

Willse was responsible for the day-to-day operations of the *News;* however, the

British-appointed Arthur Andersen administrators of Robert Maxwell's private holdings could, at a minimum, oversee, if not overrule, the decisions made by Willse and other *News* executives as well as union leaders. Who had final authority to operate the *News* at this time was unclear because of the different bankruptcy laws and related operating procedures found in Britain and the United States. In Britain, administrators are appointed by the court to be responsible to the creditors, and these individuals are enabled to restructure the debt, or sell part or all of the organization to repay debt.

Under Chapter 11 protection in the United States, management remains in control in the restructuring of the company and has 120 days to come up with a viable survival plan. Willse did not publicly indicate which laws and related personnel (British accountants or *News* management) would prevail, but he did note that the British administrators were pleased about how the newspaper was being operated. This situation was confirmed by John Talbot, an Arthur Andersen administrator, who had taken control of Maxwell's private companies that owned the *News* and indicated that there was no conflict with the paper's directors. He said, "We're sitting down quietly with them to find a way forward."

Willse also noted that the first meeting of the creditors' committee appointed under United States' bankruptcy proceedings would meet December 30. This meeting occurred against the backdrop of financial uncertainty and urgency. Kheel estimated that the *News* would lose $1.8 million in December and had only enough cash to continue through January 1992, when he thought the newspaper would be sold or closed. These pressures could be exacerbated by the traditional January decline in advertising revenues after the Christmas holidays. Kheel's comments were modified by Barry Lipton, who wanted to obtain a fix on the true financial condition of the newspaper, and related management sources of savings such as office rents, management salaries and staffing levels, and suppliers' contracts before considering further job cuts of union members.

Two meetings between *News* executives and union representatives were in fact held on December 30, 1991. A meeting with the planning committee (which included Kheel and Keilin as the union representatives) was held in the morning to consider balancing the newspaper's costs with revenues. In the afternoon, the first meeting involving the creditors' committee (with four union representatives) was also conducted.

Kheel indicated that the meeting generated some $8 million in annual savings, which gave the parties some "breathing room"; however, he further noted that union and management representatives could not relax and enjoy prosperity over this situation. The savings came from management concessions and initiatives such as cutting executive bonuses, curtailing advertising and promotion, and renegotiating vendor's contracts. The *News* would also attempt to renegotiate leases for office space because staffing reductions from 4,500 to 1,800 employees meant that only 150,000 square feet instead of the originally leased 250,000 square feet would be needed. Union members apparently faced no wage cuts or layoffs as a result of these meetings, at least for the short term.

Management also announced after these meetings that Coopers and Lybrand was conducting an audit of the *News* since Robert Maxwell had been paid $60 million in March 1991 to take over the newspaper. The audit, to be completed in several weeks, represented necessary information for potential purchasers of the *News*. Shortly after this arrangement, *News* management retained the investment banking firm Salomon Brothers to assist the *News* reorganization under U.S. bankruptcy protection. Willse thought Salomon Brothers had extensive expertise in both corporate restructuring and media. Moreover, the *News* had $8.9 million as of January 5, 1992 and adequate cash flow to continue operations through March 1. A few days later, the newspaper secured an addition $10 million in debtor-in-possession financing from Sterling National Bank and Trust Company, which was subsequently approved by U.S. Bankruptcy Court Judge Tina Brozman. Barry Lipton maintained that the *News*'s financial situation as it entered 1992 was "secure for the moment" with no "anticipated crisis."

NOTES

1. Rose Marie Arce, "Bittersweet Settlement for News Employees," *Newsday,* March 13, 1991, 3-A. Dialog File 638, item 06075020.

2. Scott Ladd, "Union to Try 140 Members for Deserting News Strike," *Newsday,* May 19, 1991. Dialog File 638, item 06143306. Capeci's attitude regarding fines for crossovers notwithstanding, the NLRB, in late February 1993, charged that union officials violated employees' rights when they informed them they could not resign from the union immediately prior to or during the strike. The eventual impact of this initial finding on crossovers' fines will be approached at an NLRB hearing scheduled for September 8, 1993.

3. *Playboy* Interview: Robert Maxwell, *Playboy,* October, 1991, 76.

4. Scott Ladd, "New Owner, Old Woes at News, Maxwell's Tabloid Regains Some Advertisers But Still Loses Money," *Newsday,* June 27, 1991. Dialog File 638, item 06182182.

5. Tom Robbins, "2 Newspapers, Union Raided," *New York Daily News,* January 16, 1992 (Located in News Bank), Med. 2: E-11.

6. A year after the *Daily News* strike ended, the Audit Bureau of Circulations reported readership of all the New York daily newspapers was 325,000 less on weekdays and 275,000 less on Sundays. *Newsday*'s reported circulation for its New York and Long Island editions was 766,000, down from the 826,000 figure reported at the strike's end. The *Post*'s circulation dropped from 630,000 to 471,000 for the time period, while the *New York Times'* daily circulation dropped about 1,500 copies, to 1.2 million. The *Daily News* reported daily and Sunday sales of 782,000 and 983,000 respectively, compared to figures at the strike's end of 1.2 million and 1.5 million a year before the strike. Alex S. Jones, "Papers Losing Readers Since Strike at the News," *New York Times,* April 28, 1992, B-2.

7. "Bloated Empire: Media Mogul Maxwell Reveled in Growth, Now Must Scale Back," *Wall Street Journal,* September 13, 1991, A-1.

8. Kate McKenna, "The Daily News: Too Tough to Die?" *Washington Journalism Review* (March 1992): 28.

9. "Goodbye Captain Bob," *Editor and Publisher,* November 9, 1991, 35.

10. Edward Klein, "The Sinking of Captain Bob," *Vanity Fair,* March 1992, 180, 182, 183–86, 238–41.

11. These figures were $1.72 billion revenue and $2.33 billion debt from Maxwell Communication for the fiscal year that ended March 31, 1991; 1990 revenue of $885 million and debt of $548 million (as of June 30, 1991) from Mirror Group Newspapers; and unknown 1990 revenue but more than $250 million of 1990 debt from Robert Maxwell Group Limited, which included the *Daily News.* Ken Wells and Patrick M. Reilly, "Maxwell Death Clouds Empire's Future," *Wall Street Journal,* November 6, 1991, B-1 and B-4. The $4.38 billion debt estimate came from "The Family Takes Command," *Newsweek,* November 18, 1991, 52.

12. James Cox, "Few Answers, Big Headlines Feed Rumors," *USA Today,* December 16, 1991, 2-B. For additional financial considerations and strategies experienced shortly before Maxwell's death, see Ken Wells and Tony Horwitz, *"Drowning Man:* Frantic Last Months Show Robert Maxwell Knew End Was Near," *Wall Street Journal,* December 19, 1991, A-1; "What The Banks Knew," *Newsweek,* December 23, 1991, 34 and 35; Mark Maremont and Mark Landler, "An Empire in Trouble," *Business Week,* December 23, 1991, 70–73; and Cotton Timberlake, "Unraveled Empire: How Robert Maxwell Lost at His Own Shell Game," December 23, 1991. Dialog File 258, item 02578052.

13. Alex S. Jones, "Daily News to Continue, Its New Publisher Says," *New York Times,* November 6, 1991, C-20.

14. "Robert Maxwell's Shell Game" (editorial), *New York Times,* December 12, 1991, A-30.

15. "Ad Rebate Added to 'Daily News' Debt," *USA Today,* December 12, 1991, 8-B.

16. D. D. Guttenplan, " 'Miracle Max,' and the Marveling Media," *Columbia Journalism Review* (May–June 1992): 48.

8

Labor-Management Negotiations Under Bankruptcy Proceedings

Barry Lipton's perspective regarding labor–management tranquility soon had to change as collective bargaining became shaped by bankruptcy proceedings and concerns and potential outside purchasers. Mortimer Zuckerman emerged as the eventual publisher of the *Daily News* but not before encountering peripheral bargaining dimensions involving the typographers' union and the Newspaper Guild.

INITIAL CONSIDERATIONS

Differences in Collective Bargaining

Union officials had to approach negotiations with potential purchasers with far more trepidation than they had experienced with Robert Maxwell. The Supreme Court's *Bildisco* decision enabled management to disregard the existing labor agreement and the union representative when filing for bankruptcy. These actions are not automatically permitted, however, as management must show pervasive evidence of financial trouble, and the removal of the labor agreement's provisions is "necessary" to aid the reorganization and is also "fair and equitable." Congress had also passed amendments to the federal bankruptcy code (P.L. 98–353) in June 1984 that made it more difficult for employers to abdicate labor agreement prescriptions:

In general, the law requires that a company propose contract modifications which are necessary to the reorganization to its union(s) and provide the union(s) with relevant information by which to evaluate the proposal. Only if the union(s) rejects the company's proposal "without good cause" and the "balance of equities . . . clearly favors" termination of the unexpired labor contracts can a bankruptcy court approve the company's modifications. If the court fails to act within 30 days after a hearing is held on the company's request, the company then is free to unilaterally impose new contract terms.[1]

Thus, bankruptcy proceedings represent two major peripheral departures from traditional bargaining relationships: (1) unions' rights might not be fully recognized under traditional protections afforded under the National Labor Relations Act; (2) moreover, outside individuals such as creditors and the bankruptcy judge could sharply modify, even eliminate, collective bargaining issues and relationships.

George McDonald maintained the same coordinated posture of the nine *News* unions in the Allied Printing Trades Council which excluded the typographers: all had to accept a potential purchaser's bargaining proposal or there would be no agreement involving any of the unions. Yet this solidarity had to be undermined by some, if not all, union officials, who realized that a holdout under bankruptcy proceedings might result in the removal of their members and organizations. Dissension among some of the unions had occurred shortly after the bankruptcy filing. Barry Lipton of the Newspaper Guild, Jack Kennedy of the pressmen's union, and Douglas LaChance of the drivers' union wanted to curtail Theodore Kheel's role in assessing potential *News* purchasers. One leader of a newspaper union, who spoke to a reporter on the condition of anonymity, indicated that Lipton and Kennedy were concerned that Kheel was 77 years old and had not been active as a lawyer for some time. Kheel labeled the unidentified union leader, who made the internal dispute public, a "jackal." McDonald indicated that Kheel would continue in his advisory capacity although there were few public statements made by Kheel for the next year.

Union employees at the *News* were not debilitated by the December 5, 1991 filing for Chapter 11 bankruptcy. Many were proud that they had survived previous setbacks and adopted a "try-and-kill-us" attitude. Richard Sisk, a *News* reporter, suggested this resolve was further enhanced by revenge against the paper's former owner as well as by purchaser loyalty in a "union town."

It's a bit of orneriness, a need to stick it to the bloodless buffoons at the Tribune Company who did this to us. . . . They drained this paper dry, taking all the money back to Chicago. Now at least we've gotten rid of those leeches and can try again. . . . Despite all the ridiculous things that have happened . . . [*News* readers] love the paper and they just would not buy a scab newspaper. . . . They stood by us, and we're going to stand by them.[2]

Employees' efforts at the *News* met, at least briefly, Robert Maxwell's prediction that the *News* would show a profit within a year of his purchase. The *News* did turn a profit of $63,000 for the busiest time period for newspapers, December 5–29, although it lost $2.8 million during operations in January 1992. *News* spokespersons indicated that January's loss was less than projected and that the newspaper was on schedule to break even or make a profit by the end of 1992. This later prediction was quickly canceled, however, when February's losses of $1.5 million were twice management's previous projection.

News circulation figures in March 1992 (800,000 daily; 1.1 million Sunday) approached its prestrike readership and were higher than those of its major rivals, the *New York Post* (600,000 daily circulation) and *New York Newsday* (which slipped from its midstrike high of 340,000 daily copies to 297,000). However, the *News* reported more than $5 million losses for the first-quarter 1992, and its publisher, James Willse, said that the newspaper had used some of its $10 million line of credit but was in "no danger" of running out of cash.

Potential *News* Purchasers

Willse's remarks were not intended to eliminate the *News's* purchase by an outside party. Indeed, *News* management requested that potential purchasers of the newspaper formally submit their intentions and related plans by April 10, 1992. Information supplied concerning amount of purchase, proposed creditor payments, and proposed labor cost reductions would be analyzed by Salomon Brothers then presented to the working committee of the *News's* creditors and management and union representatives. The proposals would be regarded as "starting points" instead of "firm offers." April 10 did not represent an absolute deadline; it only indicated who would have an exclusive time period until May 26 to arrange an agreement in principle for the *News* purchase. This time frame enabled *News* management to pursue other potential purchasers and its other option, emerging from bankruptcy proceedings, under its continued independent organization. The newspaper had until June 30 to present a reorganization plan to a U.S. bankruptcy court judge.

Three individuals responded to this invitation—Peter Kalikow, Mortimer Zuckerman, and Conrad Black. Kalikow, a real estate developer and owner of the *New York Post,* indicated that a merger involving the *News* and his newspaper represented the "surest" and perhaps only opportunity for the *Daily News's* survival. Employees at the *Post* were both surprised and cynical to hear of Kalikow's purchase intentions. One *Post* reporter compared this action to "a man who cannot swim jumping in to save a drowning dolphin." *Post* reporters also wondered where Kalikow could find the necessary money since they were working four day weeks with little overtime and were also experiencing other austere working conditions (for example, they had been implored by a memo to stop dialing 411 for information so often). Kalikow's remarks were also not enthusiastically received by *News* management employees and union officials. *Daily News* publisher James Willse said that the *News* was a "healthy franchise" that could "live a long and prosperous life on its own." Willse, aware of Kalikow's involvement in personal bankruptcy proceedings, further opined, "I'd rather be where we are than where he is." Willse and other *News* executives were concerned that another purchaser could replicate an unneeded and complicated mine field, even the "psychodrama" that had been embodied by Robert Maxwell.

Reporters at the *News* thought that years of competition against the *Post* would make a joint venture difficult. At least one reporter thought there would be major differences in quality since the *Post* had "completely deteriorated" and was currently "not a worthwhile read." Even Kalikow indicated that the bankruptcy court would be very apprehensive about his ownership unless the unions came to him enthused about the sale and ready to make significant labor concessions. He thought this situation might occur as a result of abilities he demonstrated in 1990 to bargain directly and openly with *News* unions to keep the *Post* operating.

Union leaders such as George McDonald, however, did not heartily endorse Kalikow's overtures. Some were concerned that Kalikow wanted the *News* for only its Sunday edition and would shut down the daily operations of the newspaper. James Kennedy, president of the pressmen's union, concluded that Kalikow "doesn't look like a white knight at this point." Kalikow did not make a formal proposal because Salomon Brothers refused to open the *News* books to him unless his rival *Post* reciprocated. He did, however, suggest a continuing purchase interest in the *News* that might be further initiated in bankruptcy proceedings.

Mortimer Zuckerman, also involved in real estate and owner of *The Atlantic* and *U.S. News and World Report,* indicated his interest in purchasing the *News,* but also noted uncertainties concerning shut-down liabilities, how Maxwell handled the money he received from the Tribune Company, and current newspaper operating costs. Zuckerman's apprehension over the *News's* financial situation and intertwined relationships with other companies in the Maxwell empire was well founded and indicative of how Maxwell may have deceived bankers. For example, Maxwell Communication consisted of 138 companies in 27 countries. An executive who ran one of these companies, Investment MGN, also was a representative of the *Daily News's* largest creditor, Donahue Paper Company, partially owned by Maxwell, and he noted, "Investment MGN Canada is a wholly owned subsidiary of Mirror Group Newspapers. It owns 49 percent of a company called Mircorp, which owns 54 percent of Donahue, and I'm on the Donahue board. . . . Kind of hard to follow, isn't it?"[3] Yet Zuckerman expressed continued interest in the *News* because a long delay in resolving its ownership would reduce its property value.

Conrad Black, a Canadian publisher and controlling shareholder of Hollinger Inc., which owns more than 200 small daily newspapers throughout Canada and the United States, also responded to the *News* purchase decision. Black was regarded as a "bottom line guy," who, unlike Robert Maxwell, would ignore idealism, sentiment, and vanity, and instead base his purchase decision on whether the newspaper could become profitable. For example, Black's purchase of 58 percent of the *Telegraph* in 1986 featured lower wages, longer hours, and severance payments up to $100,000 for employees, a situation that resulted in an annual saving of $50 million and a reduction of printing jobs, to 639 from 1,637.[4]

Black believed that the *News* represented "a fundamentally good enterprise" because of the newspaper's "excellent, competitive circulation position . . . in one of the world's great trading zones." His purchase intention and plan were dependent upon receiving at least a 25 percent profit in his first year of owning the *News.* Union concessions represented a necessary element of this plan, and Black thought they would be attainable under the current bargaining situation:

When the Tribune got completely exasperated and in effect threatened to shut the place, everyone knew it was a rich company and would have had to pay generous severances to the laid-off workers. . . . Now that the technical owner is the receiver for Bob Maxwell, who doesn't have any resources at all, those people have got to know that if the paper goes down, they're not going to get anything. That does create a somewhat different atmosphere.[5]

Hollinger received the exclusive time period to obtain new labor agreements with the union, and representatives from Black's organization proposed the following:

1. Reductions of 100 management and 600 union positions. (The deepest union membership reductions—49 percent or more—would come from the pressmen, mailers, paperhandlers, plate engravers, stereotypers, and the International Typographical Union. The Newspaper Guild and the drivers would face membership cuts of 33 percent and 28 percent respectively, while smaller cuts would come from the electricians and the machinists)[6];
2. Closing the *News* printing facility in Kearny, New Jersey;
3. Severe limitations on previous severance packages and seniority rights within some unions; and
4. Long-term labor agreements, at least through 1999.

In return, Black's organization indicated a willingness to purchase the *News* for $75 million, including $22 million for creditors and assumption of $8 million in liabilities such as vacation pay for continuing employees, missed payments to unionized employees' pension and welfare funds, and missed contributions to employees' Section 401(k) plans. Some $45 million would also be available for immediate operating improvements, early retirement and severance programs, and working capital needs. Black also indicated that a $200 million color printing plant would be constructed somewhere in New York, with improvements made to the existing facility.

Union leaders were not enthused about these proposals, but regarded them as a start. George McDonald, for example, indicated that the unions would negotiate, but not agree to, reductions "anywhere near" those proposed by Black's representatives. Any bargaining settlement also appeared to be conditioned on a commitment from Black to replace the outdated Brooklyn printing facility with a new operation.

No agreement between Hollinger and the unions was reached by the time limit. Black joined the unions in face-to-face meetings in late July 1992 for the first time since he had initiated efforts to purchase the paper five months previously; however, no results were forthcoming.

Mortimer Zuckerman had also been involved with the unions on an informal basis about a month before Black's meeting. These discussions had not been very specific, although Zuckerman indicated that he would immediately build a modern color printing plant if he were successful in purchasing the *News*. Zuckerman had proposed a smaller reduction of pressmen and drivers than mentioned in Black's proposal; however, he appeared to single out the Guild for major, in some cases unusual, concessions. For example, Zuckerman wanted the right to evaluate the *News* staff for 18 months and to replace those he regarded as not meeting standards of journalistic excellence. He also sought the transfer of advertising employees out of the Guild's jurisdiction, a cap for severance pay at eight weeks, and elimination of arbitration for dismissed employees.

Barry Lipton of the Newspaper Guild, aware that Zuckerman asked no other union official for the right to unilaterally dismiss members without regard to seniority, regarded this proposal as "a package of deal killers." However, union officials who represented the pressmen, drivers, and mailers were reportedly "upbeat" about Zuckerman's plan, and regarded it as being likely better than that offered by Black.

Bargaining Developments in August 1992

Neither Black nor Zuckerman made any substantial progress with the unions through July 1992. At this time, Silver Screen management also proposed an unsuccessful settlement that would spend $25 million at the *News* and give management and unions a 40 to 50 percent ownership in the *News* in exchange for $40 million in work rule concessions. Union officials were no doubt leery about furnishing "final" concessions to one potential purchaser only to have them used as a starting point for another *News* owner.

Tina Brozman, a U.S. bankruptcy court judge responsible for related proceedings involving the *News,* was concerned about this lack of progress particularly given the newspaper's poor financial experiences at this time. The *News* had lost $300,000 in June, and more than $6 million since January 1992. Moreover, advertising is typically slowest in the summer, and bankruptcy fees were costing the *News* about $350,000 a month. James Willse, *News* editor and publisher, thought the newspaper would face a cash shortage in September or October unless actions could be taken that would cut costs and/or increase financial reserves. Brozman gave the *Daily News* a ten-day extension through August 10 to file a reorganization plan but urged the involved parties to "galvanize their efforts" and break any log jam. She also suggested that she might change the status quo if changes were not made in these directions.

Top management officials at the *News* appeared to prefer Black's Hollinger, and a deal between the two organizations appeared forthcoming around August 6. James Kennedy of the pressmen's union reiterated his preference for Zuckerman's proposal, however, and further indicated, along with the Guild's leaders, that any agreement Black reached with management was meaningless because it excluded these two organizations. The arrangement was not consummated. This situation prompted Judge Brozman to issue another one-week extension (until August 17) along with harsh words for creditors, management, and union officials, who were "all going in different directions":

You are teetering on the brink of a very large precipice unless you are able to make a great deal of progress in the next several days. . . . You may be jeopardizing my ability to keep this newspaper alive. . . . The time has come for headlong progress to be made.[7]

The drivers were leaning toward Zuckerman; however, some unions were not happy that the pressmen had already reached a tentative verbal agreement with him. An official of the Guild noted that Zuckerman had not changed his earlier desire for a free hand in dismissing news staff: "As of today [Zuckerman's] dead. . . . He thinks he's the cock of the walk." The Guild appeared to be leaning toward Silver Screen's previously described employee stock ownership proposal.

News management preferred Black's Hollinger, largely because Zuckerman's terms of purchase included only $18 million in cash payments; however, many union officials were also angered that Black requested a $1.5 million reimbursement fee in the event that he was unable to purchase the *News*. The creditors committee (which represented dozens of businesses and some unions owed $35 million) was split, with some favoring Black, some Zuckerman, and others Silver Screen. Black's proposal would give creditors 40 cents on the dollar while the proposals by Zuckerman and Silver Screen were not detailed enough at the time to compute comparable figures.

George McDonald indicated that the unions would meet Wednesday and Thursday with all prospective buyers, and use "real collective bargaining" to reach agreement on one name by 2 P.M., Friday, August 14. *News* publisher James Willse indicated that management expected to go into court with an agreement and that the newspaper's board of directors could ratify the choice as early as the evening of the fourteenth.

The unions reserved several rooms at the Grand Hyatt hotel for August 12, where they hoped to have intensive, around-the-clock meetings with potential purchasers. There were not many negotiations by 5 P.M.; indeed, no representatives from Silver Screen ever attended. Mortimer Zuckerman, who apparently reached previous agreement with the pressmen, met with the drivers' union, whom he regarded as the only union capable of preventing the newspaper from publishing should a subsequent strike occur. The drivers and the pressmen reportedly informed Zuckerman that they would use their clout in the APTC to persuade the Guild and other unions only if Zuckerman improved his offer to the Guild. Zuckerman did not meet with the Guild or other unions at this time, however.

Representatives of Conrad Black only met with the mailers', drivers', and stereotypers' unions. By 4 P.M., only three of the nine unions represented by the APTC had met with either Black or Zuckerman, and one observer noted, "Most union officials spent the day sitting around long rectangular tables in private rooms and roaming the long corridors, making it seem more like a big card game than a major negotiation session."[8]

Little bargaining progress occurred the next day. The only specific proposals generated through these meetings concerned the typographical union, which was not represented by the APTC and had worked during the strike to preserve its "lifetime employment" provisions in the labor agreement. Zuckerman reportedly wanted the court to reject the union's job guarantees and would keep 30 of the 166 members, while Black had proposed reducing the union to 40 members. Black indicated that negotiations were proceeding on a slow perhaps nonexistent course because he would not let his organization be sent to the guillotine.

The lack of bargaining progress culminated in the unions' inability to agree on a *News* purchaser on Friday, August 14, 1992. Union officials at the meeting said that six of the unions favored Zuckerman, and three of the unions favored Black; however, strong sentiment was only evidenced by three unions: the Guild, which supported Black; and the drivers and pressmen, which supported Zuckerman. The other unions apparently could vote for either purchaser, depending upon the will of the majority. A meeting of the APTC was scheduled for the morning of August 17, before the 4 P.M. meeting with bankruptcy judge Tina Brozman. No formal negotiations with potential negotiators were scheduled for the weekend.

The APTC did call the *News*'s 13-member creditors' committee, which, in addition to the paper's board of directors acting on behalf of the owners, threatened to select a purchaser if the unions were unable to do so. These actions without the unions' agreement were likely meaningless; however, they were intended to focus attention on negotiations between the unions and one purchaser. Both the creditors' committee and the newspaper's board of directors agreed to delay any endorsement of a buyer until August 17, although both groups were expected eventually to endorse Black.

Neither the unions nor the creditors' committee could agree among themselves on an eventual purchaser on August 17. However, Judge Brozman accepted *News* management's reorganization plan, which favored Conrad Black's Hollinger Incorporated as the purchaser of the newspaper and assured Black that he would receive up to $1 million in expense reimbursement if someone else purchased the newspaper. Black's proposal noted that if he could not reach agreement with the typographers, he would have no obligation to honor their lifetime-employment guarantees, but he would then add $4 million to the purchase price. The deal would have to be concluded by November 30, 1992.

Judge Brozman also set a deadline of September 8, by which a definite agreement with Hollinger had to be filed with the court. If unions had not reached agreement on Black or Zuckerman by this time, she could press *News* management to preserve the newspaper's assets through wage reductions and/or employee layoffs. By September 11, another court hearing would determine the amount of Hollinger's interim financing of the newspaper's cash shortfalls. This figure could be as much as $3 million and was conditioned on Black reaching agreements with at least six labor unions, including the pressmen, drivers, and the Newspaper Guild.

A representative of Hollinger contended that this situation meant, "The unions . . . hold the whip hand," an assessment further explained by *New York Times* reporter, Alex S. Jones:

In most bankruptcy proceedings, the court would have the threat of liquidating the company to create pressure on the parties to reach agreement. But in this case, the company—The News—has no value except its franchise and its labor agreements. In effect, without the unions, there is no News and the unions are well aware of their power to make or break a deal.[9]

George McDonald indicated that negotiations between potential *News* purchasers and the union were still uncertain with Black and Zuckerman representing very close alternatives. He and other union officials also stressed that they would continue to talk to Zuckerman along with Black (an action Brozman found legally appropriate), and acknowledged that in the past they did not act decisively until faced with a rigid deadline. *News* management shared the unions' uncertainty over Black as a potential purchaser. James Willse noted that Judge Brozman's acceptance of the *Daily News's* reorganization plan neither included labor agreements nor eliminated the cash crisis facing the newspaper. Willse added, moreover, "It does not preclude a better, subsequent offer from another party."

Perhaps the most significant bargaining development as of August 17 occurred among the unions in the APTC. Published accounts before this date indicated that no labor agreements would be reached with a potential purchaser unless the nine unions in the APTC were satisfied. This attitude extended to the four union representatives on the creditors' committee, who said they would have abstained from endorsing a purchaser if a vote had been taken because they had agreed that their decision would be unanimous. However, McDonald publicly suggested for the first time after the August 17 meeting with Judge Brozman, that the APTC had not formally adopted such a requirement of unanimity. Douglas LaChance, president of the drivers' union, reiterated his aversion to a purchaser settlement that did not include Guild support, and stressed that he would not leave the Guild "in the street." But his statement did not appear intended as an unconditional guarantee that the drivers would not settle with management until the Guild reached an agreement.

James Willse, publisher of the *News,* may have further fissured unanimity among unions on August 30, when he announced that he would ask Judge Brozman to approve a 10 percent across-the-board wage cut on September 13 if the unions could not agree on a purchaser by this date. Willse's statement might have been intended to persuade unions to select Black and his $3 million payment conditioned on obtaining labor agreements with six unions, which could prevent the wage cuts. It may have also prompted the APTC to assign higher priority to collective bargaining closure than to unanimity among all APTC unions.,

On September 4, 1992, the APTC formed a committee to monitor and assist negotiations between its unions and potential *News* purchasers. The committee included George McDonald and representatives of unions representing the drivers, pressmen, and machinists. Barry Lipton and his Guild represented a notable exclusion. This action might have been reinforced by continuing and discouraging financial information covering the *News,* which had lost $7.6 million through

July, and was projected to lose another $2.7 million by November 1. There also appeared to be a real softness in new printing plant commitments from Black and Zuckerman. Both potential purchasers indicated they would either pay employees $5 million or put $10 million in escrow for a new facility. Unions contended that these amounts did not represent stiff enough penalties if this significant bargaining issue was forfeited.

ZUCKERMAN'S EMERGENCE AS LIKELY *NEWS* PURCHASER

Black's About-Face and Other Negotiations

On September 10, 1992, Conrad Black rather abruptly withdrew from negotiations with the unions. He would not match Zuckerman's offers made to the drivers and pressmen because they would forego any management progress with work rule changes, and return the *News* to pre-Maxwell managerial limitations that, he thought, would destroy the newspaper. Black maintained his "radical" bargaining proposals needed to be stressed up front because the previous *News* strike revealed local politicians, Cardinal John J. O'Connor, and even the Police Department would side with the unions if a long, peripheral bargaining situation/impasse occurred.

Black contended that Zuckerman's offer represented "very little money for a property that is worth very little" and that Zuckerman's negotiations with the unions benefiting future *News* operations would be difficult and long. "[Zuckerman is] going to have to either go for increased cost savings, negotiating with unions whose sense of avarice and inflexibility have been whetted and confirmed by this experience, or he's going to preside over an inexorable, continued decline of that franchise."[10] At least one business associate of Zuckerman, Robert Manning, editor of the *Atlantic Monthly,* suggested that Zuckerman would be involved in a lot more collective bargaining before labor agreements were reached. Manning's advice to *News* unions: "Get the money up front. . . . [Zuckerman's] got this knack for signing deals, shaking hands, and then, after it's all done, to say, 'now the negotiations begin.' "[11]

Only one union, the photoengravers, had reached an agreement with Black by this date. Most of the nine unions went to Zuckerman's law firm after Black's announcement. George McDonald subsequently indicated that the nine unions were in "complete unity," and would reveal their position in the scheduled September 11 court hearing.

Judge Brozman adjourned this meeting and scheduled another for September 17. She also noted that it would be near impossible to receive another adjournment unless substantial tangible progress was made. The unions were given this time to reach a settlement with Zuckerman or another purchaser such as Silver Screen Management, who claimed to have understandings with five or six *News* unions, and offered creditors a return similar to Black's proposed 40 cents on the dollar. If these negotiations were unsuccessful, *News* management would likely ask Judge Brozman to invoke wage reductions greater than 10 percent on September 17, however, Zuckerman indicated he would agree to a $3 million bridge loan that would make this action unnecessary should he reach agreement with the unions.

These negotiations were not expected to be simple. In addition to interunion differences, the *News* lawyer indicated that Zuckerman had not made an offer found acceptable by either the debtor or the trade creditors. Zuckerman's likely proposal to them (14 to 17 cents on the dollar) was much worse than that offered by Black; therefore, his proposal could be blocked by the creditors even if agreements were reached with the unions. Peter Kalikow used this opportunity to publicly reassert his interest in the *News,* expecting both the unions and creditors to turn to him eventually. Even Black indicated to the unions that his offer remained on the table although he was withdrawing active pursuit of the newspaper. He would only resume interest if the unions' bargaining proposals, particularly that of the pressmen (the only union with which he had not previously recorded significant bargaining progress), clearly justified his building of a new printing plant.

By September 15, the Whitman Group, involving several New York investors, appeared to replace Silver Screen Management as the "stand-alone" option to Zuckerman. The Whitman Group proposed to place $25 million of equity financing into the *News* as part of a management buy-out with a 40-percent-ownership stake. Also included was a $3 million bridge loan and a revenue-sharing provision by which employees would receive 35 cents of every dollar the newspaper earned over a level based on its circulation before the 1990–91 strike. The Whitman Group also offered more return to the creditors than the Zuckerman proposal and announced that it had agreements in principle with six unions although not the pressmen and the drivers. Barry Lipton of the Newspaper Guild no doubt favored the Whitman Group over Zuckerman's discharge-at-will approach; however, Lipton indicated that he would begin "torturous" negotiations with Zuckerman on September 15.

Lipton entered these negotiations under the specter of a 10 percent-or-greater wage reduction, which, in turn, placed pressure on the unions to urge a Guild settlement. One senior-level negotiations participant indicated, on the condition of anonymity, that Zuckerman would still provide the $3 million loan, which would prevent wage cuts, even if no agreement were reached with the Guild. But Zuckerman would do so only if the other major unions, particularly pressmen and drivers, would agree to crossing a Guild picket line if that became necessary. Douglas LaChance of the drivers' union said his members would be angered if a wage cut occurred and implied that the other unions might break with the Guild if it made unreasonable bargaining demands.

Negotiations between the Guild and Zuckerman continued through September 16, and the union's bargaining position seemed to improve when Guild negotiators were accompanied by an APTC subcommittee comprised of leaders from three other unions. McDonald contended that this action's message stressed that the unions were unified. Yet the subcommittee may have helped ensure, as well as reflect, unity among all unions, particularly as the salary reduction deadline approached. An eventual labor agreement appeared likely as both Zuckerman and the Guild seemed willing to make concessions. Zuckerman discussed eliminating his previous request that advertising employees be removed from Guild jurisdiction. He also proposed to enhance severance payments to employees who volunteered to resign and, if necessary, to dismiss others in a layoff by seniority. He sought cuts of 70 to 80 editorial employees from a base of 300 and promised to put 50 of them on a recall list.

The Newspaper Guild indicated it would consider giving Zuckerman more discretion over the "unborn"—Guild members hired after the labor agreement was settled. The new employees would likely be subject to dismissal without arbitration for a probationary period of one year instead of the previously agreed-upon 90 days. Lipton indicated that many items were still subject to negotiation, particularly the number of staff reductions, but he also expressed optimism that an agreement could be reached. Perhaps Lipton's expression was influenced by the realization that the other unions thought the time and terms as well as the conditions were right for all unions to reach an agreement. The next day, George McDonald predicted that Mortimer Zuckerman would be the new owner of the *Daily News* while Michael Connery, lawyer for the APTC, indicated this transition would occur by Thanksgiving.

James Willse, publisher of the *News,* agreed with his union counterparts, saying "as far as we're concerned, it's done."[12] These union–management endorsements temporarily scuttled a Whitman Group proposal made on September 16 that clearly surpassed Zuckerman's offer to creditors and that also included a $3 million bridge loan to the newspaper provided the creditors' committee and the *News* Board of Directors endorsed them as purchaser. Douglas LaChance of the drivers' union denounced the Whitman Group offer as a last-minute effort by an unknown buyer to derail extensively negotiated agreements with Zuckerman's organization.

While no labor agreements were ratified at this time, Zuckerman proposed a cash payment of $18 million for the *News* and additional payments of $7.25 million to assume liabilities for accrued vacation pay and up to $1 million to assume obligations for contributions to welfare and pension payments. He would also honor the current severance policy for exempt noncontract employees, with exempt employees held to no more than six months' salary. Drivers received assurances that they would deliver all of the newspapers instead of having some of their work performed by wholesalers.

The proposed offer also called for the reduction of 200 jobs from a base of 1,400 through buy-outs at the Newspaper Guild and layoffs in the craft unions. The remaining employees would have their job security guaranteed through their labor agreements running through the year 2005. A 3 percent wage increase would be applied after the first year, followed by annual wage increases of no more than 3 percent. Zuckerman stated that these increases would amount to half of the year's rise in the consumer price index, with half of that amount to be funded with cash and the other half contingent on productivity improvements. The proposed labor agreements also included no strike provisions.

Zuckerman acknowledged that both unions and creditors had to make some real sacrifices if this transaction were made. Creditors were also very much concerned about the $4.1 million payment possibility to him if the deal fell apart. Judge Brozman considered the creditors' objections and deferred her decision on Zuckerman's proposal until September 23. By this time, the creditors' committee had endorsed Zuckerman's *News* purchase plan, in part because he reduced his $4.1 million breakup payment possibility to $3.2 million. The committee preferred to support the Whitman proposal, which offered them 34 to 40 cents on the dollar compared to Zuckerman's 13 to 18 cents creditor return; however, the creditors realized that Zuckerman had necessary union backing that was not automatically transferable to the Whitman Group. Douglas LaChance perhaps reflected the sentiment of his drivers' union and the rest of the APTC at this time when he opined that the Whitman offer came from "a vulture fund looking to pick meat off the bones" of the *News*. Moreover, he stressed that Whitman had neither a credible plan nor a demonstrated ability to operate the newspaper.

Judge Brozman okayed Zuckerman's $3.2 million breakup fee and his $3 million bridge loan to the *News* at the September 23 meeting. Zuckerman would pay $500,000 at this time and another $500,000 on October 22, when the court expected to finalize the transaction. Brozman indicated that an auction of *Daily News* assets could be held on this date between Zuckerman and another potential purchaser such as the Whitman Group.

Lewis Kaden, attorney for the Whitman Group, realized that Zuckerman's "contracts" with the union were nonexclusive and that the unions could take a different position any time between September 23 and October 22. However, Judge Brozman did not grant a request by the Whitman Group and the creditors who sought disclosure of Zuckerman's union agreements. She responded that it was unnecessary that the Whitman Group negotiate "identical" labor agreements and inappropriate to have a bidding war over the employees. Guild president Barry Lipton indicated that Zuckerman remained the most likely candidate to own the newspaper but added, "It can't really finish unless we're on board. Zuckerman is going to need to come to an acceptable conclusion with us."[13]

On October 4, 1992, the pressmen's union ratified its settlement with Zuckerman by a 2-to-1 margin, but the APTC asked the other *News* unions to postpone any labor agreement settlements with Zuckerman. George McDonald was concerned that Zuckerman had not yet detailed his plans for building a new color printing facility in his purchase or labor agreements. In fact, the only place Zuckerman had described his new printing facility intention was in one paragraph in an August 14 letter to *News* directors. Zuckerman's partner, Fred Drasner, retorted that the new printing facility was no longer an issue because "our commitment hasn't changed from day one"; moreover, eight union leaders had reviewed the letter and then signed the labor agreement.

McDonald also did not want Zuckerman to have ratified labor agreements until a settlement was reached with the Newspaper Guild. McDonald thought this situation could be attained within a few days, particularly if the other unions in the APTC "beat up on Zuckerman" as hard as they could to get a contract with the Guild. McDonald clearly qualified the APTC's support of the Newspaper Guild, however, by saying, "At this moment the Allied is 100 percent united to see that the Guild gets a contract. That's today."[14]

Interunion tensions were further increased in early October when a *Newsday* article revealed that the pressmen's and drivers' unions received "secret" bonuses of $1 million and $1.5 million respectively for signing their labor agreements. Many union leaders were surprised and angered at this revelation. Pat Flannery, president of the paperhandlers' union, was "disappointed" at these "unfair" agreements because they were not shared with other unions. James Grottola, president of the Typographers Union, was also concerned: "I live in the real world too. If Zuckerman is crying poverty here and looking to annihilate my bargaining unit, and he gives to other people $2.5 million, am I being asked to finance that?"[15] George McDonald expressed his surprise about this development and indicated that if it were confirmed, he would expect the same arrangement with the other unions in the APTC.

Fred Drasner responded that these bonuses were tied to productivity increases in lieu of wages. For example, the drivers' bonus was tied to reduced newspaper returns and fewer corresponding expenses. McDonald subsequently downplayed his opinion of the bonuses, indicating that they were given in exchange for concessions on retirement plan provisions and were not "secret" since they were printed in the tentative contracts distributed to union members. McDonald further blamed Zuckerman's negotiators for failing to disclose these arrangements with other union leaders, including himself, who requested information for "me too," collective bargaining agreement language. McDonald concluded, "Everybody negotiates something for what they give up, if they can get it. That leaves the other unions to try to achieve that in our areas."[16] He intended to seek an equivalent bonus arrangement for his mailers' union, but was vague on what would occur if these provisions were not granted.

Seven of the nine unions in the APTC had ratified the labor agreements as the October 22 purchase approval date approached, with the eighth union, the photoengravers, expected to ratify its agreement shortly thereafter. (The terms of these 13-year labor agreements containing no strike provisions were discussed earlier.) Suffice it to say that these settlements would result in the elimination of 200 positions (not including those in the Newspaper Guild and Typographer's union) when Zuckerman assumed ownership. The *News*'s loss of $9 million for the first three quarters of 1992 further impelled the sale of the newspaper to Zuckerman.

Two unions, however, typographers and the Newspaper Guild, posed purchase obstacles. Both reflected peripheral bargaining considerations: the typographers became entangled with external judicial activities, and the Guild faced a bargaining issue derived from principle.

Judicial Considerations of Zuckerman's Bargaining Stance with the Typographical Union

The typographers' annual payroll of $8 to $10 million was honored in 1991. Zuckerman contended that he offered the union "a number of jobs"; however, he also stressed that he would not honor their lifetime job guarantees and would not purchase the *News* if the courts ordered him to do so. James Grottola, president of the typographers' union, indicated that as of early October 1992, he had had "no meaningful negotiations" with Zuckerman and maintained that Zuckerman's bargaining position was that his union "must get wiped off the face of the earth."

Grottola wanted an arbitrator to resolve a grievance, filed July 31, 1992, that sought enforcement of the lifetime employment security provisions before the intended October 22 sale of the *News* to Zuckerman. Some evidence of bargaining had occurred by this date. Grottola noted that the union's concept of lifetime job guarantees was changed to assure a certain number of shifts that could mean reduced work weeks for his members. The union's proposal reduced the number of work shifts from 770 to 500 a week. If this meant more employees than shifts, then the employees' work weeks would be reduced. Grottola though this procedure would reduce the number of employees from 100 at time of purchase to 40 in six years of a proposed 13-year labor agreement. The typographers also sought early-retirement incentives.

Zuckerman's written proposal, the first ever received by the union, was given the night before the October 22 hearings. It reduced the union membership to 80, working 400 shifts after Zuckerman's purchase; these conditions would be further streamlined to 15 members and 75 shifts after four years. No early retirement incentives were included in the proposal, although $1 million would be given to the union toward a medical fund. Zuckerman contended that his proposal reflected extensive negotiations and was more than reasonable since it would cost $30 million. This position was backed by the creditors, who also wanted Judge Tina Brozman to void the typographers' labor agreement. The creditors reasoned that a remaining labor agreement would not make the *News* attractive to any buyer, thereby resulting in the newspaper's liquidation.

Judge Brozman initially agreed with the union on October 22, and instructed both union and management representatives to continue bargaining since she was not convinced the parties were at impasse. On October 26, however, she decided that Zuckerman could purchase the *News* by December 31 without having to consider the typographers' labor agreement including lifetime employment guarantees. Zuckerman would be obligated for some $36 to $38 million, paying $18,250,000 in cash and assuming $8,250,000 in specific liabilities such as vacation and retirement pay and another $12 million for production materials like paper and ink. She gave several reasons for her decision, including her determination that Zuckerman had "negotiated fairly . . . and in good faith" with the union. Brozman also maintained that new technology rendered the typographers' jobs "superfluous"; therefore, continuing the lifetime employment guarantees would "kill" the *News* since no potential purchaser would acquire the "bleeding dinosaur" with this large, unnecessary expense. She concluded:

Allowing a debtor to reject a collective bargaining agreement can never be an easy decision. Yet Congress and the courts have clearly recognized that within the context of reorganization proceedings, this avenue for relief may be a debtor's only viable chance for successfully reorganizing. Still, in enacting section 1113 of the Bankruptcy Code, Congress has made clear its intent to have the court approve such motion only after finding that the debtor has surmounted the procedural and substantive hurdles mandated by the Code. The Debtor has met those burdens.[17]

Zuckerman was obviously pleased with this decision and also indicated that he would offer typographers some "real work" not "featherbedding" (watching television at work, for example) even though the decision did not obligate him to do so. Typographers' union president Grottola responded to Judge Brozman's decision in an equally predictable fashion: "We were slaughtered. . . . That means that 167 people, who had lifetime job guarantees are now headed toward the guillotine."[18] The union appealed this decision at both the state and federal levels; it filed a $240 million suit in state court, charging Zuckerman and the pressmen's and drivers' unions with conspiracy to undermine typographers' rights. Zuckerman countered that this effort had "no connection with any reality that I know about" and represented a futile attempt to accomplish what the union had failed to gain with Judge Brozman.

The typographers also appealed the decision through the federal courts. If unsuccessful in these efforts, they intended to file a $60 million priority claim representing the value of its labor agreement against *News* sale proceeds. The union also indicated that it would challenge Zuckerman's "rampant featherbedding" charge in its appeal, since his hired productivity consultants investigating *News* operation had found much higher excess employment among the pressmen, who were not bound to make any immediate staffing cuts in their collective bargaining agreements with Zuckerman.

Judge Lawrence M. McKenna of the United States District Court for the Southern District of New York boosted the typographers' hopes for continued collective bargaining on December 3, 1992, when he in part reversed Judge Brozman's decision and remanded the case to the bankruptcy court for proceedings consistent with his opinion. He agreed with Brozman that the following two of three conditions established by U.S.C. 1113 for voiding a labor agreement under bankruptcy proceedings had been met:

• the trustee [defined to include a debtor in possession] has, prior to the hearing, made a proposal that fulfills the requirements of subsection (b) (1); and
• the balance of the equities clearly favors rejection of such agreement.

McKenna, however, did disagree with Brozman's ruling that the following third legal prerequisite for eliminating the typographers' bargaining agreement under bankruptcy proceedings had been met: the authorized representative of the employees has refused to accept such proposal without good cause. Consideration of this legal requirement is also necessary to the thesis of this book, which suggests that movement from traditional bargaining to peripheral bargaining is counterproductive to both parties.

McKenna maintained that Brozman had erred when she only considered the content of management's bargaining proposal without examining and establishing related proof concerning the process in which it was presented to the union. He stressed that the typographers had good cause to refuse Zuckerman's proposal because it was made late in the evening before the October 22 purchase approval date, and caught the union off guard, particularly since it withdrew any inducement of any kind for early retirement:

Had Debtor's final proposal been made several days earlier, or had it reflected a further adjustment of the elements that had been under discussion since October 14 — abandonment of lifetime job guarantees for all members of the Printers with a reduction in required shifts over a period of some years coupled with some consideration for the loss of job guarantees in the form of inducements for early retirement — the printers might have been expected to have responded with a counterproposal. The shift in direction of Debtor's proposal, however, in particular its abandonment of its own proposal of October 15 of the addition of years to age at retirement and years of service at the Daily News, quite obviously put the Printers in a position where, in order to make a meaningful counterproposal, more time was needed than the few hours remaining before the October 22 hearing. At issue for the Printers was not a relatively simple matter such as a wage rate, but the ability of members trained in the composing room and in or approaching their sixties to survive.[19]

Judge McKenna also found the actions of Zuckerman's partner and chief negotiator, Fred Drasner, to have been incompatible with good-faith bargaining since Drasner was on record as indicating Zuckerman would walk away from the *News* transaction if the typographers' labor agreement was not rejected. McKenna further scored Zuckerman's insistence on voiding lifetime employment guarantees, which he regarded a nonissue since the union officers in their first response (October 14) made it clear that lifetime guarantees were negotiable, and had not insisted on it since.

Daniel Englestein, attorney for the union, called McKenna's decision "a significant victory" since it defined the "good cause" requirement in the bankruptcy law and indicated that good faith bargaining in a bankruptcy situation must meet "more than just the necessity test." This decision nullified the December 6 *News* sale date and Zuckerman's payment of $18 million to purchase the newspaper the next day. Zuckerman and the typographers planned to resume negotiations the following week. Marc Kirschner, the bankruptcy lawyer for the *Daily News*, hoped that Judge Brozman would declare a bargaining impasse if no agreement had been reached by this time and then void the typographers' collective bargaining agreement so that the *News* sale could be consummated on December 13. Zuckerman sent the typographers a six-page letter on December 8 that included a reduction of the same number of employees indicated in a previous proposal already rejected by the union, but that also reinstated some early retirement incentives.

Zuckerman's purchase agreement enabled him to walk away from the *News* sale after December 31, 1992 if agreement was not reached. After receiving Judge McKenna's decision, he refused to extend this deadline even though the paper was profitable in the fourth quarter of 1992, more so than expected. Since Zuckerman had also indicated that he would not accept the typographers' lifetime employment guarantees, APTC union officials focused attention on *News* Management Inc.'s appeal of Judge McKenna's decision. Related anxiety occurred over whether the appeal decision would favor the debtor and Zuckerman and whether it would be reached before the December 31 deadline.

Both questions were issued in the affirmative as Judge Richard J. Cardamone, a veteran of the U.S. Navy, placed the *News's* bargaining situation into the following external perspective.

The circumstances confronting the debtor and the printers are like those facing a Navy ship torpedoed at sea. Drastic damage control instituted at the site seals off that portion of the vessel, with a disproportionate loss of those ill-fated to be in that section. These measures are necessary so that the ship and its remaining crew might survive. The present debtor, like the ship, is in danger of foundering, eliminating not only the typesetters' jobs, but also costing the 1850 other employees their livelihoods as well. Modification of the collective bargaining agreement, like naval damage control, is not something good or pleasing to contemplate, but without it this newspaper will sink.[20]

Cardamone also reversed District Court Judge McKenna's ruling on the manner in which Zuckerman made his final offer to the union because the union had never complained about not having enough time to respond to the employer's proposal. He maintained that union and management officials typically negotiate for many hours under deadlines, and that ten hours is "ample time" to consider and respond to a proposal. He therefore found that Bankruptcy Judge Brozman correctly concluded that the union rejected the employer's proposal without good cause.

Judge Cardamone, while throwing out the typographers' lifetime employment guarantees, indicated the December 22, 1992 decision was conditioned on Zuckerman leaving his previously described final offer on the table. This proposal, including buy-outs of 50 jobs, would cost Zuckerman $30 million over the proposed 13-year labor agreement, or 90 percent of the typographers' last offer, and the union indicated it would not appeal Judge Cardamone's decision. A *News* attorney maintained the decision cleared "the last major obstacle to closing the deal."

Zuckerman and The Newspaper Guild

Maybe the *News* attorney's optimism pertaining to collective bargaining and Zuckerman's purchase of the newspaper was correct; however, Zuckerman's purchase was not consummated in the remaining nine days of 1992. Zuckerman agreed to extend this time period partly because of the Court of Appeal's decision. Also, he and the Newspaper Guild had established and maintained a bargaining impasse during 1992's fourth quarter, a situation largely created by Zuckerman's principled embodiment of labor–management negotiations:

I'm not in this thing to cut costs and just make money. I'm in it principally because of the editorial product and the editorial challenge.[21]

Zuckerman had approached this principle in his previous purchase of the *Atlantic*. Under his ownership, the magazine increased its circulation from 325,000 in 1981 to 400,000 in 1991; advertising revenue increased from $1.8 million in 1981 to $12.3 million in 1991; and the magazine won five National Magazine Awards and received 24 National Magazine Award nominations during this time period. Yet Zuckerman, while spending some $40 million on the *Atlantic,* has yet to experience a profit from the magazine.[22]

Editorial enhancement, while a possibly appropriate publishing objective, is difficult to translate into collective bargaining proposals/provisions that are accepted by both union and management officials. Consider, for example, Zuckerman's operationalization of this objective when Judge Brozman initially awarded the *News* purchase to him on October 26: "No other people care about their city as much as New Yorkers do, and the *News* is going to capture the tone and flavor of that New York voice."[23] Zuckerman also attempted at this time to align this issue with a traditional bargaining concept, seniority:

We are seriously committed to establishing editorial control over the editorial product, while at the same time we will respect seniority. . . . The only way you control the editorial product is to be able to be satisfied that you have talented editorial people. We intend to make those judgments, as best we can, on the basis of merit.[24]

Confusion over this bargaining principle was heightened by tensions between other unions and the Guild as well as within the Guild membership. The APTC's support of the Guild turned into an armed truce at the time of Judge Brozman's initial purchase decision. Barry Lipton indicated that his Guild was unhappy with the actions of other APTC unions but preferred to obtain a collective bargaining agreement rather than dwell on interunion differences. McDonald reaffirmed the APTC's support of the Guild but gave no indication of what form, if any, this support would take if the Guild did not reach an agreement:

There's been no betrayal of the Guild, no more than the Guild betrayed the other unions when they said they were opposed to going ahead with the sale. There are two sides to the coin.[25]

As was true with previous bargaining experiences since the October 1990 strike, differences arose among Guild members over what would constitute an appropriate settlement. One reporter backed Zuckerman's bargaining objectives and, presumably, subsequent labor agreement provisions:

There are questions about what he's going to do but at least we know it's going to stay open. . . . And we have someone with a good reputation in publishing who really wants to keep this paper open and alive and wants to put out a quality product.[26]

However, at least one prominent writer, David Haberstram, questioned Zuckerman's journalistic qualifications, much as Pete Hamill had done of Chicago Tribune executive Charles Brumback several years earlier:

[Zuckerman] likes to think of himself as a journalist. . . . He's not. He's a real-estate person who has bought a series of very vulnerable publications, and it gave him a social legitimacy that he very, very badly wanted.[27]

Other reporters thought Zuckerman's offer was "punitive" and counterproductive since the only reporters he could hire without job-security provisions would be "novices" and "has-beens." Many union members, while not sure of the extent their seniority rights would be eroded under Zuckerman's bargaining principle, realized that the union could be weakened or disappear as current members eventually left the organization. One Guild lawyer indicated that as of Judge Brozman's initial purchase decision Zuckerman wanted to reduce the 541-member union by 173 people, or 32 percent. This figure would involve some 100 more Guild members than that given in Zuckerman's earlier proposal. Depending on who left the *News,* management's severance-payment obligation would increase from $3.8 million to $7.3 million. Zuckerman also sought to eliminate arbitration rights for new employees if they were fired for "lack of competence."

Bargaining between Zuckerman and the Guild became increasingly public in November and December. A rally was held outside the *News* headquarters on November 17 to protest the lack of management's bargaining efforts, and it included some 200 members of the Guild along with union representatives of municipal workers, teachers, restaurant workers, and Local 1199. Reporter Juan Gonzalez addressed the crowd in now all too familiar terms:

Even though Mort Zuckerman thinks we don't have any fight left and we don't have any friends left, we're going to let him know as we taught (former owner) Tribune Company . . . from a business viewpoint it's not worth it to try and break us.[28]

The rally had no immediate, direct impact on collective bargaining as management indicated at this time that Guild members would have to reapply for their own jobs if a collective bargaining agreement was not reached by December 6, another possible closing date proposed by the courts. Zuckerman indicated that this statement represented a necessary step in the "editorial rebuilding process," not a scare tactic "bargaining ultimatum."

Guild members were not receptive to Zuckerman's explanation. One reporter regarded this tactic as "back-door union busting" since reapplication would mean reporters were on a two-year probation, which would mean no job security and related union bargaining power. Another reporter thought Zuckerman took this action to threaten reporters and force them to capitulate.

Juan Gonzalez attempted to express his dissent by writing a newspaper column — which was never published — in which he labeled Zuckerman a "bully" and revived the memory of James Hoge, who, he claimed, had spent more money in union-busting efforts than the newspaper could lose in a generation. Gonzalez also related the *News*'s bargaining situation to that experienced by other unions across the country, and claimed that Zuckerman's reception in bankruptcy court represented one more indignity heaped on his fellow union members since

Mr. Zuckerman somehow found a way to reach fair contracts with several other unions. One of the unions signed minutes before the district attorney arrived to take its leader to jail for parole violation and indict a bunch of the other leaders.

But for some reason Zuckerman has decided to treat the Newspaper Guild, the largest and most squeaky clean of the unions, differently. He wants to get rid of 179 out of 540 members. This is on top of a one-third reduction we took when Maxwell assumed control. He wants the right to fire, without impartial outside arbitration, any new workers he deems unproductive.

In short, he wants to gut our union and leave us the carcass.

Admittedly, this is a personal opinion.

It also happens to be accurate.[29]

News publisher James Willse acknowledged that he "killed" Gonzalez's potential column because it represented a conflict of interest. Willse maintained that Gonzalez was involved in the labor dispute and should not extend it through the *News*'s pages.

At an emergency meeting on December 2, about 200 Guild members voted unanimously to fill out *News* employment applications "under protest." This action was taken reluctantly and angrily since members thought it demeaned them. Indeed, one question on the application was "Have you ever worked for the Daily News?" Nor were the Guild members appeased by Zuckerman's statement at the time, "I'd rather negotiate with the Palestinians than the Newspaper Guild."[30]

Two weeks later, the Newspaper Guild filed an unfair-labor-practice charge with the National Labor Relations Board against Zuckerman, claiming that he did not negotiate his latest proposal concerning severance pay with the union but instead presented it directly to the employees. Tom Pennacchio, the Guild's secretary-treasurer, termed Zuckerman's buy-out offer "one of the worst we've seen." "Regular, active" Guild members electing buy-outs would receive $2\frac{1}{2}$ weeks pay for each year of service up to 20 years, then three weeks pay for every additional year. Permanent employees who left the company would be entitled to 18 months of health benefits at a group rate; however, the remaining employees would have a new health policy and 25 percent payment of related premiums as opposed to other labor agreements including the former *News* full payment of these benefits.

Pennacchio further indicated that Zuckerman had not held a collective bargaining session with the Guild since November 30, an inaction that circumvented the collective bargaining process and had the "smell of union busting." Zuckerman would later retort that he had had over 30 collective bargaining meetings and 300 hours with the Newspaper Guild without any productive results; however, his claim was modified by reporter Don Singleton, who contended that the union could not understand or respond to Zuckerman because he had never put a final offer on the table. Union officials were also concerned that Zuckerman refused to meet with them with or without a mediator and that he was backing off from his previous negotiation stance that he would not lay off members without regard to seniority.

Guild members were to respond to Zuckerman's offer by January 28, 1993. However, Barry Lipton told them not to submit the forms. Union officials suggested that they would not strike, although they and some 150 Newspaper Guild members indicated that the following external steps would be taken: a letter would be sent to Mayor David Dinkins asking him to intervene in the dispute; and authorization would be given to spend $100,000 to pay for a professionally organized boycott to drive down circulation by 100,000 a day by the end of January. Ray Rogers, who had been involved in related union campaigns against J. P. Stevens, Hormel, American Airlines, and International Paper, would head the boycott activities against the *News*. His major objective was to extend the union's peripheral bargaining influence beyond the picket line, to organizations' board members and financiers, who might place pressure on management to resolve its differences with the union.

My goal is to get the Guild a fair settlement. We are developing a multidimensional strategy that is national in scope. Zuckerman has a farflung empire: real estate development, the U.S. News and World Report, the Atlantic Monthly. We have to look at his areas of vulnerability and take the fight into those areas.[31]

Related tactics included galvanizing members of the union local by employing them as foot soldiers in raising the consciousness of other unions, and soliciting funds from some 55,000 individuals and organizations on his mailing list. It moreover would include many facets such as artwork, fund-raising, leafletting, telephone banking, local and nationwide mailings outreach to the labor community in New York and around the country, and lobbying political officials. Guild member Jerry Capeci thought this external strategy, which did not work against Brumback, might significantly persuade Zuckerman since Zuckerman was a "little boy" who did not have the Tribune Company's "deep pockets." One of Rogers's opponents in a previous corporate campaign against Hormel Company contended that Zuckerman could have a real problem standing up to intense "negative trashing" which is a strong feature of the corporate campaign. A related theme considered for use was the allegation that Zuckerman did not pay any federal income taxes for the years 1981 to 1986. *News's* co-publisher, Fred Drasner, countered that his organization had reached agreements with nine of the ten unions and that the Guild's efforts represented a "sideshow" that could adversely affect the 1,535 positions perceived at the newspaper.

The union also voted to explore whether Zuckerman and the other *Daily News* unions conspired to put the Newspaper Guild in this nonbargaining situation, and if so, determine appropriate lawsuits. Fred Drasner responded that this bargaining vacuum was created by the previous court battle with the typographers' union. He moreover observed that he had not received a proposal from the Newspaper Guild, "and nothing's ripened."

Two days later, January 7, 1993, bargaining between Zuckerman and the Newspaper Guild had most likely rotted. Zuckerman assumed ownership of the *News* at this time, not in a public signing ceremony, but instead through transferring documents among law firms. Fred Drasner acknowledged that tough decisions were made, but also indicated his pleasure that the jobs of 1,535 employees were saved. George McDonald, of the Allied Printing Trades Council, also attempted to place a positive spin on this event, particularly in light of the previous three years marked by peripheral bargaining.

Over the last several years, our membership has endured a devastating strike, bankruptcy, and almost daily uncertainty about their futures at the newspaper. We now look forward to a long, prosperous and stable future under Mort and Fred's leadership at the *New York Daily News*.[32]

Zuckerman offered Newspaper Guild employees the previously discussed buyouts which were contingent on waivers of rights to sue the employer or return to the job. An alternative, available without the waivers to those not offered jobs, represented regular severance of one week per six months of service. Employees could waive their severance pay claims from the *News* under Maxwell's operation and retain seniority, or they could preserve their severance claims and work as a new employee with two years probation and benefits accrued through previous work experience. The Newspaper Guild maintains that all members should be entitled to severance payments (a position which might be decided in arbitration) and that remaining employees should maintain their seniority under Zuckerman. However, Zuckerman and previous *Daily News* management indicated that severance payments would only be paid to employees who restart work as a new employee with no subsequent severance rights unless they are won in court rather than at the bargaining table. The *News's* organization, with no labor agreement with the Newspaper Guild, terminated payments into the union's health funds. Newspaper Guild employees who continued to work for Zuckerman would be covered by a new health fund, although benefits of recently dismissed employees and retirees, who were covered through the union's health benefits, might be at risk. A week later management effected another implication of the Newspaper Guild's nonlabor agreement status when it stopped deducting members' dues from their paychecks.

Some 200 employees represented by the Newspaper Guild (100 reporters and editors and another 100 members in circulation and advertising) were also released at this time through notification in manila envelopes. A thick envelope meant employees had a job with the *News*, although at sharply reduced rates, while a thinner one meant they were out of work and should leave the building immediately, and return over the weekend to collect their belongings. Computer passwords were changed, and telephones had been cut off in the circulation department on that day and the night before, presumably to eliminate sabotage opportunities. However, one Guild reporter, speaking shortly before receiving his envelope, noted,

It's going to be a bloodbath and it's unfortunate someone is imposing such a tragic theater. It is people's lives, after all. I'm sure there must have been a more humane way to do it.[33]

One *News* photographer for 40 years noted "I just read the words, 'we regret to inform you,' and I didn't read the rest. . . . I feel discarded."[34] Reporter, Jerry Capeci, who was offered a job with the *News*, maintained,

This is the most horrible thing I've ever gone through . . . To see someone duck into an alleyway so no one sees him crying, it's terrible.[35]

Publisher James Willse was also discharged, but stayed until the last reporter left the newsroom. He took some solace in believing the *News* would survive since "It's the most resilient organization I know." Lipton acknowledged that Zuckerman had the right to reduce the Newspaper Guild staff. However, he urged that any staff reductions and related buy-outs be based on seniority instead of managerial discretion. Some Newspaper Guild members who received employment contracts were supposedly thinking about conducting a wildcat strike to protest management's depersonalized approach to labor relations.

Drasner responded that there was no easy way to lay off employees, an attitude echoed by Zuckerman who said he was "investing" in the *News* while his predecessors, Maxwell and the Chicago Tribune Company respectively, had "raped" and "milked" the newspaper. Zuckerman intended to hire some 100 new reporters and editors to replace those who were dismissed, and maintained that this firing and hiring discretion represented

an absolute precondition for turning the paper around. If I'm going to put in a new printing plant, I have to have the ability to put words on paper that will provide a compelling reason to continue to buy the *Daily News*.[36]

He further noted that the first Sunday *News* published under his ownership would have a statement of principles to readers.

Zuckerman did at least suggest the possibility that some mistaken personnel decisions might have been made in a meeting he held with remaining Newspaper Guild members the day after he purchased the *News*. However, he also suggested that any mistakes would be corrected by himself, not through negotiations with the Newspaper Guild, which had neither reduced the number of layoffs nor exercised any control over who would be separated from the *News*.

Some Newspaper Guild members were concerned that Barry Lipton was unable to reach a settlement with Zuckerman. One noted that the Newspaper Guild was completely unprepared to deal with Zuckerman when the organization was spun off from the other unions. Reporter Jerry Capeci maintained that no one could have likely obtained a settlement from Zuckerman, who from the beginning, "did not want to make a deal."

Other Newspaper Guild criticism focused on Lipton's inability to obtain at least a face-saving deal which would have prevented several members' humiliation of being called "deadwood," and for being late in employing the external efforts against Zuckerman. Tom Robbins, for example, maintained that Lipton's

fatal flaw is he can never make up his mind what to do. He hasn't got the guts to fight, and he lacks the courage to tell other people the cause is lost and you have to bite the bullet. Barry was at the steering wheel when our car drove off the cliff, and I hold him personally responsible for the fact that longtime *Daily News* employees never got a chance to leave this place with dignity.[37]

Robbins, Capeci, and Gonzalez wanted Lipton to take aggressive action against Zuckerman (hiring Ray Rogers, for example) in September, 1992, when the drivers' and pressmen's unions obtained collective bargaining settlements with the *News*.

Lipton did, however, encourage active members who were rehired to remain on the *News* so the Guild could fight related battles within the organization. This situation appeared particularly urgent and necessary since 8 of the 13 bargaining committee members were not offered jobs with the *News*. The Newspaper Guild reiterated its emphasis on its external boycott, an action Barry Lipton hoped would send Zuckerman the following message: "We've got to tell Mr. Zuckerman that he can't get away with behaving like this. This is not 1850 and we still have unions."[38] According to one account, Zuckerman attempted to meet Lipton's concern by having a bodyguard accompany his movements through the *Daily News*. However, rebuttal of Lipton's remarks came not from Zuckerman but from George McDonald, who stressed that he and other leaders believed Zuckerman and Drasner never attempted to break the Newspaper Guild, as they had bargained in "complete good faith" from the beginning. McDonald further intimated that the APTC was the "best friend the Guild ever had," but would not support peripheral bargaining efforts such as reader boycotts initiated by a "reactionary group," the Newspaper Guild, because it could jeopardize the jobs of 1,535 people (including 350 Guild positions) preserved by Zuckerman's sale agreement. "That's like shooting yourself in the foot. We want to save the paper, not kill it."[39]

A subsequent vote by the 24-person executive board of the Newspaper Guild on January 12, 1993, withdrew its long-established relationship (more than 40 years) with the APTC. Barry Lipton indicated that McDonald's criticism against his organization was "misdirected," and contended external actions against the *News* were taken to force Zuckerman back to the bargaining table, not to destroy the *News*.

McDonald retorted that the APTC was on the Newspaper Guild's side in obtaining an agreement with Zuckerman; moreover the Newspaper Guild would in the long run realize the "many great things" received from the APTC and rejoin the organization. However, two days after the Guild's withdrawal decision, the APTC voted to send a resolution to the national and state AFL-CIO and a city labor council, condemning the Newspaper Guild's planned readership and advertising boycott against the *News* because the jobs of 1,535 union employees, including 350 members of the Guild, would be endangered.

The Newspaper Guild received external and temporary support from civil rights leaders and other unions operating in New York City while its dispute with other APTC unions continued. Zuckerman's dismissals after the *News's* purchase included nine out of ten black newsroom employees, a situation labelled by Barry Lipton as "ethnic cleansing." The Guild's final employment tabulations contended 182 of 544 members lost their jobs "without any regard" for seniority or other labor agreement provisions. It further charged that Zuckerman's unilateral job reduction violated equal employment opportunity in several instances, since 41 percent of all black employees (54 percent of black males), 40 percent of Latin females, and nearly half of the employees over 50 years of age lost their jobs. Management contended that its current occupational distribution of blacks, Asians, and women were better than those obtained under previous *News* executives, including Robert Maxwell. Zuckerman further maintained that fewer minorities would have been retained by the *News* if management had used two Guild selection proposals based on job classification or employment seniority. His publicized statement on the issue reaffirmed the organization's future commitment to aggressively recruit minorities.

When pressed on his dismissal of all six black male reporters Zuckerman responded that his layoffs were determined "purely on a merit-basis review," and that this employment category was artificially created by the union since laws prohibited layoffs based on race, ethnicity, gender, or union activity. He charged the Guild with being completely hypocritical on this issue since 25 percent more minorities would have lost their jobs if the Guild's seniority system were used. Zuckerman's position was rejected by the National Association of Black Journalists, which was outraged over "the disproportionate layoffs of African-American and other journalists of color." The Rev. Al Sharpton and other civil rights activists also expressed concern over the *News's* racially tainted layoffs. Sharpton threatened to don his protest running suit and lie down in front of *News's* delivery trucks unless a labor agreement with the newspaper was reached.

Thirty-nine labor leaders including national and local police, firefighter, electrical, utility, and hospital employees' unions, as well as 100 volunteers, helped to boycott Zuckerman's *News* and other publications. Many agreed to distribute 200,000 leaflets at busy street corners and public transportation sites. One flier portrayed Zuckerman with a machine gun and the logo: "Mort Massacres 180 Jobs" while another branded the *News* as "New York's Hometown Racist Newspaper." However, this external support sources efforts were likely dampened a day later (January 28, 1993) when the state AFL-CIO affirmatively responded to the APTC's request and opposed the Guild's boycott actions against the *News.* As of May 1993, the peripheral bargaining efforts had exerted no measurable impact on the *News,* and a labor agreement between management and the Newspaper Guild had not been reached.

NOTES

1. Linda LeGrande, "Labor Problems at Eastern Air Lines," Congressional Research Service Updated, February 22, 1989, 2–3. For insights into Congressional adjustment of the *Bildisco* decision, see U.S. Senate Committee on Labor and Human Resources, *Oversight on the Taft-Hartley Act, the Railway Labor Act, and the National Labor Relations Act,* 98th Cong., 2nd sess., September 13 and 18, 1984; Senate Committee on Labor and Human Resources and the Committee on the Judiciary *Oversight of Collective Bargaining Agreement and the Bildisco Decision,* 98th Cong., 2nd sess., April 10, 1984; and U.S. House of Representatives Committee on Education and Labor, *Oversight Hearing on Effect of Bankruptcy Actions on the Stability of Labor–Management Relations and the Preservation of Labor Standards,* 98th Cong., 1st sess., October 5, 1983.

2. Kate McKenna, "The *Daily News:* Too Tough to Die?" *Washington Journalism Review* (March 1992): 28.

3. James Cox, "Few Answers, Big Headlines Feed Rumors," *USA Today,* December 16, 1991, 2-B.

4. For additional financial considerations affecting Black's proposed purchase, see Richard Siklos, "Hollinger Plans to Raise $500 Million," *Financial Post,* (Toronto, Ont., Canada), May 19, 1992, 14. Dialog File 635, item 0298490.

5. "No Deal Without Concessions, Says Daily News Suitor," *Newsday,* April 30, 1992. Dialog File 638, item 06623224.

6. William Goldschlag, "Black's Bid for News Tied to Deep Cut in Work Force," *New York Daily News,* May 20, 1992. (Located in News Bank) SUP, 250: C-1.

7. Edward R. Silverman, "News Factions Told to Stop Bickering," *Newsday,* August 7, 1992. Dialog File 638, item 06724144.

8. Elizabeth Sanger, "Last Round for News Suitors," *Newsday,* August 13, 1992. Dialog File 638, item 06730059.

9. Alex S. Jones, "News Unions Still Divided on Buyer," *New York Times,* August 18, 1992, B-1 and B-2.

10. Tim W. Ferguson, "Press Lords Haven't Put Daily News to Bed," *Wall Street Journal,* October 6, 1992, A-19.

11. Jill Dutt and Elizabeth Sanger, "The News Man. Can Dealmaker Mort Zuckerman Save the Tabloid?," *Newsday,* October 19, 1992. Dialog File 638, item 06798047. For insights into Zuckerman's controversial negotiations style and related interpersonal rela-

tionships see Jeanie Kasindorft, "Citizen Mort," *New York,* October 5, 1992, pp. 40, 42, and 45–47.

12. Alex S. Jones, "Zuckerman Is Choice to Buy New York Daily News," *New York Times,* September 18, 1992, A-1.

13. AP News. September 28, 1992. Dialog file 258, item 02801912.

14. "Negotiations Continue with Guild, Zuckerman in Agreement Involving New York Daily News," Bureau of National Affairs Inc., *Daily Labor Report,* Number 199 (October 14, 1992), A-7.

15. Elizabeth Sanger, "News Unions Rap Bonuses," *Newsday,* October 7, 1992. Dialog File 638, item 06786132.

16. "Negotiations Continue," A-7.

17. Maxwell Newspapers, Inc., d/b/a Daily News, Debtor, Case No. 91-15531 (TLB), 23 Bank. Ct., Dec. CRR 999, Oct. 27, 1992 (1992 Bankr. Lexis 1736).

18. "Judge Approves Sale of Daily News to Publisher Zuckerman," *Reuters North American Business Report,* October 21, 1992. Dialog File 611, item 1187262.

19. New York Typographical Union v. Maxwell Newspapers Inc., d/b/a/ Daily News, 92 Civ (LMM) D. New York, Dec. 3, 1992 (U.S. Dist Lexis 1736).

20. *New York Typographical Union No. 6 v. Maxwell Newspapers Inc.,* 1992 U.S. App. LEXIS 33587.

21. Dutt and Sanger, "The News Man."

22. Kasindorf, "Citizen Mort," 42.

23. Elizabeth Sanger, "News Sale Deadlocked," *Newsday,* October 24, 1992. Dialog File 638, item 06802198.

24. "Judge Approves *Daily News* Sale to *U.S. News* Owner Zuckerman," Bureau of National Affairs Inc., *Daily Labor Report* 208 (October 27, 1992): A-11.

25. Ibid.

26. Jon Nordheimer, "Judge Approves Daily News Sale," *New York Times,* October 27, 1992, C-17.

27. William Glaberson, "At Daily News, A New Owner, Old Difficulties," *New York Times,* January 7, 1993, C-17.

28. Elizabeth Sanger, "They're Mortified. Guild Members Rap Zuckerman," *Newsday,* November 18, 1992. Dialog File 638, item 06828198.

29. Wendy Lin, "Labor Talks at News Stall, Paper Kills Column Blasting Zuckerman," *Newsday,* December 2, 1992. Dialog File 638, item 06843158. Gonzalez must be referring to Douglas LaChance, president of the drivers' union, who was arrested on October 23 and charged with violating the terms of his parole.

30. Wendell Jamaieson, Elizabeth Sanger, and Pat Wechsler, "News Guild Acts Under Protest," *Newsday,* December 3, 1992, Dialog File 638, item 06844068.

31. Kenneth C. Crowe, "Contract Put on Zuckerman. Guild Hires A Labor Guerrilla Warrior to Take on Boss," *Newsday,* January 12, 1993. Dialog File 638, item 0701290.

32. Elizabeth Sanger, "Union to Daily News Buyer: Bargain or Face Boycott," *Newsday,* January 6, 1993. Dialog File 638, file 07006077.

33. Elizabeth Sanger, "Costly Rescue, Zuckerman Buys News, Sacks 200," *Newsday,* January 8, 1993. Dialog File 638, item 07008011. According to one account, Zuckerman relied on Arthur Browne, a longtime managing editor, to compile the performance appraisals used in the retain/discharge decisions. Zuckerman subsequently discharged Browne one day before his 20th anniversary at the *News.* Some News Guild members were "ecstatic" about the move while others charged Zuckerman with using Browne as a

"scapegoat" so that he could cozy up to the retained News Guild members. Doug Vaughan and Anthony Scaduto, "Inside New York," *Newsday,* February 22, 1993. Dialog File 638, item 07053151.

34. Wendy Lin, "For Some, Bad News. Many Longtime Workers Fired," *Newsday,* January 8, 1993. Dialog File 638, item 07008019.

35. Ibid. Capeci and two other reporters mentioned frequently in the book, Juan Gonzalez and Tom Robbins, remained with the *News;* however, Don Singleton accepted a buyout option but returned to the newspaper on a part-time basis. Dave Hardy, a 20-year *News* veteran who won a previously mentioned 1987 racial discrimination suit, was released. On February 1, 1993, Mike McAlary, dissatisfied with *Post* management returned to the *News,* and the *Post* reciprocated by publishing his salary ($275,000, which was higher than the "common people" he claimed to represent) and negative remarks he had previously made about Zuckerman.

36. Howard Kurtz, "Zuckerman Takes Over Daily News. 175 Guild Members Fired by New Owner," *Washington Post,* January 8, 1993. Dialog File 146, item 2112995.

37. Kenneth C. Crowe, "Daily News Has Been Bad News for Newspaper Guild Chief," *Newsday,* February 7, 1993. Dialog File 638, item 07038006.

38. Bureau of National Affairs Inc., "Newspaper Guild Hires Consultant to Lead Campaign Against *Daily News,*" *Daily Labor Report,* Number 6 (January 11, 1993), A-13.

39. Robert D. McFadden, "Smaller Staff at *Daily News,*" *New York Times,* January 10, 1993, A-15.

9

Observations

The concept of peripheral bargaining was presented in this book's introduction and applied to the *New York Daily News* dispute in the subsequent chapters. Through such a bargaining approach, union and management officials involved with related behaviors and attitudes focus on their respective organizations instead of on superordinate goals and the strengthening of relations. The officials lose any value gained from a more traditional bargaining approach, particularly in a competitive atmosphere where management should at least consider employee involvement in corporate decision making and shared profits, and union officials should ensure their members' jobs by helping to maintain, even strengthen, corporate long-term financial well-being. Indeed, the only participants who might benefit from the peripheral bargaining experience at the *Daily News* might be a few executives with substantial severance payments and individuals providing legal/financial services.

This final chapter will approach three characteristics of peripheral bargaining at the *Daily News:*

- the lack of flexibility exhibited by union and management negotiators
- bargaining emphasis on principles and personalities instead of measurable bargaining-table issues; and
- the negotiators' susceptibility to external influences.

First, union negotiators basically assumed a defensive posture in negotiations. With the exception of indicating the possible application of the *New York Post* labor agreement to the situation at the *News,* union leaders took little initiative in presenting proposals of their own. To be sure, union leaders are more subject to pressures from their memberships than management is to their stockholders, at least in the short term. Few, if any, members would endorse a union leader who volunteered employee layoffs. However, union officers could have more specifically indicated what conditions, information, and possible management trade-offs would facilitate union adjustments to employment-level reductions and technological change. Further discussions could have tied these possible arrangements to past financial/labor–management experiences at the *News* and could have related future indicators/projections.

News management, particularly that associated with the Chicago Tribune Company, also demonstrated bargaining inflexibility. Indeed, there is little, if any, evidence to suggest that management sought union bargaining proposals at formal negotiation meetings. Bert Pogrebin represented Mortimer Zuckerman in efforts to purchase the *News,* and he did not fault *News* management for its "confrontational" style with the unions, a style he thought might be needed to convince unions that change was warranted. However, Pogrebin blamed management for not having attendant flexibility in its bargaining approach—they should not have tried to change deeply embedded work rule traditions (staffing levels, for example) in one fell swoop.

Second, union and management negotiators also focused on personalities and principles during the *News* dispute instead of on specific, measurable issues. Jack Kennedy of the pressmen noted that more than two years of "negotiations" took place before actual staffing levels were discussed by management. The only bargaining issue receiving any consistent attention was management's insistence on an open-ended, all-inclusive management rights clause. *News* management was probably correct that this type of clause is rather common in American industry, yet management's principle of "directing the work force" was already in part attainable through existing labor agreement provisions, which they were unwilling to implement. Principle was also stressed more than traditional bargaining when management attempted to impose the management rights clause, which went against a particular bargaining relationship, without first seeing if tangible progress to management's satisfaction could have been made on staffing, overtime, and other issues. An even more dubious example of principle was management's rationalization of strike replacements in terms of equal employment opportunity. Indeed, union and management arguments over equal employment opportunity appeared based on ephemeral convenience as no lasting gains in this area appeared sought or realized.

Interestingly, no bargaining issues were publicized at the strike's initiation, only those bargaining actions claimed by each side against the other. Management contended that employees walked out of the plant, while the union countered that its members were being replaced. The publicized emphasis on bargaining behaviors instead of on bargaining issues continued throughout the dispute.

Union leaders also stressed some principles in their bargaining dispute; more specifically, that they, rather than management, wanted to avoid a strike at all costs, and that management wanted to "bust" the unions, particularly through the use of strike replacements. The leaders intensified this latter principle through continuous and contemptuous reference to various *News* management representatives, such as Charles Brumback, James Hoge, and Robert Ballow.

When the newspaper was sold to Robert Maxwell, Don Singleton, an active, striking reporter for the *News,* reflected on how principles and personalities could overcome traditional bargaining issues:

It's like two prizefighters who've been in the ring for 35 rounds. Both of them are covered with blood. But one of them is on his back, unable to move—that's the News—and the other one's still on his feet. That's us. We may be beat up, but we still won.

And we won on a more important level, too. Until he came up against us, Bob Ballow looked like a real winner, like a new secret weapon for newspaper managements all over the country. But we showed him up for what he really is—a law thug whose tactics, when they backfire, can destroy a newspaper faster than any union could.

If we get our jobs back, great. . . . But even if we don't, we can feel good about saving a lot of workers on other newspapers a lot of trouble down the line.[1]

Focusing on principles and personalities instead of issues may generate and sustain a strike, but it does not facilitate an agreement, and, if one were reached, it debilitates the interactions between union and management officials that are necessary for an effective relationship.

Finally, negotiators in a peripheral-bargaining situation become susceptible to, in some cases are controlled by, external influences that can basically pertain to either the union or management organizations or to both. The nine unions in the Allied Printing Trades Council received much indirect support (rallies) and direct contributions (financial and effort) from other unions that assisted them during the dispute with *News* management.

The emphasis on a "victory" or "loss" for the national–labor movement, however, is deceptive at best, destructive at worst. One New York labor relations attorney for management clients suggests that there were "no real winners" in the strike and that few, if any, employers will be guided by bargaining behaviors and results at the *News*. There are over 160,000 labor agreements negotiated between management and union officials in the United States. The National Labor Relations Act has indicated that the union is the exclusive bargaining representative for employees in designated, appropriate bargaining units in these instances. Time, focus, efforts, and emotions necessary for effective bargaining involving these units are diverted by a national emphasis. Even if a national tally book/scorecard indicating unions' victories/losses could be constructed, it would not be directly applicable to local bargaining conditions.

News management did not appear to be significantly influenced by its constituents in the investment community. The strike was relatively short, occurring over two quarters of earnings statements before the *News* was sold to Robert Maxwell. Management might not have been able to calculate break-even points and apply them to collective bargaining decisions in this time frame or, if they did have these calculations, the unions did not appear aware of them. It is also difficult for the union to mobilize investors or indirect members of the financial community (analysts), within a six-month period, particularly if the struck unit only represents a portion of the organization's operations.

Management was far more affected by a partially external influence, its 1985 bargaining experience involving the Chicago Tribune Company. This influence and why it did not extend to the *News's* bargaining results as management had hoped has been discussed in full and will not be repeated here. Management at the *News* did, however, make a major miscalculation when it assumed that it could as easily deliver newspapers in New York City as it had in Chicago.

Community opinion in New York City made a substantial contribution to management's distribution problems while at the same time supporting these attitudes and actions of *News* unions. A "union town" label, even in New York City, is controversial and limited. Some, for example, would contend that two possible dimensions of a union town—electing politicians at all levels of government, and getting union-friendly legislation passed (such as revocation of a provision of Taylor Law that outlaws strikes by public employees)—has been weak, even nonexistent. Moreover, the number of New York City citizens who are union members, while comparatively high for U.S. cities, does not represent a majority of the population.

The *News's* unions did benefit from two characteristics of a "union town," however, namely, support from other unions, and citizens ignoring, if not condoning, their tactics, strike, and related violence. Public tolerance/support may have been generated for several reasons. Jimmy Breslin observed that the *News* strike represented the first labor dispute in decades that caught the public interest in New York City:

It is one thing for the unions at the Daily News to be selfish and dumb, but it is another for the owners to be openly evil. Because of this, the strike is becoming a test of the character of New York City at this time.[2]

Management compounded a negative community attitude when it quickly hired strike replacements to operate the facility and the homeless to sell newspapers. Some potential readers did not buy the *News* because they would visibly signal their betrayal of the strikers to others by a folded newspaper under their arms. Others did not want to become involved in a confrontation between strikers and hawkers, particularly when substitute newspapers were available. While there were no polls taken concerning the extent the public supported unions' actions, there were no public counterdemonstrations against the strike and related violence either. Still, there is no reason to think that the community's reaction in this situation would be transferable to other labor–management disputes in New York City.

The media represent another external influence potentially affecting both union and management. Related organizations seemed to transmit accounts of the *News* dispute in an objective fashion but represent business nonetheless. James Hoge thought that related coverage and downplaying of union violence and "conspiracies" by *New York Post* and *Newsday* were because they were business competitors of the *News*. Yet Hoge and other *News* management officials should have realized that the business orientations of these and other newspapers did not generate one editorial endorsement of the union's role in the dispute. Regardless of predisposition, the media neither helped resolve the "bargaining impasse" nor shape the terms of the labor agreement. Reporter Dennis Duggan noted that the *Daily News* strike, like almost all strikes, was "not going to be settled in the headlines, but in the bottom lines."[3]

Government officials and agencies represent another frequently considered, if not influential source in peripheral bargaining. Elected government officials were not effective in the *Daily News* dispute in any demonstrable sense since there were no tangible results or progress as a result of their actions.

Mediation appeared to offer a potential for bargaining settlement, but it came too late, and perhaps without the appropriate participants. It seemed that management did have an opportunity to engage in serious collective bargaining with federal mediator William Usery from February 15 to 27, 1991, when it made its settle-or-sell decision by March 4, 1991. Management may have been reluctant to settle because they thought Robert Maxwell or someone else would purchase the newspaper for $60 million. Whatever management's inclination to settle the dispute, their decision to have Robert Ballow remain as chief negotiator at this time, while James Hoge was present at the negotiations, reinforced, even enhanced, past union officials' hostilities, which gave them no hope that a bargaining settlement could be reached.

Bankruptcy Court Judge Tina Brozman (supported later by Judge Richard Cardamone) was perhaps the only outside individual having a direct influence on *News* labor–management relationships and output. There were no publicized criticisms of her conduct of the preliminary hearings made by union and management officials; however, neither party seemed to be particularly concerned with deadlines during the last six months of 1992, since delays seemed to be associated with judicial proceedings.

Based on the *News* experience, unions should make concerted efforts to avoid bankruptcy proceedings. In addition to unpublicized but substantial legal costs surrounding these efforts, unions can become embroiled in a tangled mess of interunion priorities and staggered bargaining with different potential purchasers that shift over time when some actively enter negotiations, and others pull out, or remain on the sidelines. Unions rather quickly agreed to concessions with Robert Maxwell, which were possibly greater than they would have had to give to *News* management (Chicago Tribune Company), because Maxwell made sure he was the unions' absolute last chance. This situation and union concessions were compounded (greater than those given to Maxwell) in bankruptcy proceedings when potential purchasers acted at several times as if they were the union's last chance.

A union's worst case scenario in bankruptcy proceedings occurs when the organization's existence and previous bargaining accomplishments, as embodied in past labor agreements, are ruled irrelevant. This experience nearly happened to the International Typographers' Union, which did not strike the *News* to protect its lifetime job guarantees negotiated in 1974. James Grottola, president of the union, stated, "We are being excluded from the process," a situation that basically remained after Judge Brozman's decision and subsequent appeals. The Newspaper Guild also experienced this exclusion in large part because Brozman indicated that Zuckerman did not have to reach agreement with all ten unions.

Will peripheral bargaining at the *News* presage future labor–management negotiations at the newspaper or elsewhere? Let us hope otherwise.

NOTES

1. Don Singleton, New York Forum About The News-II. "The Strikers Won Weeks Ago," *Newsday,* March 15, 1991. Dialog File 638, item 06077175. It should be noted that one at least quasi-principal issue, safety, that was stressed by McDonald at the beginning of negotiations appeared to evaporate as labor agreements were eventually reached by nine unions.

2. Jimmy Breslin, "News' Battle Plan: Crackers and Scabs," *Newsday,* October 28, 1990. Dialog File 638, item 05807356.

3. Dennis Duggan, "News New York Diary. Firebrands of '60s, Wimps of the '90s: Labor's Love Lost," *Newsday,* October 30, 1990. Dialog File 638, item 05809182.

APPENDIX

List of Journalists Whose Articles Served as Data Base

Appleson, Gail — *Reuters North American Business Report*
Arce, Rose Marie — *Newsday*
Arena, Michael — *Newsday*
Armstrong, Larry — *Business Week*
Astor, David — *Editor and Publisher*

Baker, Bob — *Los Angeles Times*
Barron, James — *New York Times*
Barsky, Neil — *Wall Street Journal*
Battle, Bob — *Nashville Banner*
Berkowitz, Harry — *Newsday*
Bernstein, Aaron — *Business Week*
Bernstein, Harry — *Los Angeles Times*
Bessent, Alvin E. — *Newsday*
Blair, William G. — *New York Times*
Blumenthal, Ralph — *New York Times*
Bowles, Pete — *Newsday*
Bray, Nicholas — *Wall Street Journal*
Breslin, Jimmy — *Newsday*
Breznick, Alan — *Crain's New York Business*
Broderick, Don — *New York Post*
Brown, Keith M. — *Newsday*
Bunch, William — *Newsday*

Bunis, Dena—*Newsday*
Burke, Cathy—*New York Post*

Carmody, Deirdre—*New York Times*
Carper, Alison—*Newsday*
Carter, Bill—*New York Times*
Case, Tony—*Editor and Publisher*
Cauchon, Dennis—*USA Today*
Cheliotes, Arthur—*Newsday*
Cohen, Laurie—*Chicago Tribune*
Cohen, Richard—*Washington Post*
Cohen, Roger—*New York Times*
Cox, James—*USA Today*
Crowe, Kenneth C.—*Newsday*
Crowley, Kieran—*New York Post*

Dalglish, Brenda—*Maclean's*
Davis, Robert—*Chicago Tribune*
deCourcy Hinds, Michael—*New York Times*
Diamond, Edwin—*New York*
Donaton, Scott—*Advertising Age*
Duffy, Susan—*Business Week*
Duggan, Dennis—*Newsday*
Duke, Lynne—*Washington Post*
Dutt, Jill—*Newsday*

Egan, Timothy—*New York Times*
Ehrlich, Dan—*Editor and Publisher*
Ellis, James—*Business Week*
Enrico, Dottie—*Newsday*

Fan, Maureen—*Newsday*
Ferguson, Tim W. —*Wall Street Journal*
Finder, Alan—*New York Times*
Fitzgerald, Mark—*Editor and Publisher*
Foderaro, Lisa W.—*New York Times*
Foran, Katherine—*Newsday*
Frankel, Bruce—*USA Today*
Friefield, Karen—*Newsday*

French, Mary Ann—*St. Petersburg Times*
Friendly, Jonathan—*New York Times*

Gambaradello, Joseph A.—*Newsday*
Garcilazo, Miguel—*New York Post*
Garneau, George—*Editor and Publisher*
Gelman, Mitch—*Newsday*
Glaberson, William—*New York Times*
Goldman, Kevin—*Wall Street Journal*
Goldschlag, William—*New York Daily News*
Goldstein, Marianne—*New York Post*
Gonzalez, David—*New York Times*
Goodstein, Laurie—*Washington Post*
Goozner, Merrill—*Chicago Tribune*
Gopsill, Timothy—*New York Times*
Gottlieb, Martin—*New York Times*
Greenwald, John—*Time*
Guttenplan, D. D.—*Columbia Journalism Review*
Guy, Pat—*USA Today*

Hamill, Pete—*Esquire*
Hammer, Joshua—*Newsweek*
Harney, James—*USA Today*
Harpaz, Beth J.—*Boston Globe*
Healy, Robert M.—*Chicago Tribune*
Henican, Ellis—*Newsday*
Hess, John L.—*Los Angeles Times*
Hevesi, Dennis—*New York Times*
Horwitz, Tony—*Wall Street Journal*
Howe, Irving—*New York Times*

Jamaieson, Wendell—*Newsday*
Jones, Alex S.—*New York Times*

Kandel, Bethany—*USA Today*
Kasindorf, Jeanie—*New York*
Kempton, Murray—*Newsday*
Kennedy, Randy Alan—*New York Times*

Kerwin, Ann Marie—*Editor and Publisher*

Kessler, Glenn—*Newsday*

Kifner, John—*New York Times*

Kilborn, Peter K.—*New York Times*

King, Jeanne—*Reuters North American Business Report*

Klein, Edward—*Vanity Fair*

Klose, Kevin—*Washington Post*

Kolbert, Elizabeth—*New York Times*

Kurtz, Howard—*Washington Post*

Labaton, Stephen—*New York Times*

Ladd, Scott—*Newsday*

Lambert, Bruce—*New York Times*

Lander, Mark—*Business Week*

LaRosa, Paul—*New York Daily News*

Lavan, Rosemary Metzler—*New York Daily News*

Levin, Doron—*New York Times*

Levine, Richard—*New York Times*

Lin, Wendy—*Newsday*

Locin, Mitchell—*Chicago Tribune*

Lohr, Steve—*New York Times*

Lombardi, Frank—*New York Daily News*

Lowery, Mark—*Newsday*

Lucas, Caryl R.—*Newark Star-Ledger*

Maremont, Mark—*Business Week*

Martin, Alex—*Newsday*

Martin, Douglas—*New York Times*

McCarthy, Sheryl—*Newsday*

McCartney, Robert J.—*Washington Post*

McCoy, Kevin—*Newsday*

McDarrah, Timothy—*New York Post*

McFadden, Robert D.—*New York Times*

McGee, Susan—*Wall Street Journal*

McKenna, Kate—*Washington Journalism Review*

McKinley, James C., Jr.—*New York Times*

McQuiston, John T.—*New York Times*

McShane, Larry—*New York Daily News*

Montez, Roqua, IV—*USA Today*
Moses, Jonathan M.—*Wall Street Journal*
Moses, Paul—*Newsday*
Murray, William J.—*Wall Street Journal*

Neuffer, Elizabeth—*New York Times*
Nieves, Evelyn—*New York Times*
Nordheimer, Jon—*New York Times*

O'Connor, Helen—*New York Daily News*
Oliver, Chris—*New York Post*
O'Neill, Michael J.—*New York Times*
Oreskes, Michael—*New York Times*
Otwell, Ralph—*Chicago Tribune*

Parks, James B.—*AFL-CIO News*
Payne, Les—*Newsday*
Perez-Rivas, Miguel—*Newsday*
Perry, James M.—*Wall Street Journal*
Pines, Deborah—*Reuters North American Business Report*
Pitt, David E.—*New York Times*
Polich, John—*Editor and Publisher*
Prial, Frank J.—*New York Times*
Prokesch, Steven—*New York Times*
Purdum, Todd S.—*New York Times*

Queen, Joseph W.—*Newsday*

Radolf, Andrew—*Editor and Publisher*
Reilly, Patrick M.—*Wall Street Journal*
Rhoden, William C.—*New York Times*
Richter, Paul—*Los Angeles Times*
Riley, John—*Newsday*
Rist, Curtis—*Newsday*
Rivera, Elaine—*Newsday*
Robbins, Tom—*New York Daily News*
Rodriquez, Yolanda—*Newsday*
Rosen, Richard—*New York Daily News*
Rosenstiel, Thomas B.—*Los Angeles Times*

Roth, Norm — *Labor Today*
Rothmyer, Keith — *Newsday*
Ruben, George — *Monthly Labor Review*
Ruffni, Gene — *The Nation*

Salpukas, Alex — *New York Times*
Sanger, Elizabeth — *Newsday*
Scaduto, Anthony — *Newsday*
Scanlon, Michael — *New York Times*
Schanberg, Sydney H. — *Newsday*
Schmidt, William E. — *New York Times*
Schwartzman, Paul — *New York Times*
Seligman, Daniel — *Fortune*
Shain, Michael — *New York Post*
Sheinkman, Jack — *Wall Street Journal*
Shipp, E. R. — *New York Times*
Siklos, Richard — *Financial Post*
Silverman, Edward R. — *Newsday*
Simons, Marlise — *New York Times*
Singleton, Don — *Newsday*
Sloan, Alan — *Newsday*
Solomon, Digby — *New York Daily News*
Specter, Michael — *Washington Post*
Stanley, Alessandra — *New York Times*
Steir, Richard — *New York Post*
Sterling, Guy — *Newark Star-Ledger*
Stetson, Damon — *New York Times*
Stevenson, Richard W. — *New York Times*
Strong, James — *Chicago Tribune*

Tabor, Mary B. — *New York Times*
Taranto, James — *Wall Street Journal*
Taylor, Curtis T. — *Newsday*
Teinowitz, Ira — *Advertising Age*
Treadwell, David — *Los Angeles Times*

Vaughan, Doug — *Newsday*

Warren, James — *Chicago Tribune*
Weber, Bruce — *New York Times*

Wechsler, Pat—*Newsday*
Weiner, Steve—*Forbes*
Wells, Ken—*Wall Street Journal*
Whitney, Craig R.—*New York Times*
Widder, Pat—*Chicago Tribune*
Wieghart, James G.—*New York Times*

Yarrow, Andrew L.—*New York Times*

Zonana, Victor F.—*Los Angeles Times*

Bibliographic Note

To retrieve references to approximately 1,000 articles on the *New York Daily News* strike and the subsequent negotiations for the sale of the newspaper, literature searches were performed through Dialog Information Services, Inc., a data base vendor located in Palo Alto, California, which provides fee-based on-line access to around 400 data bases in a broad range of disciplines. The WESTLAW online information retrieval system was searched for citations and text of court cases. Searches were also performed through NewsBank and Business News-Bank on CD-ROM produced by NewsBank, Inc., in New Canaan, Connecticut. The electronic version of NewsBank contains indexing to 200 newspapers published in the United States between 1981 and the present. Business NewsBank indexes over 600 publications published in the United States between 1985 and the present.

Seven major Dialog data bases were searched for bibliographic citations and abstracts for articles published from October 23, 1990, through October 30, 1992, in journals, magazines, newspapers, and wire services. The National Newspaper Index was searched for articles published between 1979 and 1989 on the *Daily News* and contract negotiations. On occasion, when articles were not available in the University of North Florida Library, the complete text of articles was retrieved on-line. Following are descriptions of the data bases that were searched.

ABI/INFORM (File 15) indexes over 800 publications in business and related fields. National Newspaper Index (File 111) provides indexing of the *Christian Science Monitor,* the *New York Times,* the *Wall Street Journal,* the *Washington Post,* and the *Los Angeles Times.* Newsearch (File 211) contains records received for the current month for articles from over 1,700 newspapers, magazines, and periodicals; 100 local and regional business publications; and the complete text of PR Newswire. At the end of the month, the month's records are transferred from Newsearch to other files. AP NEWS (File 258) provides full text of the coverage by Associated Press of national, international, and business news. PR Newswire (File 613) is produced by the PR Newswire Association, Inc., and contains the complete text of news releases from various sources. Business Dateline (File 635) contains full-text articles from regional business publications from the United States and Canada as well as the Crain News Service, nine daily newspapers, and BusinessWire, which provides business-related news releases. Newsday (File 638) provides full-text indexing of articles appearing in the newspaper, *Newsday,* with emphasis on business and government in the New York metropolitan area.

In addition, a complete search of the Bureau of National Affairs Inc., *Daily Labor Reports* was made from January 1, 1985, through January 1, 1992. Also helpful were decisions of the National Labor Relations Board and various hearings from the United States Senate, which are identified in the chapter endnotes.

NOTE

The author is grateful to Sarah Philips for devising and describing this systematic, computerized, and thorough search of items related to the *Daily News*'s bargaining situation.

Index

About the Author

KENNETH M. JENNINGS is a professor of industrial relations at the University of North Florida. He is the author of several books including *The Labor Relations Process* (fourth edition) and *Balls and Strikes: The Money Game in Professional Baseball* (Praeger, 1990).